Photography

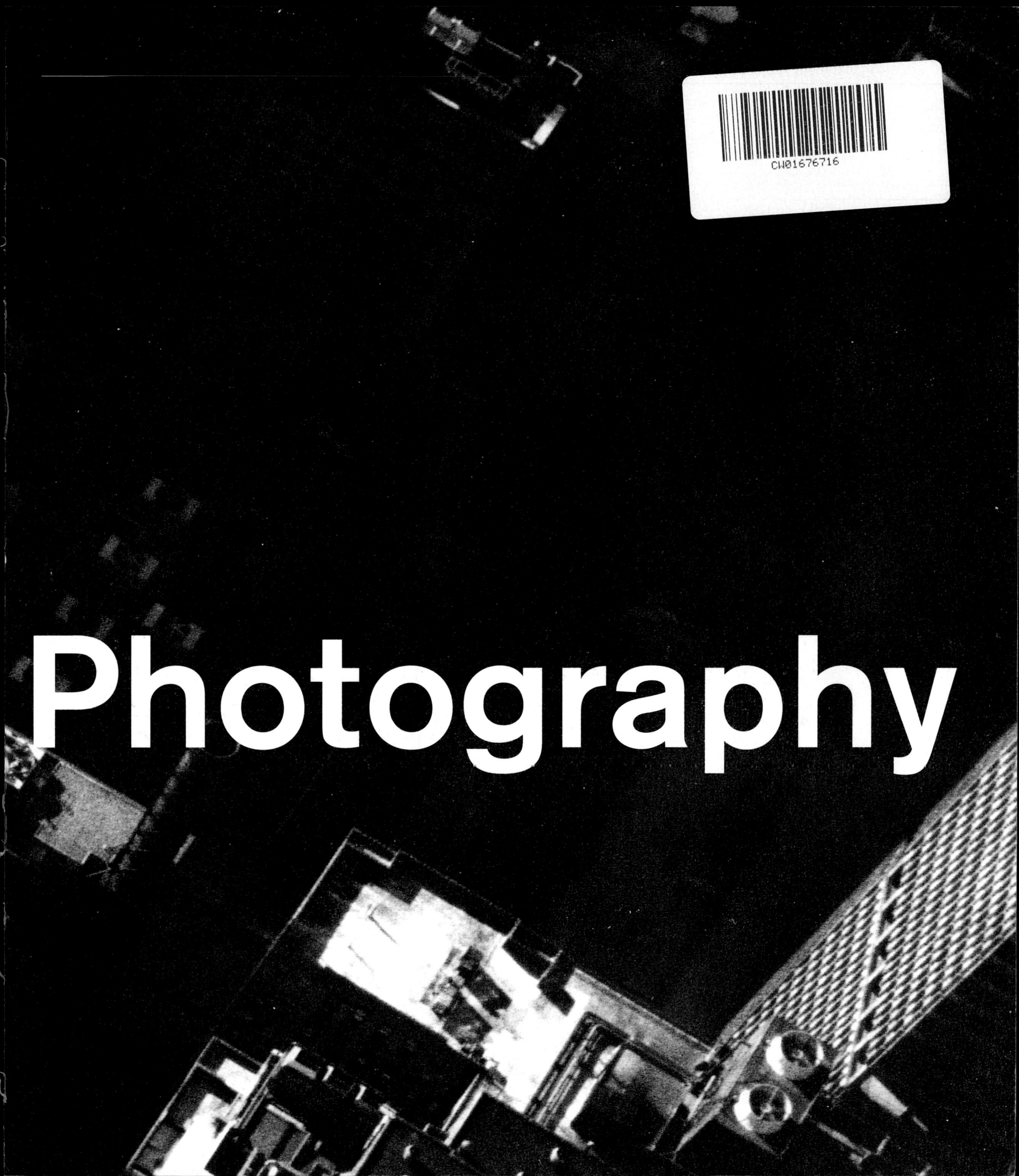

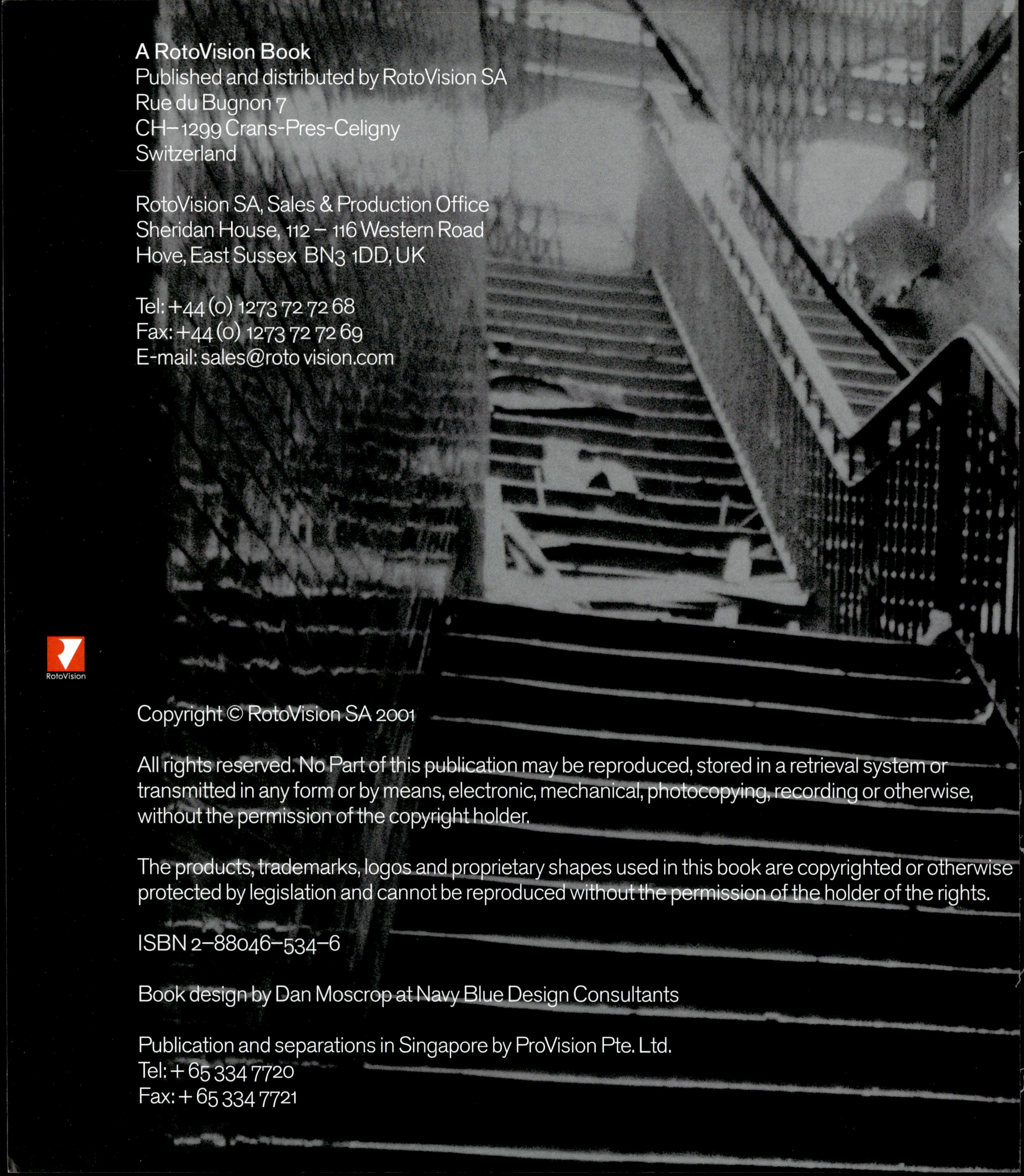

A RotoVision Book
Published and distributed by RotoVision SA
Rue du Bugnon 7
CH–1299 Crans-Pres-Celigny
Switzerland

RotoVision SA, Sales & Production Office
Sheridan House, 112 – 116 Western Road
Hove, East Sussex BN3 1DD, UK

Tel: +44 (0) 1273 72 72 68
Fax: +44 (0) 1273 72 72 69
E-mail: sales@roto vision.com

ISBN 2–88046–534–6

Book design by Dan Moscrop at Navy Blue Design Consultants

Publication and separations in Singapore by ProVision Pte. Ltd.
Tel: + 65 334 7720
Fax: + 65 334 7721

This is a book that's as much about images as it is about technique. It's as much about having an eye for a picture as it is about having a mastery of the technicalities of black and white. And hopefully, as well as all the things that are passed on through the words of the photographers who created this collection of incredible images, one of the main benefits of the book will be its ability simply to inspire. If, having seen the quality and the sheer breadth of imagery that make up these pages you feel the irresistible urge to pick up a camera and to go off and try some of the ideas for yourself, then the book will have achieved its purpose in style.

Architecture has so many aspects to it that in many ways it's difficult to produce just one book that will cover all of them. Certainly it would be almost impossible for a single photographer using his or her own pictures as examples to try and explain the variety of ways that this subject can be tackled. An architectural study can be many things, as you'll see throughout this book. It could be a beautifully observed and executed interior, such as the picture of Che House in Australia by Anderson & Low, that builds on the architect's vision for the sweep and flow of a building, and which understands the role of natural light in defining structure. It could also be an interpretation of a building and the character that surrounds it. A photographer such as Adrian Ensor, for example, looks for the shape and tone of a structure, such as the extraordinary Guggenheim Museum in Bilbao, and then picks out just a section that is then used to express the overall impression that the building creates. The viewer gets a real feel for what it must have been like to stand in front of the place and to experience its atmosphere, and the result is far more emotive than a mere record shot could ever be.

An architectural study could be the poignant remains of a charred cherub, still hanging on the wall of a gutted building in the aftermath of a terrible fire, or it could be the slowly decaying interior of a once proud and grand structure that has fallen on hard times. It could be a detail that reveals something hitherto unsuspected and beautiful about an everyday building or, through the lens of one of the world's great masters such as Ralph Gibson, it could be a seemingly trivial moment that has, through skilful observation, been turned into a classic architectural study, through the interaction of form and light.

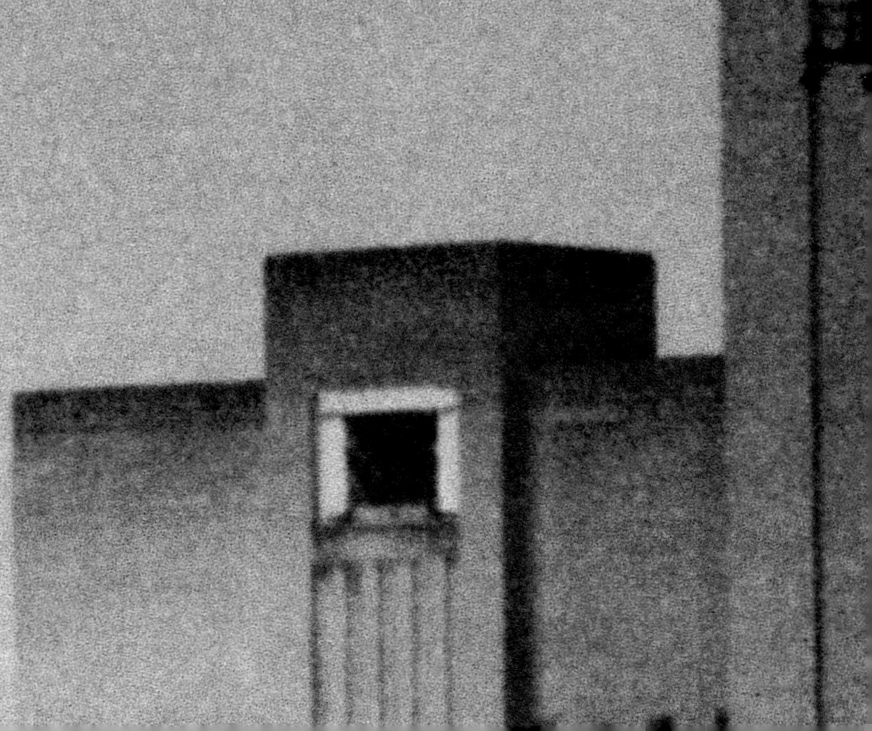

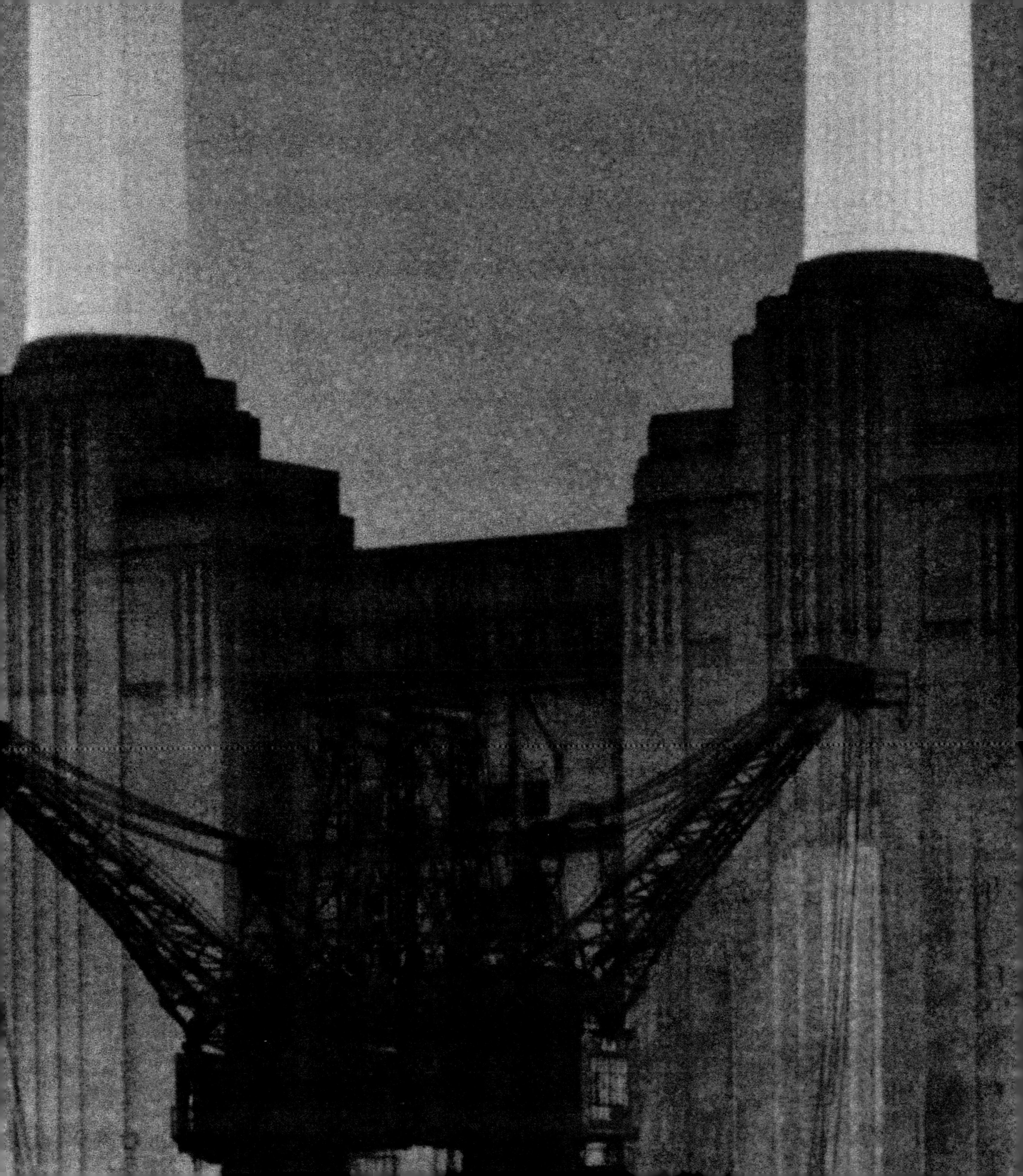

Architecture can be seen as pure structure and form or as something that has a personality and that can be approached in a way that will reveal some facet of its character, good or bad. Simon Marsden builds on ghostly legends to add a sinister aspect to his work, utilising the characteristics of infrared film to add an unworldly and mystical feel to his pictures. Others photographers, such as the great Edward Steichen, have looked more to natural elements, such as fog and the shroud of darkness, to add atmosphere to early 20th century studies of New York street life.

Above all, the photographic interpretation of architecture is about an individual's feeling for a place and the effect that it has on him or her. And, as we see from the contrasting views from Frederick Evans (Wells Cathedral) and Simon Norfolk (Auschwitz), sometimes it's the knowledge that we ourselves have about a place that fills in the details. Both pictures feature as their focal point steps whose worn appearance bears silent witness to the heavy use that they have suffered, and our imagination tells us the story of the unseen people who once passed through here in such numbers.

Architectural pictures can be meticulously planned, they can be 'found,' they might be an instant that is over in 1/125sec and is never repeated or they could be a regular scene that is simply interpreted in an individual manner. They could even be part of a series that will keep a photographer occupied for years, and which will continue to stimulate and inspire for all that time. That's the beauty of this and so many other photographic subjects: the individual can make of it what they will, there's no set agenda that has to be followed. Even the golden rules that others have established over the years for photographers to follow are there to be broken and turned on their heads, as so many of the photographers featured here take the greatest delight in proving over and over again.

So much for the subject: what about the medium? What is it about black and white that makes it so enduring? Sheer logic should dictate that, with colour film so accessible and of such high quality now, black and white should have been relegated to the history books long ago. But instead the opposite has happened. It's taken on a new life of its own, and is gaining a steady and growing following across the world.

Black and white is now seen as the natural medium for fine art prints and, as the digital side of photography becomes ever more important, those who choose to indulge in silver halide and the skills of the darkroom will increasingly be seen as artists in their own right.

A whole new generation of photographers is discovering that black and white can offer them a different way of looking at the world, one in which the simplicity and subtlety of tone and shadow triumphs over the distractions of colour. Time and again black and white somehow captures a mood and a feeling that colour, for all its accuracy, simply can't. Perhaps that's exactly the point: photography is about so much more than a simple rendering of what's in front of the camera. We want to achieve an interpretation of life, and colour can sometimes get in the way.

There's also a lot more flexibility built into black and white in the way that it can be manipulated and made to become what we want it to be. Instead of the computer screen, the traditional photographer has the darkroom, where all kinds of miracles can be performed. The rediscovery of ancient toning methods and half forgotten early printing processes has provided an extra dimension, and allowed photographers to produce pictures that wouldn't look out of place in an art gallery. As a bonus, many toners will also give a print a life expectancy of well over a hundred years as well, provided that the ground rules for display are followed.

A glance through the images in this book will show that black and white, thanks to these toning methods, can be surprisingly colourful at times, and equally impressive is quite how effective the final results can be. This is photography proudly proclaiming its history and heritage, and establishing a niche for itself that technological progress in the world of imaging won't erode.

The future of black and white looks secure, and its following will continue to grow as more and more photographers discover its advantages. So, listen to what the photographers in this book have got to say, pick up your camera and get out there and find out what black and white can offer for yourself. You won't be disappointed.

Terry Hope

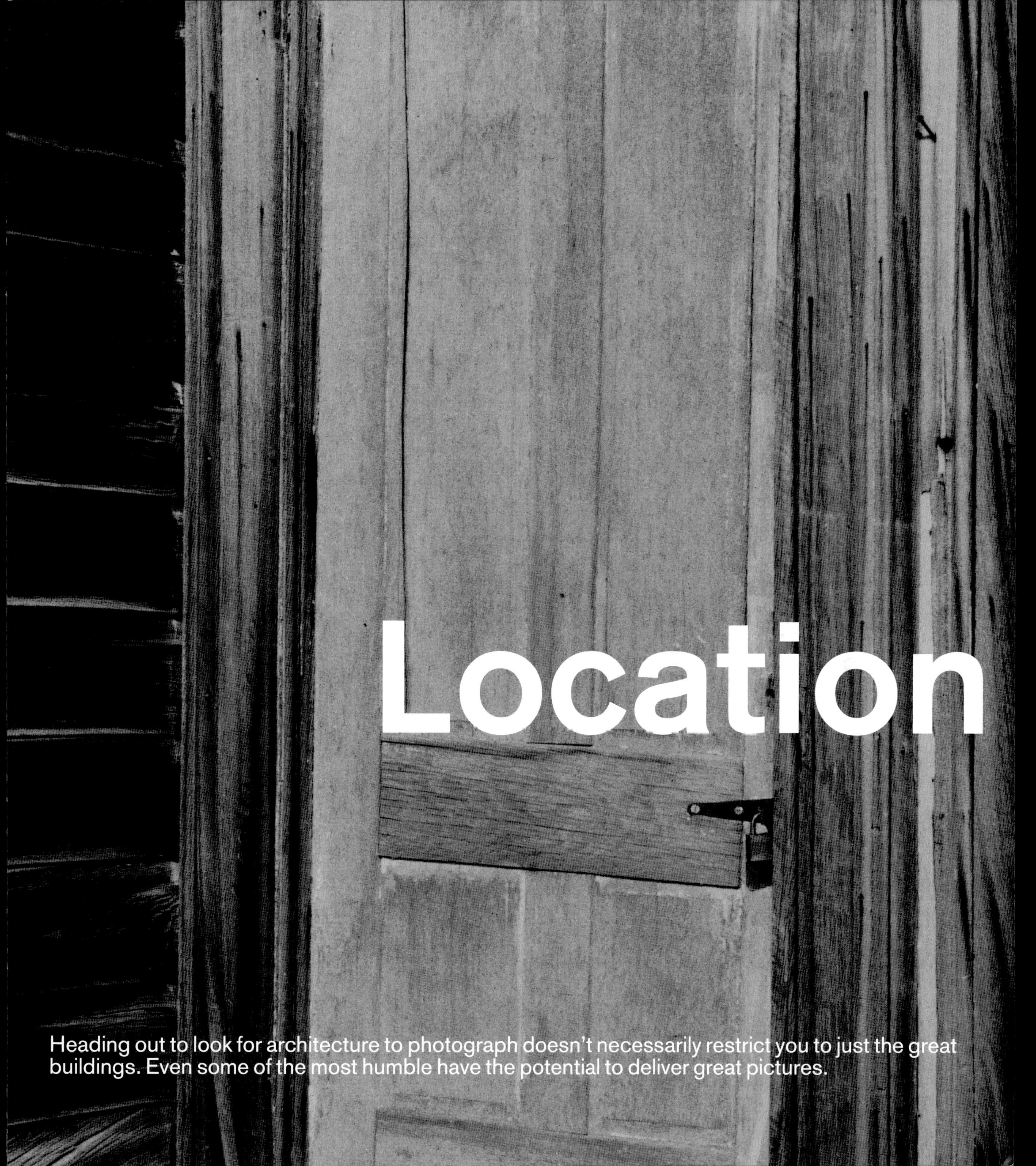

Location

Heading out to look for architecture to photograph doesn't necessarily restrict you to just the great buildings. Even some of the most humble have the potential to deliver great pictures.

Chrysler Building, New York by Jason Hawkes
Pentax 645 camera, 35mm lens, Ilford FP4 film.
Exposure 1/1000sec at f/3.5

I was commissioned to take this picture for an advertisement for Mitsubishi cars and, in some ways, it was quite easy to arrange. Getting permission to fly above New York in a helicopter is relatively straightforward – certainly easier than London, where a twin-engine helicopter is required as opposed to a single-engine version—and the Chrysler Building was only around one minute's flying time from our take off point on the Hudson River.

The door was removed from the helicopter and I was then strapped securely in and simply leaned out to take my pictures when we were in the right position. I could communicate through headphones with the pilot at all times and together we worked out what position we needed to take up. My main headache was the fact that the art director for the shoot wanted a particular perspective for the picture that could only be provided through the use of a wide angle lens. This meant I had to fit a 35mm to my 645 camera— the equivalent to a 20mm on a 35mm camera—and we had to come in really close to the building, much closer than it appears here, to fill the frame with the subject.

The pilot started each pass at around 1000 feet above the Chrysler Building and then dipped in quickly to reach a point no more than 100 feet above it. It was too dangerous to hold this position for long and so I had around ten seconds to take my pictures and generally managed around five frames in that time.

Jason Hawkes

Pointer I have tried to set my camera up on a fixed mount on occasions but it doesn't give me the opportunity to react quickly enough to the situation. As a result I prefer to hand hold and this is what I did here, setting a shutter speed that is always 1/1000sec if possible and then holding the camera as steady as I can at the moment of shooting.

Printing and Processing The picture was printed by Steve McLoud at the Metro darkrooms in London and he emphasised the impact of the Chrysler Building in the frame through holding back just a small area in the centre of the picture during the print exposure and allowing the edges to darken down to form a border around it. The procedure, known as dodging and burning, allows an expert printer to lighten or darken selective areas of a print at will by causing areas of it to receive more or less exposure. This can allow elements to be highlighted, as here, or for contrast to be evened out in a print that would otherwise be impossible to produce.

"The pilot started each pass at around 1000 feet above the Chrysler Building and then dipped in quickly to reach a point no more than 100 feet above it."

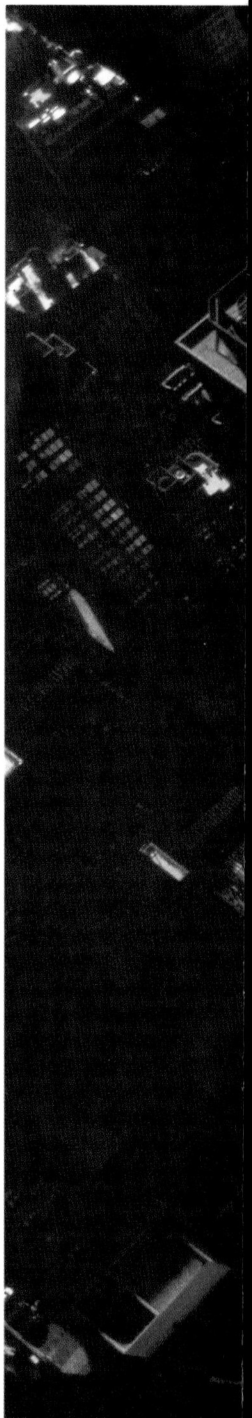

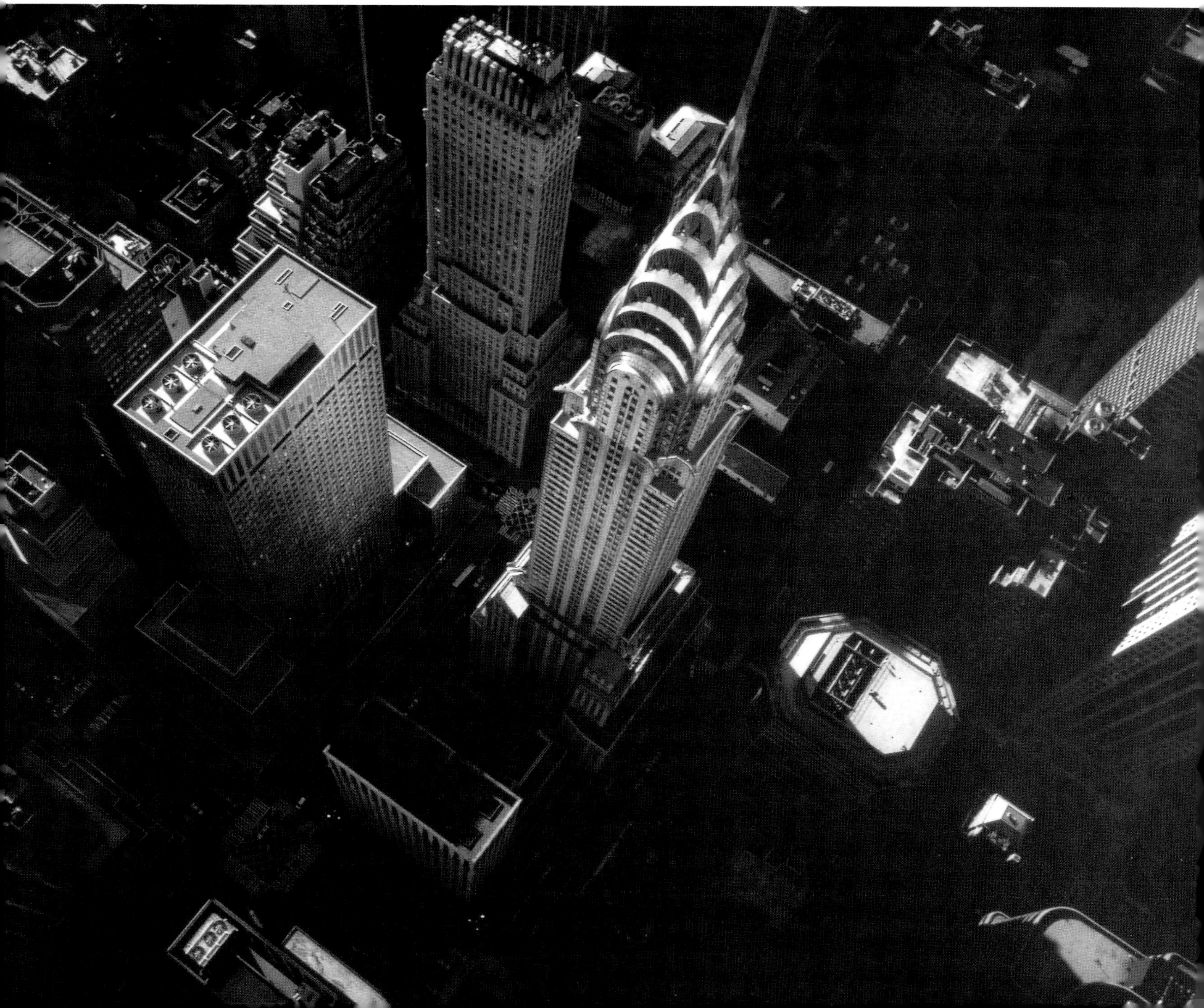

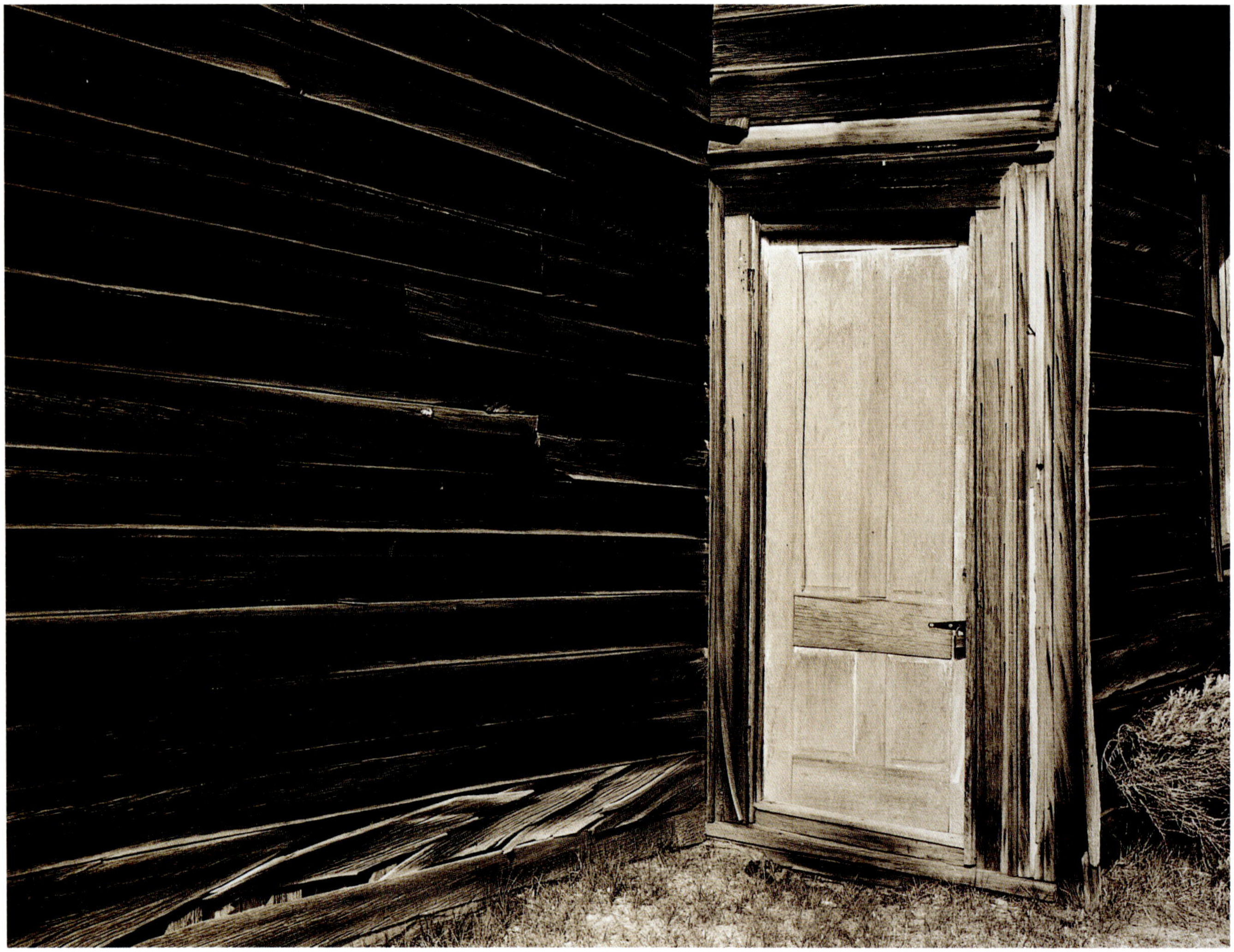

Location

I love photographing in California because of the quality of the light and the strength of the landscape that can be found there. On one of my many visits to the area I heard about the abandoned gold mining town of Bodie and it was natural for me to pay a visit to see what it could offer me in terms of a subject for the camera. It was everything that I had hoped it would be: it looked as though the people that used to live there had simply downed tools and left and everything looked exactly as must have done for decades.

I took some overall views but I also wanted to produce some detail shots to show the effect of the weathering on the wooden buildings that were still standing. The intensity of the sun was in my favour and I simply looked for areas that were receiving the kind of lighting that I was looking for, something that wasn't too flat but which would add the modelling necessary to define the shape of the structure.

I cropped this picture in-camera so that there was nothing to distract from the simplicity of the scene. Less was definitely more here: other images placed the building in the context of its surroundings but this one, by excluding details such as the roof and all but a fraction of window, concentrated the eye on the shapes and textures that had attracted me in the first place.

Ron Bambridge

Untitled IV by Ron Bambridge
Wista 5x4in camera with Sinar 6x7cm film back, 90mm lens, Ilford HP5 film. Exposure 1/125sec at f/16

Composition This doorway to one of the old houses caught my eye because the angular nature of the elements here—the upright shapes around the door and the contrasting horizontal lines created by the planking along the side of the building—helped to make up a dynamic composition. I set up the camera and arranged the picture so that the door itself fell in the right hand side of the frame, where it served to counterbalance the expanse of wooden planking to the left.

Technique I used a 5x4in camera but I decided to fit a roll film back to this because it gave me the flexibility of using roll film combined with the greater degree of control that is possible with a large format camera. Although I didn't use them with relation to this particular image I did, for example, employ the camera movements that are possible with the lens panel and the film back of a large format camera (which, when used in relation to one another, can lead to such things as increased depth of field and corrected verticals) to benefit other images that I took that day.

Hatmaker's Shop, Penang, Malaysia by Anderson & Low
Mamiya 6x7cm, 127mm lens, Kodak T-Max 400.
Exposure around half a second

Penang is still a very beautiful city but many of the buildings there are in danger of redevelopment because of recent laws that have been passed. This made us concerned to photograph as many as we could, as well as some of the traditional craftsmen who work around them, so that there was at least a record for posterity should everything be swept away in the future. All buildings have a character that, like a person, will change continually depending on what angle you photograph them from and the kind of lighting that is hitting them and when we came back to this location at two in the morning these hatmakers were still hard at work and the building behind them—a mosque—was illuminated just by street lighting and the night had added an ambience and a sense of stillness and mystery. We asked permission to take the picture but otherwise let the craftsmen carry on with their work without interference. With the camera set on a sturdy tripod, the shutter speed of around half a second was short enough to ensure that there was no serious movement from these central characters as we recorded the scene.

Anderson & Low

Technique The fact that the paintwork of this building was white was crucial because it meant that it reflected just enough of the street lighting to enable its detail to be picked out against the brighter light coming from the interiors of the shops below. A dark building would have swallowed up the light hitting it and would have made it virtually impossible to retain detail in this area of the picture.

Pointer Achieving an exposure that would allow detail to be recorded in the illuminated shop interiors and also would pick out the low light levels on the building's exterior was a matter of judgement and the exposure chosen was bracketed a stop or so either side to ensure that there were options at the printing stage. Because the scene offered such a wide range of contrast levels the ideal negative was one that offered a compromise between slight overexposure of the highlights and underexposure of the shadow areas, both of which could ultimately be corrected through careful printing.

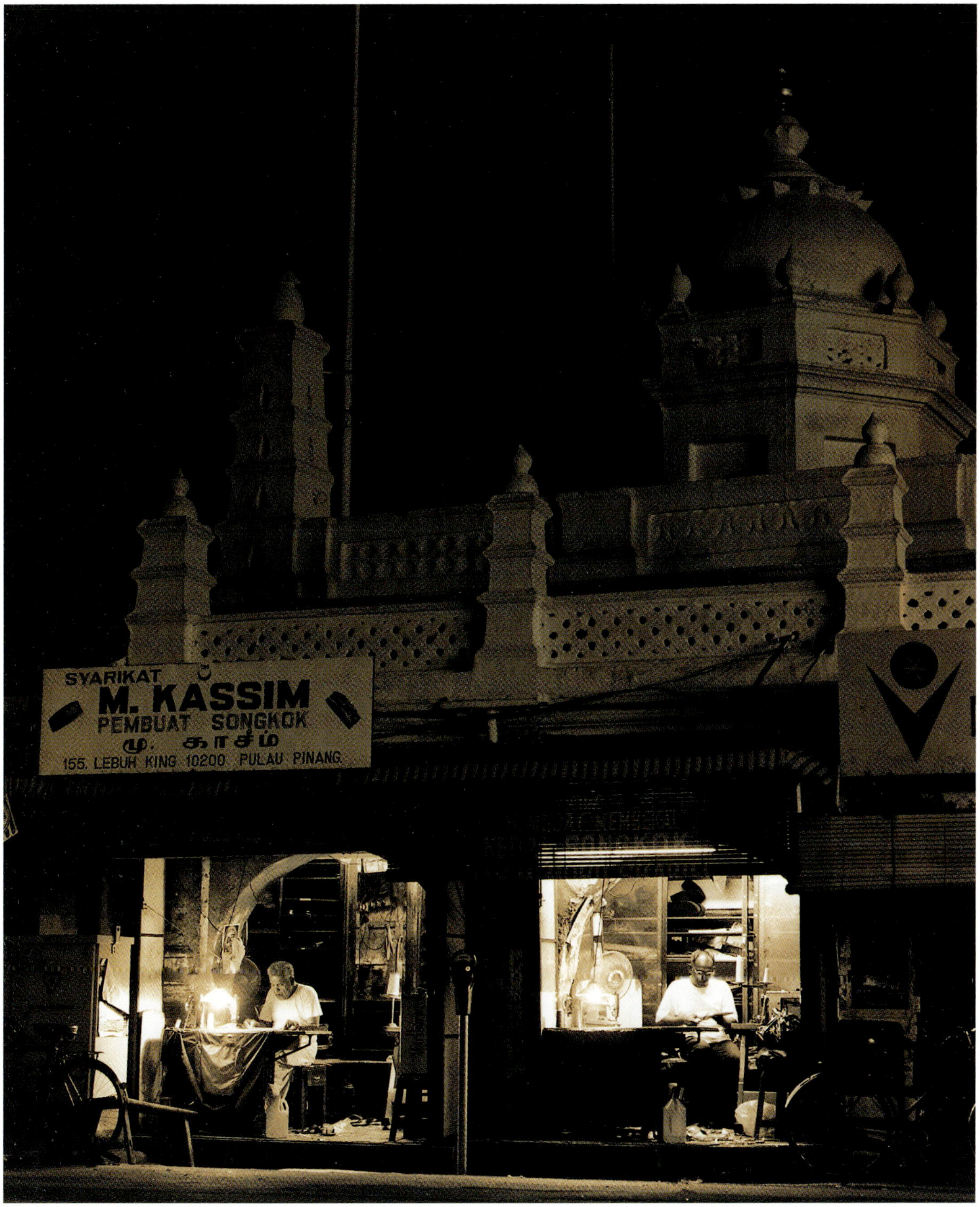
SYARIKAT
M. KASSIM
PEMBUAT SONGKOK
மு. காசீம்
155, LEBUH KING 10200 PULAU PINANG.

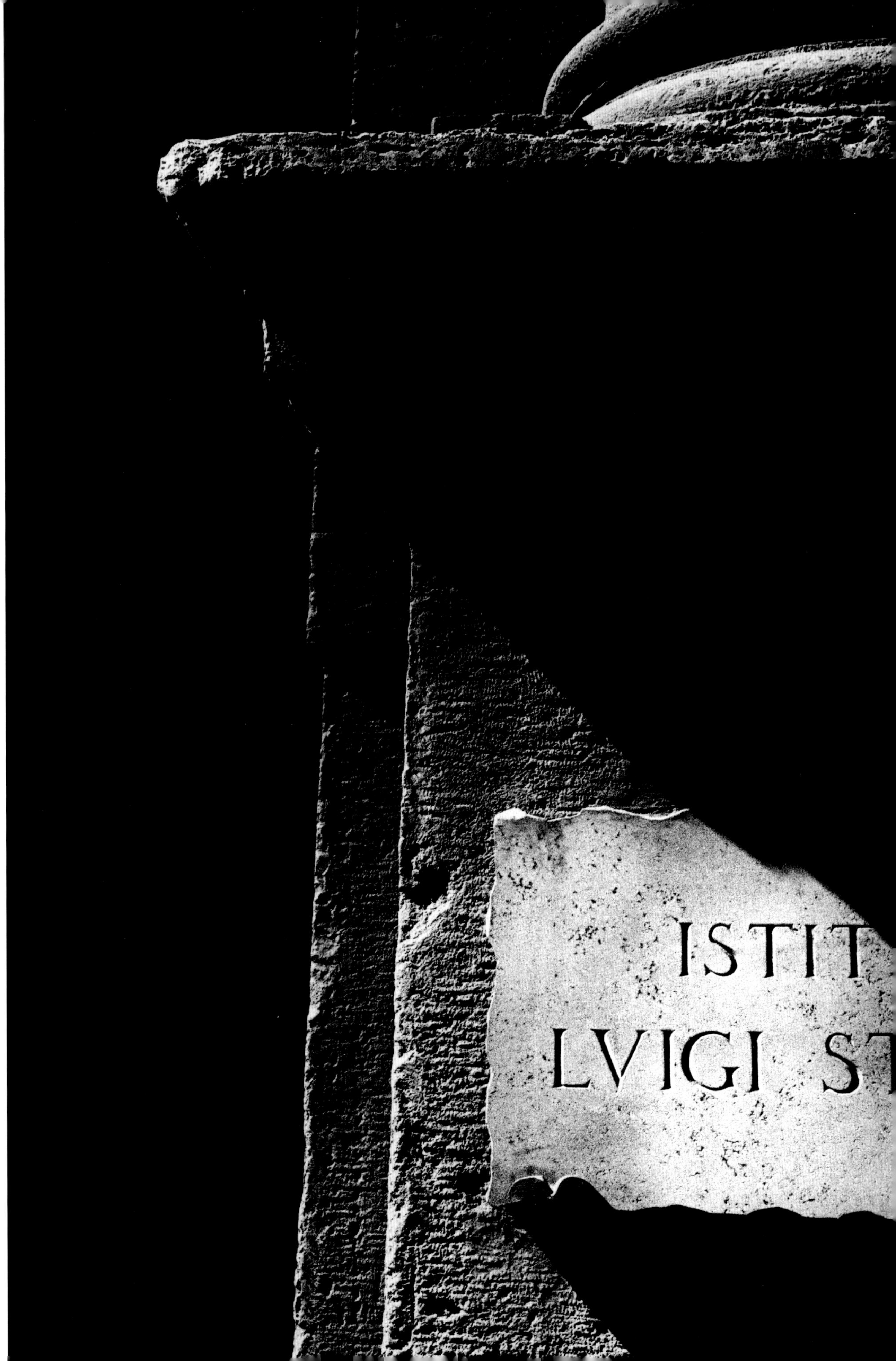
ISTIT
LVIGI ST

This was taken in Rome outside the Luigi Institute and my eye was drawn to this particular architectural detail that was being highlighted by the way that the light was hitting it. This is an example of what those involved in classical art refer to as 'chiaroscuro', the management of light and shade in a picture, and it's the basis of Renaissance as well as Lowlands painting. Caravaggio was the master of it, and light and shadow became his principle means of pictorial expression: it's something that photographers can learn to master as well. A photographer's lighting attitude must be uniquely his and it must be consistent. It's the first thing that hits the eye of the viewer. That doesn't mean that you have to restrict yourself to working only at set times of the day. Any time that my eyes are open I'm working and, indeed, I've been working on a series of pictures of Berlin taken at night so it is possible to take pictures whenever you want.

Architectural details such as this are there to be found in all kinds of places and they can be the basis for very successful pictures.
Ralph Gibson

The series of details Ralph Gibson has been working on for some time now, of which this particular image is part, has recently won him the Silver Plumb Award from the Design Trust for Public Space.

Technique There is no one set lens for shooting architectural details. Ralph Gibson generally uses either a standard or one that's slightly long but this picture was one of the rare times that he switched to a wide angle, opting for a 35mm to allow him the opportunity to step back a little from his subjects in the narrow streets of Rome.

Pointer It's not necessary for the photographer to attempt to show every element of the scene in a picture. Often it's what is suggested that is more telling and the art of capturing detail is to know what to leave out and how to use shade to break up a scene that otherwise could appear too bland and one-dimensional.

"A photographer's lighting attitude must be uniquely his and it must be consistent".

Architectural Detail by Ralph Gibson
Leica M2, 35mm lens, Kodak Tri-X film.
Exposure not recorded

I was in Utah on a commercial job, shooting a campaign for Marlboro cigarettes, and on my way to the location one morning I saw the tops of these grain silos glinting in the sun, just a short way off the road and I decided to take a small detour to check it out. When I got up close I realised that I'd been justified in taking a look: the textures and the strong dramatic shapes that they offered were the perfect basis for a picture and the lighting—although it was still only around eight in the morning—was already very strong and creating dark and dramatic shadows around them, highlighting the textures still further.

In terms of architecture, some might see this as a waste of a sheet of film, a building that is purely functional and not worth recording. To me, however, it doesn't look ordinary; it has its own beauty. There's no analysis that you can do to work out what it is that attracts you to certain places but you just know yourself as a photographer when something looks right.

John Claridge

Location

Grain Silos Utah by John Claridge
Deardorff 5x4in camera, 110mm lens,
Agfa APX 400 film. Exposure ½ second at f/22

Technique To increase the drama in the scene still further, John fitted an orange filter to his camera and this allowed the blues and the greens in the scene to register much darker on film than they actually were. This has added tone to the grass in the right hand corner but, more importantly, it's darkened down the background in the sky and consequently highlighted the clouds there, creating a striking backdrop for the silos.

Composition Faced with the solidity of this structure, John decided that his best approach would be to set the camera up looking square on to the subject, to keep the space around it to a minimum and to use the telegraph pole on the right hand side as a foil to mirror the strong uprights of the building. The effect has been to emphasise the strength of the silos and, in combination with the powerful lighting, to give them almost a majestic appearance.

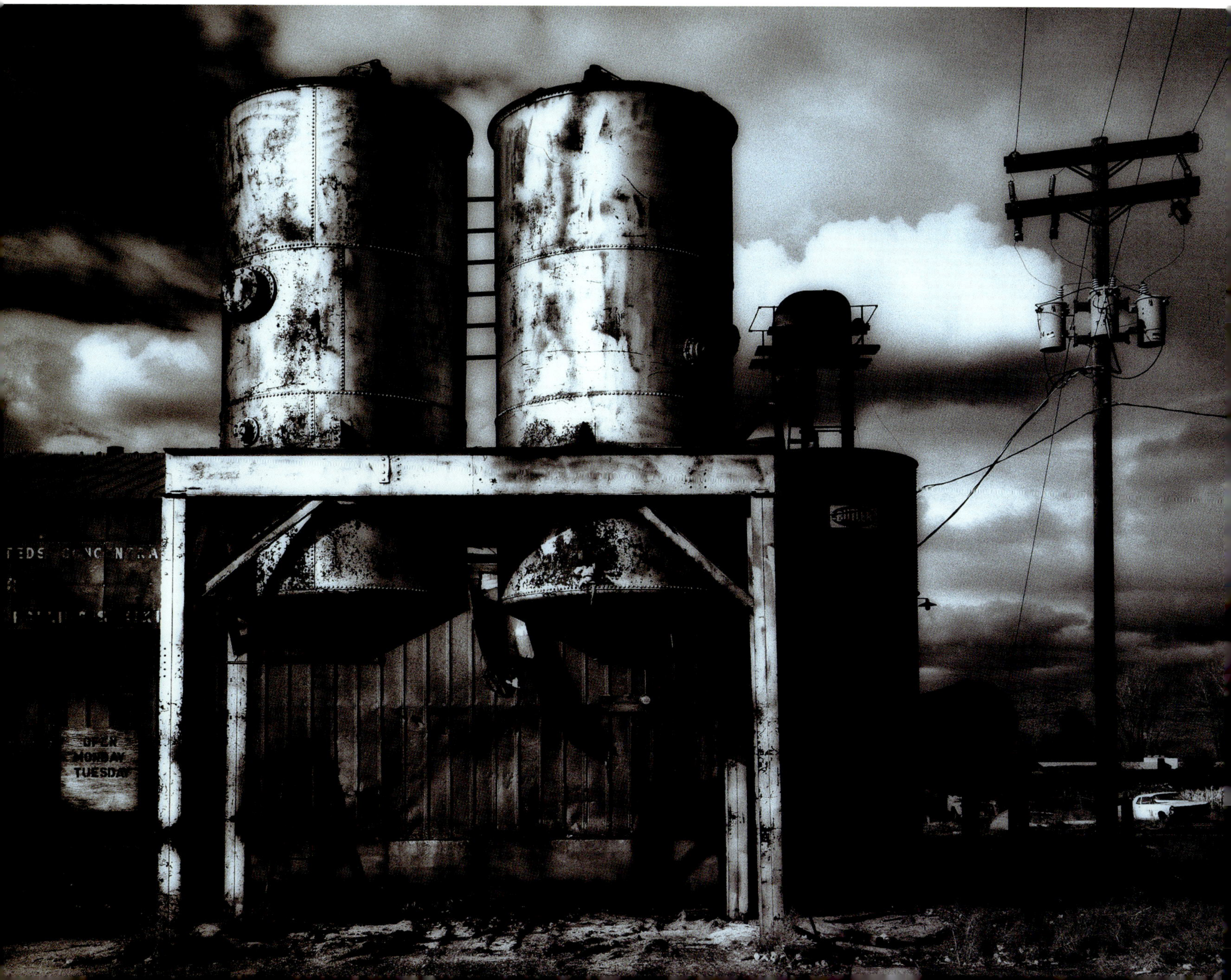
OPEN
MONDAY
TUESDAY

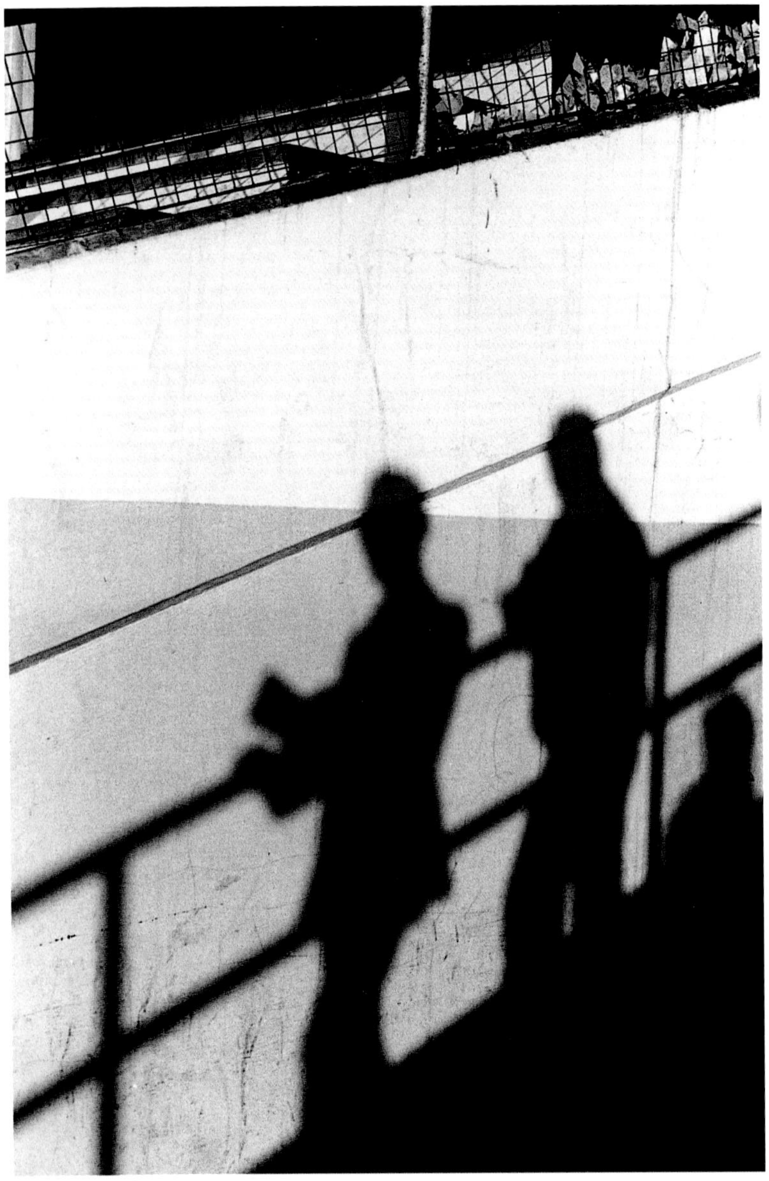

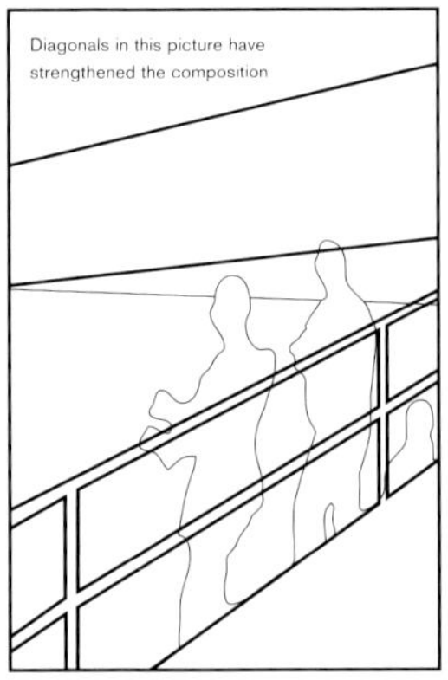

Diagonals in this picture have strengthened the composition

Greyhound Racing Track by Terry Hope
Olympus OM1, 50mm lens, Kodak Tri-X film.
Exposure 1/250sec at f/8

I decided that I would take my camera along to an afternoon greyhound racing meeting at my local stadium and expected to come back with the usual mix of action and character portraits. The day was turning out to be quite disappointing, however, and I didn't really feel that I'd done the occasion justice until, quite near the end of the event, I was walking along the pit at the front of the stands and saw these shadows being thrown on to a wall by one of the exits.

It seemed to me to capture pretty much everything that I wanted to say about the place and the people who were attending this event. There were enough of the surroundings visible to suggest something about the slightly tatty air of the stadium and its faded décor and the shapes that were being thrown on to this wall by a strong afternoon sun were beautifully defined and uncluttered. The figure in the front even had his hat and race card clearly visible and I loved the way that he was standing, relaxed against the railings, waiting for the next race to start.

To me it allowed an impression of the afternoon to be put across without the need to directly involve potentially distracting faces and characters in the mix.

Terry Hope

Composition The picture is a series of parallel diagonal lines, from the shadow in the bottom right hand corner through to the edge of the wall that runs across the top section of the picture. Repetition of strong lines such as these has given a very powerful structure to this picture and has contrasted against, and helped to set off, the upright shapes of the two figures in the centre.

Pointer Architectural photography isn't all about taking the obvious approaches. Look for different interpretations of a building and remember that, in places such as this dog racing stadium, often it's the people who make it all come alive and so try to involve them in some way if you can, without taking too much attention away from your main area of interest.

"I was walking along the pit at the front of the stands and saw these shadows being thrown on to a wall by one of the exits."

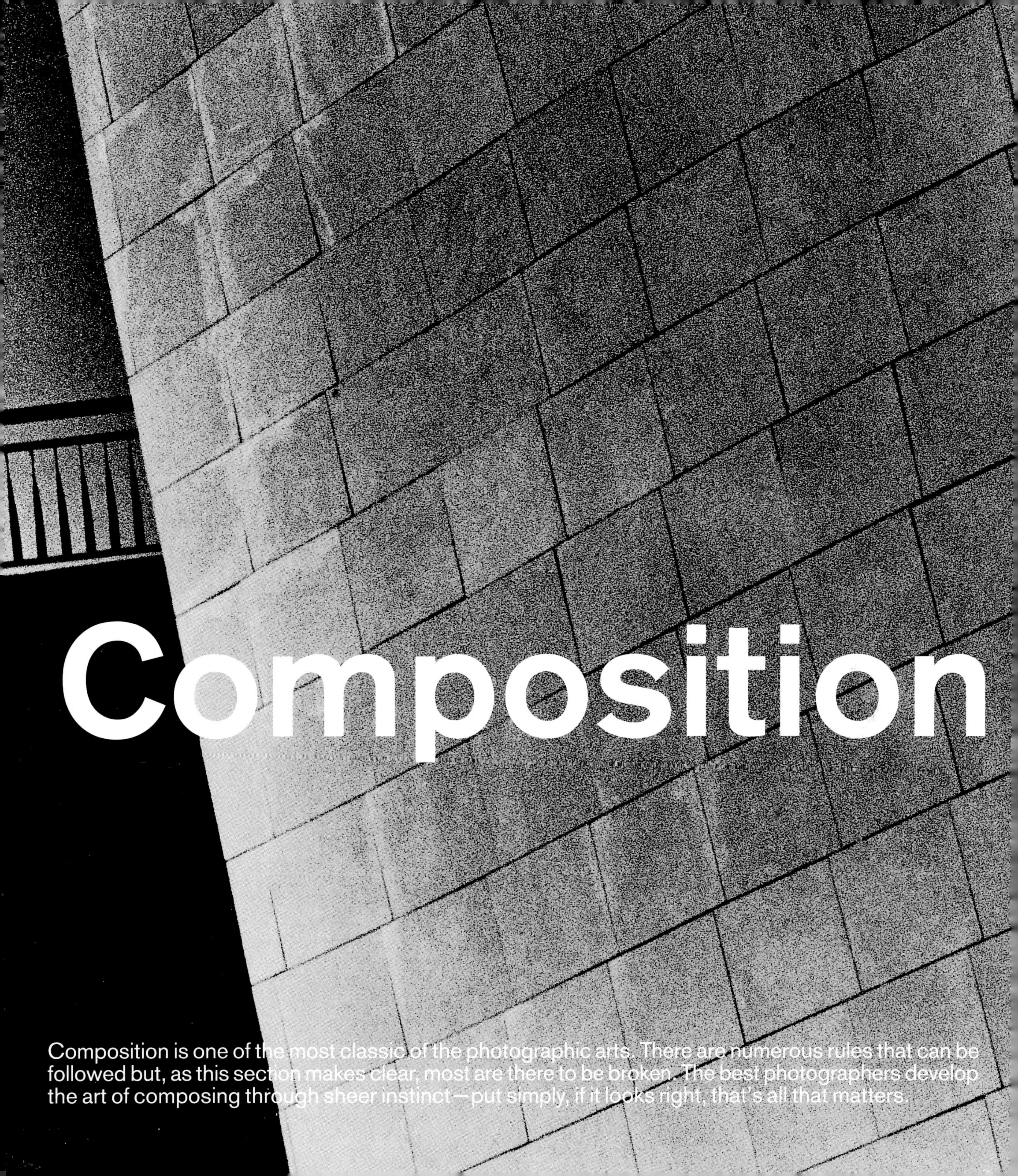

Composition

Composition is one of the most classic of the photographic arts. There are numerous rules that can be followed but, as this section makes clear, most are there to be broken. The best photographers develop the art of composing through sheer instinct—put simply, if it looks right, that's all that matters.

This is a corner of an extraordinary new art gallery, the Arken Museum, which has opened in Denmark. It's typified by a very bold and powerful design that features a free-standing main wall, around two feet wide that finishes with this striking diagonal edge. The structure reacts very strongly to natural light and, as the sun reached its maximum height in the sky, the shadows that were created defined its shape and accentuated its graphic qualities.

We set up our picture to make the most of this, picking a viewpoint that included just a segment of the wall in the left of the frame and this then became a very dominant element of the composition. The side of the wall facing us was in deep shadow while its leading edge was picked out as a bright highlight and this created a dramatic foreground, one that almost resembles a slash across the face of a canvas. In the background weakened sunlight is reflecting on to a distant wall and the fact that there's some highlight there helps to suggest a relationship between the various components of this building and ties everything together.

This is very much the way that we like to work when photographing a structure. It's rather like a portrait of a person in a way: you want to put across some of their character in the picture rather than just produce a representation of them. By the same token it's unusual for us to photograph the whole façade of a building. We would rather stand back and look for a detail that says something about what it feels like actually to experience a particular place and the lighting will be crucial in helping us to achieve that.

Anderson & Low

Composition

Arken #1 by Anderson & Low
Mamiya 6x7cm, 90mm lens, Kodak T-Max 100 film.

"It's rather like a portrait of a person in a way: you want to put across some of their character in the picture rather than just produce a representation of them."

Technique The sky was an important element of the picture here and we were lucky in that there were some excellent cloud formations around on this particular day. To emphasise them we fitted an orange filter which, by absorbing the blue light, allowed the sky to darken down considerably in the final print without affecting the tone in the clouds.

Printing and Processing This is a picture that is all about contrast level and we increased this at the printing stage by using a high grade of paper. By doing this we accentuated the difference between the highlight and shadow areas and achieved almost a pure black and white in the wall to the left to heighten its impact.

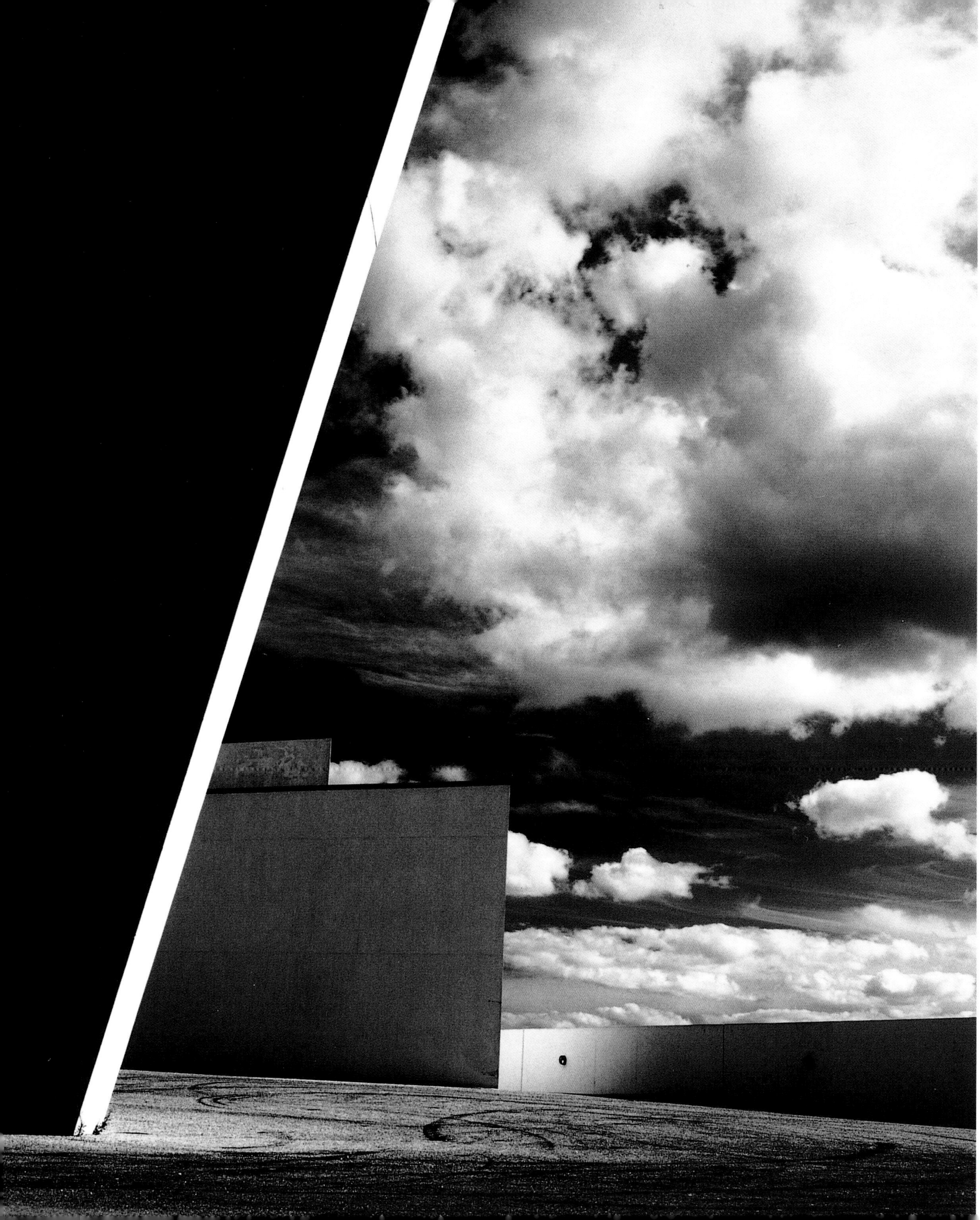

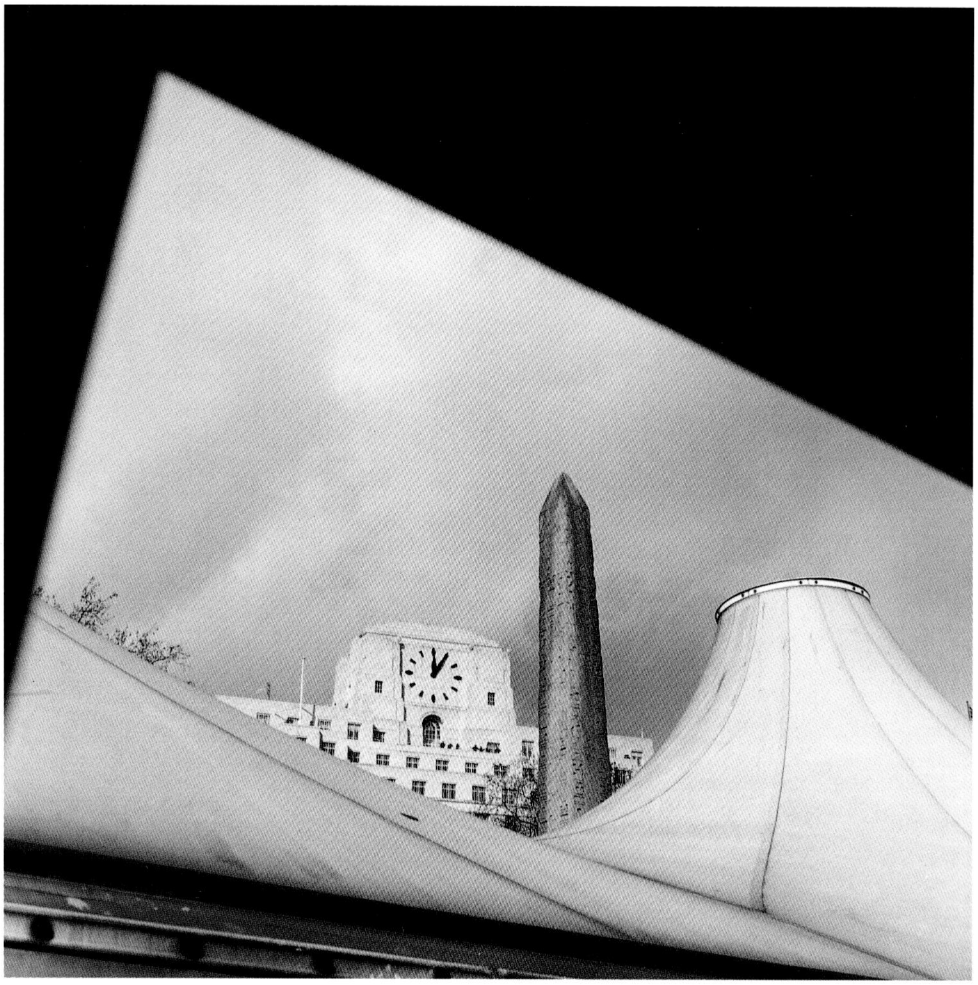

Cleopatra's Needle by Manuela Höfer
Hasselblad 500CM, 80mm lens, Ilford HP5 film.
Exposure 1/125sec at f/8

I had set myself a project to photograph famous landmarks in cities around the world in an original way, which was no easy thing to achieve because, of course, tourists are photographing these places all the time. This particular landmark is the ancient Egyptian column, housed on London's Embankment, which is known as Cleopatra's Needle. Normally it's almost impossible to get a good picture of it: approach it from the road and it's too big to fit in the frame, try to shoot from the other side of the river and it's just a speck on the horizon without a long lens.

I decided to try to photograph it from the river and booked a ticket for one of the tourist boats that was operating from a pier next to the column. I wanted to introduce something, however, that would make the composition interesting and unusual. Suddenly, as the sun came out for a moment and highlighted Cleopatra's Needle against a cloudy sky, I saw my picture, using the canvas cover that was fastened across the top of the boat as a natural frame to hold the picture in along the top and down one side.

The result is an assortment of shapes and structures that sit well together within the frame and it's certainly a view that I think is unique to me.

Manuela Höfer

Pointer This picture is part of a much wider set of pictures that I have called City Perspectives and I came up with the idea because I had noticed how many city centres around the world were now starting to look the same and even to have the same shops and services on offer. I wanted to look around and to explore new angles and I started by doing this on foot and then travelled on tourist buses and boats and also shot a series where I was looking out to the street through shop windows. It's a project that has inspired me for years and it's helped to give structure and a theme to my work.

Location Approaching a familiar landmark there's no need to look to produce the standard picture. If that's all you want then it's probably better to buy a postcard. Walk around and take in the ambience for a while and explore all the angles just using your eyes before starting to work with the camera. The more off beat your response the more unique it's likely to be: look particularly for reflections, unusual angles and, as here, natural frames that can be utilised.

Composition

Transamerica Tower, San Francisco by Tom Baril
Linhof 5x4in camera, 300mm lens, Kodak Tri-X film.
Exposure 1/8sec at f/32

The Transamerica Tower is the icon of San Francisco, probably the most photographed building in the city and it's a real challenge to tackle it and to get something that is a little different. I had no choice but to try, however, because I had received a commission from a client who wanted pictures of famous buildings to put around his office and so I tried to think how I might come up with something that was fresh.

As things worked out I just happened to see this particular scene as I was driving along. There was light cloud in the sky and the sun had got into a position where it was directly behind the tower. I saw the potential for a strong composition immediately and pulled the car over and set up this shot as quickly as I could. I used a long lens to enable me to isolate the building and I directed the camera straight up at it: I didn't want to use any perspective control because I liked the way that the building was distorting and I felt that it added to the impact.

The whole picture was simply a case of seeing a situation and reacting to it and sometimes the best architectural photography just happens to work out that way.

Tom Baril

"I didn't want to use any perspective control because I liked the way that the building was distorting and I felt that it added to the impact."

Technique Because the sun was behind the building the part that I could see was totally in shadow. I wanted to make sure that I got an adequate exposure so that I retained detail, however, and so I metered from the shadow area and then, even though I printed dark, I knew that the detail would still be contained in the print.

Pointer The basic rule of photography is that there are no rules, just guidelines that can, on occasion, be disregarded if it will result in a stronger picture. The fact that Tom Baril aimed his camera directly towards the light source should, in theory, have resulted in an unsuccessful picture but here the result is so dramatic and different that the end has justified the means.

Courtesy of Bonni Benrubi Gallery, New York.

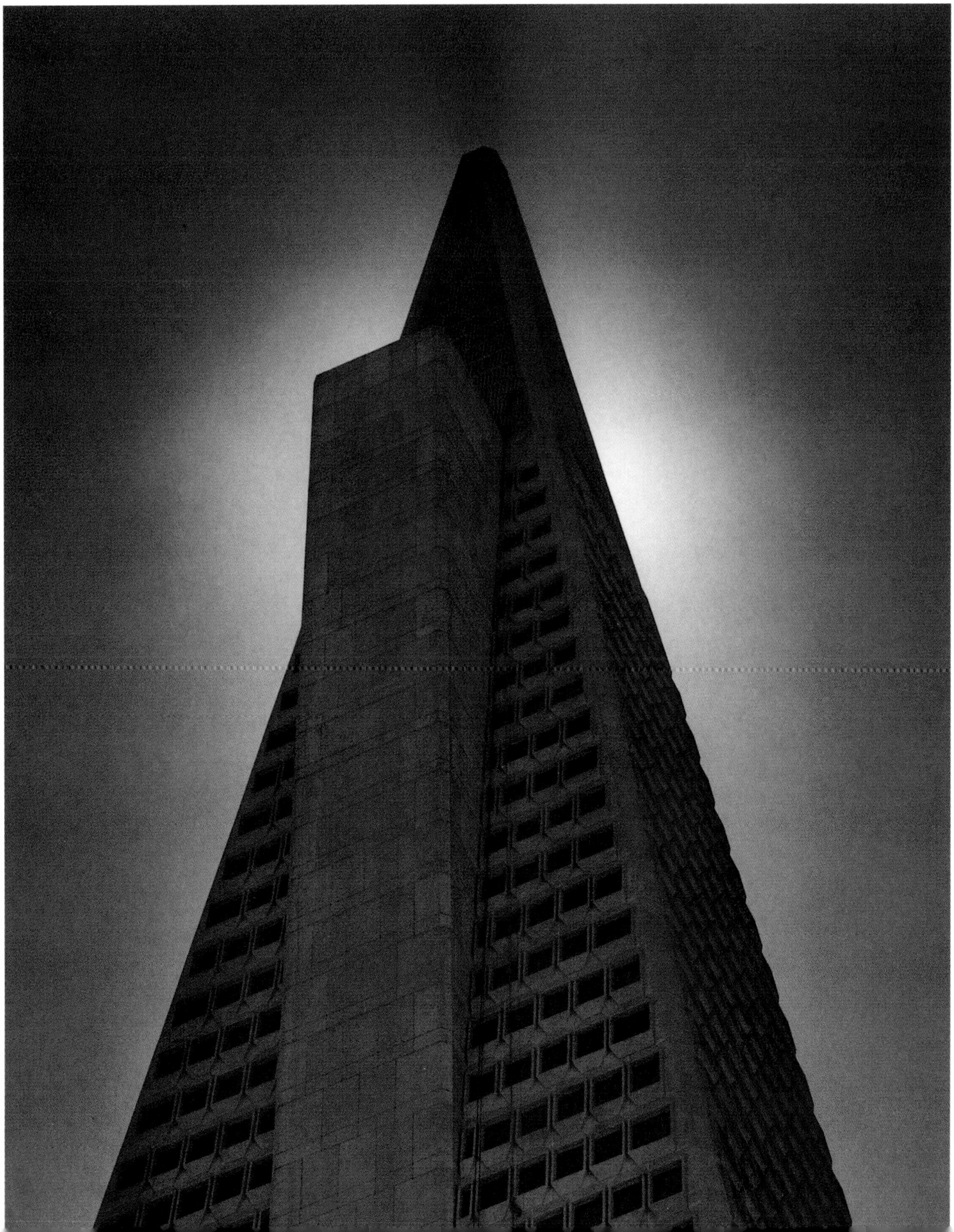

Church at Roebus, Namibia by Simon Norfolk
Mamiya 6, 75mm lens, 220 Tri-X film (ISO 320).
Exposure 1/15sec at f/16

I came across this picture perfect desert chapel at a place called Roebus, which was close to the edge of the Namib Desert in Namibia. It was a surprise discovery because it was at least 30 miles from anywhere in a region that was difficult to access because there were very few roads. I imagine that there must have been some waterholes nearby and that this chapel was built to service the needs of the people who were using these.

When I was composing the picture I had several aims in mind. I wanted to emphasise the isolation of this place but I also wanted to make a point about the history of this area and the fact that it had witnessed a terrible event during the years when it was a German colony. In what became the first genocide of the 20th century, some 80,000 members of the nomadic Herero tribe were driven into the desert and denied access to waterholes. The church played its part in the massacre and so I wanted to symbolise this by showing this building sitting under the weight of a dark and oppressive sky.

The use of a square format adds strength to a composition where the sky is dominant and I framed my picture so that the church took up no more than ten per cent of the image area, locking the camera on to a steady tripod to ensure that it didn't move. Even though it takes up such a tiny part of the composition, the church is still the focus of the picture and consequently that's where the eye goes to first.

Simon Norfolk

Technique I wanted to emphasise the sky and to build up tone in this area of the picture on the negative itself and so I took this picture through an orange filter. The use of a red would have given me a more dramatic effect but this would have been at the cost of heightening the contrast in the foreground to an unacceptable level. Orange was a good compromise, increasing the tone in the sky and giving me a good basis for further burning in of this area at the printing stage while ensuring that the detail around the church was salvageable from the negative that I achieved.

I made my print on Sterling Premium FBVC paper (now Fotospeed FBVC) and developed it in a Tetenal developer, Eukobrom, which gave me the cold tone that I wanted. I finished by immersing it in Thiocarbamide toner which I had made up to give me a chocolate-brown finish (see printing and processing section).

Exhibiting I had the idea for a project to photograph landscapes in some of the areas around the world that had suffered terrible events and yet were still, in many ways, very beautiful. It was very much something that was pre-visualised, and I knew exactly what I wanted to do, and the kind of pictures that I wanted to take. Because I hadn't mounted an exhibition before, however, it was impossible to get anyone to agree to get behind me until I had spent a year or so shooting quite a substantial part of the project, and so initially at least it was a struggle to get things moving.

I agreed a book deal for ***For Most Of It I Have No Words*** with the publisher Dewi Lewis quite early on, but getting an exhibition arranged was much harder. I've got a thick file of letters, probably around 70 or more, which details the correspondence I sent to galleries and the response was invariably negative. I even took a set of pictures to big photographic gatherings such as the festival in Arles, just trying to get some kind of feedback and I did make a few contacts this way. Notably I met up with the Blue Sky Gallery from Portland, which now represents me in America, and which recently sold an entire set of the exhibition for $15,000. I used every opportunity I had to go and see people with my pictures, because this personal contact is a hundred times more effective than just putting a selection of pictures in the post.

Eventually Impressions Gallery in York took the show on, and it opened at the end of 1998 to coincide with the 50th anniversary of the signing of the UN Convention on Genocide. From here the show has toured extensively, and I've always tried to get to the gallery concerned on the day of hanging to make sure that the pictures work together in the space and that everything is presented in the correct sequence, something that is very important with this body of work. I'll normally take some extra prints with me so that a few pictures can be swapped around if the need arises.

Putting together a project such as this one was extremely involved: I worked hard to get publicity from a variety of quarters, and I also managed to get some generous sponsorship from Fotospeed who manufacture the Sterling Premium printing paper and Fotospeed chemistry that I use. All these things were essential if the project was to be viable: I think if I put together another show at some point the fact that I've got this one behind me will make things easier for me.

Factory, New Jersey by Tom Baril
Linhof 5x4in camera, 135mm lens, Polaroid Type 55 film.
Exposure $\frac{1}{2}$ second at f/22

This is one of those locations that I've discovered in New York and I keep going back to it because I think it has so much to offer. To the people who live there and who look at this bridge and factory every single day, it's really nothing special. They're a part of their lives but they don't really see them. To me, however, they have a great beauty about them and they work very well together in a single composition: this is a niçely designed factory, as many of the older ones often are, and they're becoming harder to find these days because so many are being pulled down. I'm very attracted to it and I think, as a subject for an architectural study, it has a lot to offer.

I composed this picture so that the bridge cuts across the top of the image. It's a strong diagonal and a way of adding interest to this area and of creating a natural frame for the factory. The main reason I included it, however, was to act as a comment about the relationship that exists between industrial structures and to perhaps make people think a little about what they're really looking at.

Tom Baril

Printing and Processing I produce the majority of my prints on Kodak Ektalure paper and add tone by immersing them in a bath of cold tea, which gives them a green patina. There's no great secret to this process: I generally use about eight Liptons tea bags per gallon to make my working strength solution! The result is a subtle effect that takes the print away from a pure black and white finish.

Pointer Type 55 is one of the oldest Polaroid film materials available, and it gives the photographer both a print and a negative. It's inserted into a Polaroid back that slips into the back of a studio camera in the normal way and, on exposure, it's pulled out to release the chemicals held inside. Then it's given the usual processing time of one minute whereupon it can be peeled apart and a black and white contact print examined. This print needs to be coated quite quickly with a chemical film to prevent it oxidising, while the negative has to be cleared with a salt solution. Particular care needs to be taken, however, to frame the picture exactly as it is required because if you intend to feature the edge of the picture there's no possibility of cropping.

Courtesy of Bonni Benrubi Gallery, New York.

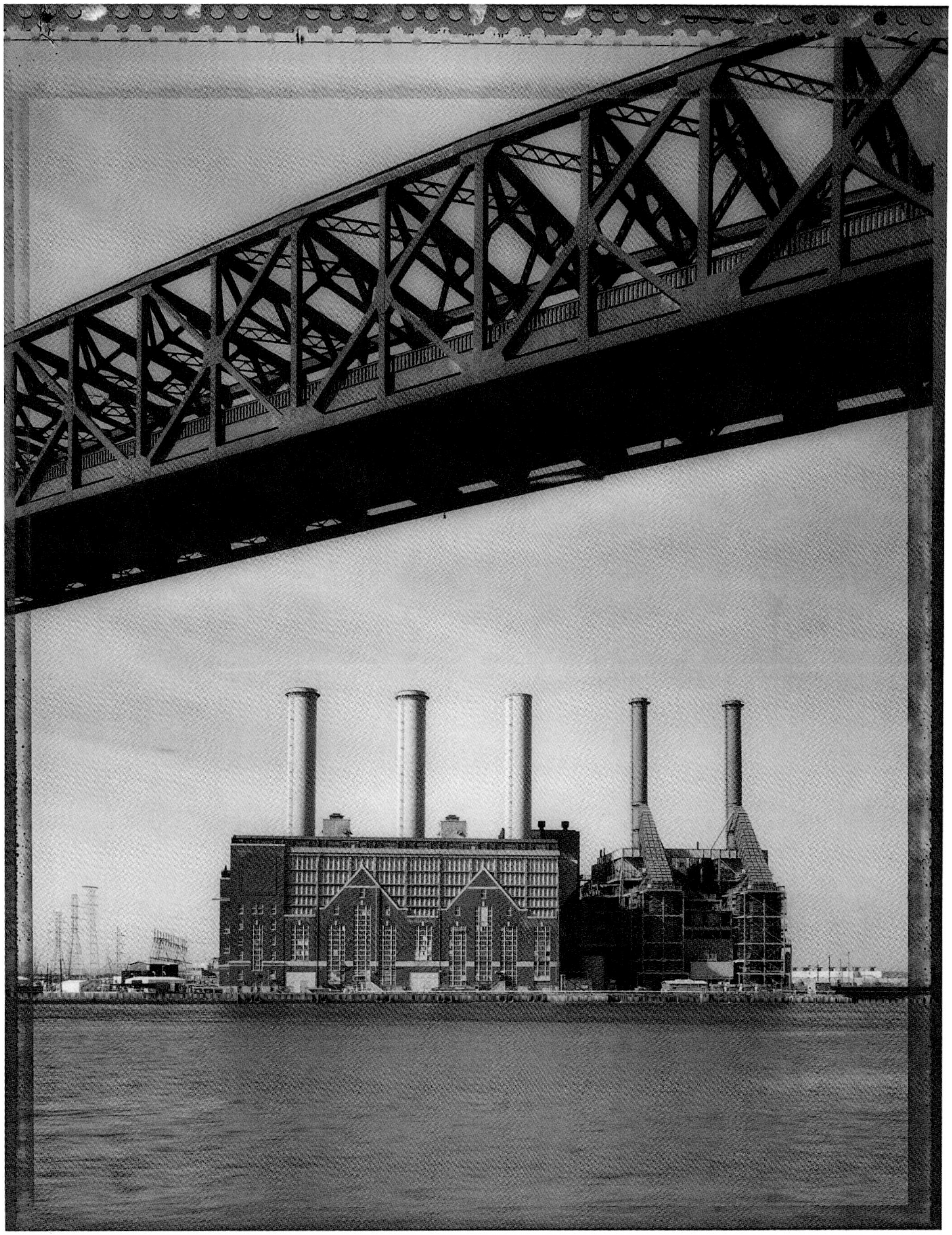

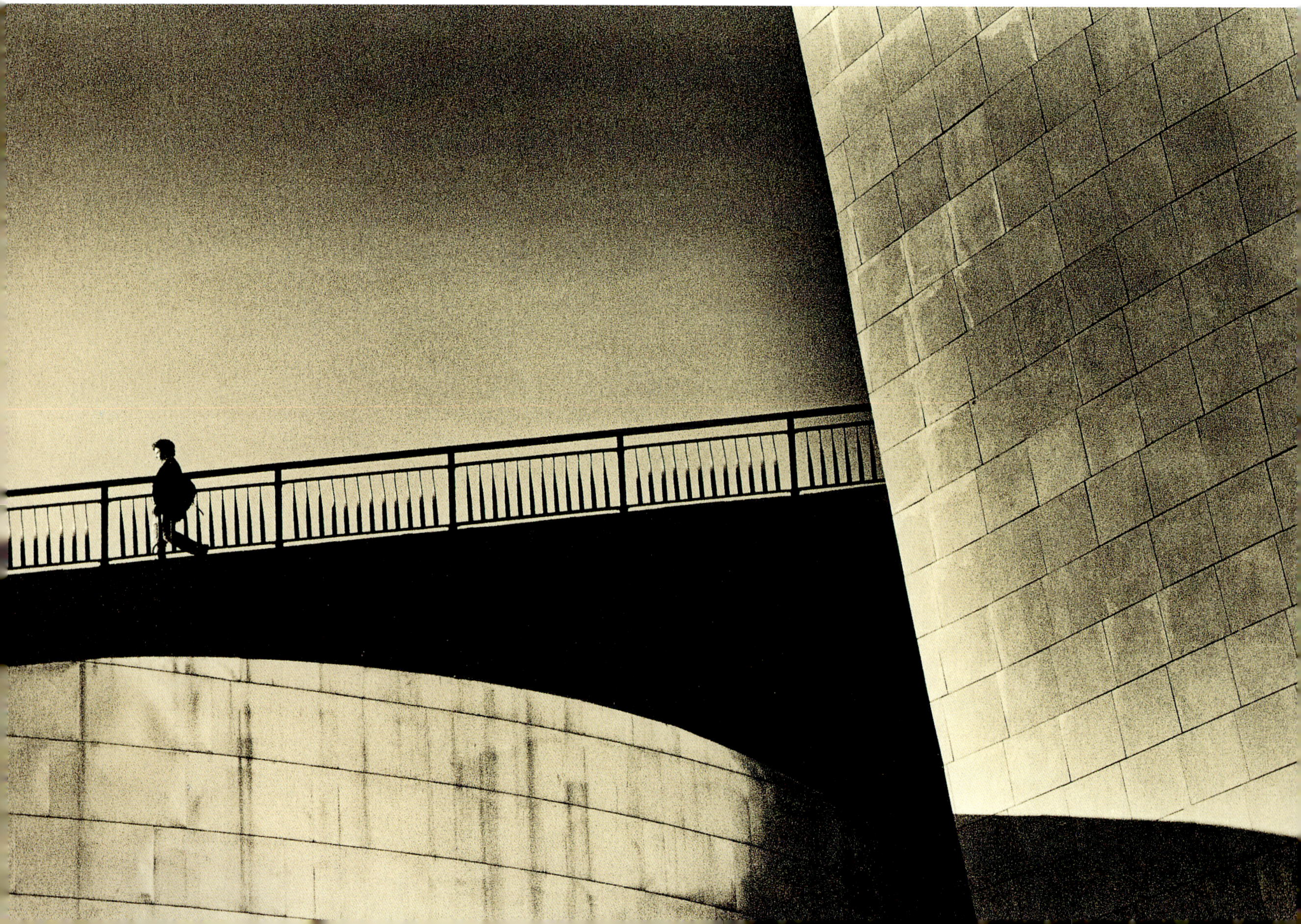

Guggenheim Museum by Adrian Ensor
Nikkormat 35mm SLR, 105mm lens, Kodak Tri-X film.
Exposure 1/125sec at f/11

The Guggenheim Museum in Bilbao, Spain, is one of the most remarkable examples of modern architecture in the world and I was inspired to pay a visit after seeing the work of other photographers. Although most of what I had seen was in colour, my prime motivation was to see what it could offer me in terms of black and white images and I spent several hours at the location, during the day and at night too, looking for details and angles that would give me something that was personal to me.

I was particularly taken with the bridge that led to the museum and felt that this had the potential to offer me something special in terms of a graphic image. Taking up a position down by the base of the building I was able to look up at it and I framed tightly using a long lens to compress the perspective a little and to pull out the angles and shapes that I wanted. There was still something missing, however, and I realised that there was nothing in the view to add the necessary sense of scale or touch of humanity.

By waiting for someone to come along the whole picture suddenly came alive and I waited for this figure to reach a point where he could be seen against a clear section of the railings and there was still some space between him and the edge of the picture. The angles within this image are all working together and they have combined to make this a very dynamic composition, one that I think says something about this building that is original to me.

Adrian Ensor

Printing and Processing I suffered a disappointment with my Guggenheim pictures because I had made a mistake with my exposure calculations and a lot of the images were quite seriously underexposed. I left them to one side for a time until Jeff Conn, one of the printers working at my darkroom, saw them and suggested that he should have a go at producing them as lith prints, a process that actually works better with negatives that are a touch thin.

It was the first time that anyone other than myself had printed my negatives and I was delighted with the results. The technique itself is straightforward enough: the picture is exposed on to a conventional sheet of paper, in this case Oriental Seagull, and then the development is carried out in lith developer. When fresh, this produces a result that is extremely contrasty and features a pink tone but when the developer starts to become exhausted the results are actually much more interesting, although you might have to wait several minutes for the print to reach the density that you want. This particular image was produced in developer that was getting quite old and the effect was to create apparent grain in the sky above the figure, which I really liked. It had the characteristic pink tone and I decided to subdue this a little by toning it in thiocarbamide, which has lifted the image and given it an almost golden appearance.

My Top Tip Instead of using the lith developer in its fresh state you can speed things up by putting sheets of fogged paper into it and then leaving them there for a period. Another way of helping the ageing process along is to add a litre of used lith developer to the fresh mix.

"The angles within this image are all working together and they have combined to make this a very dynamic composition."

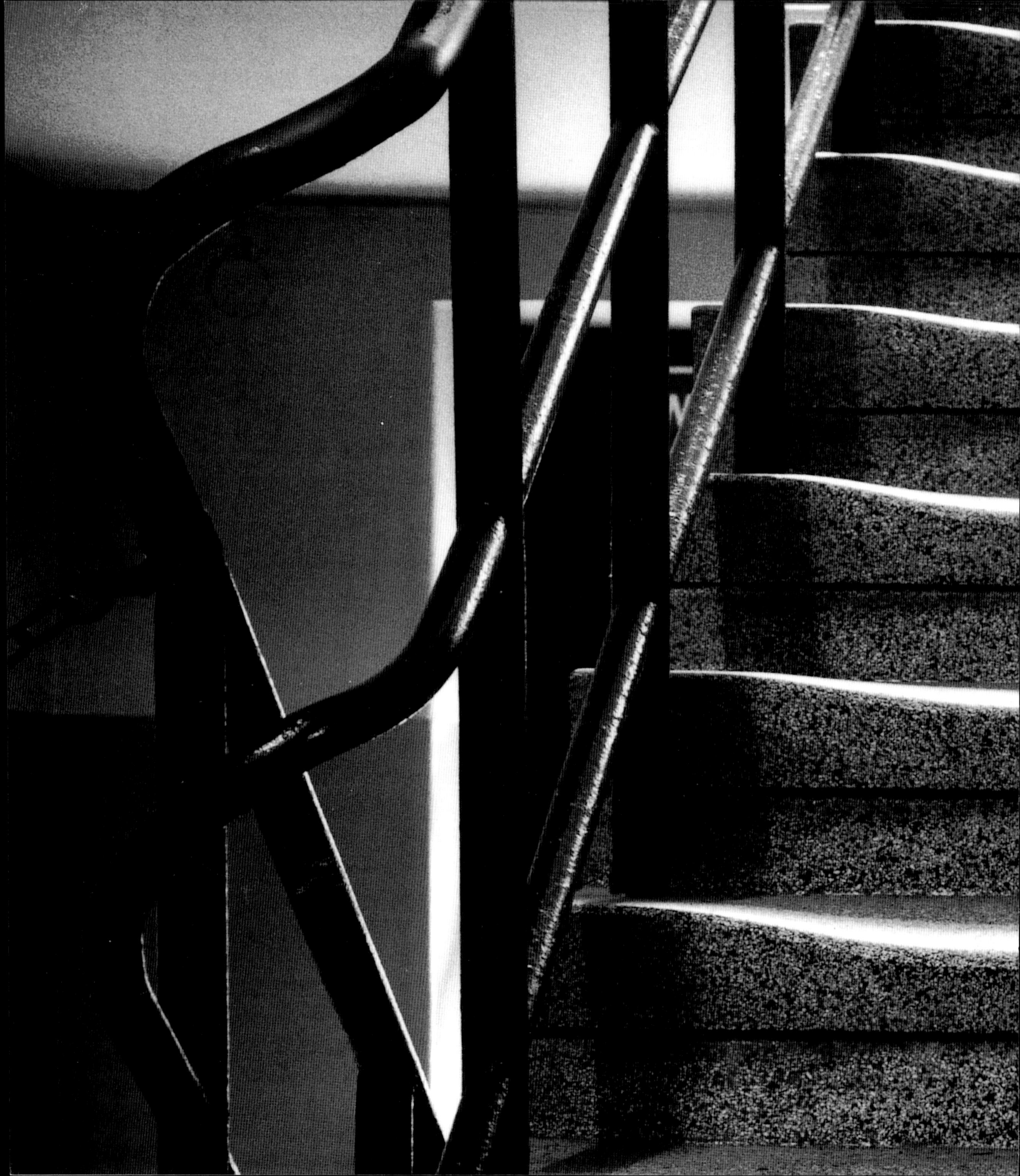

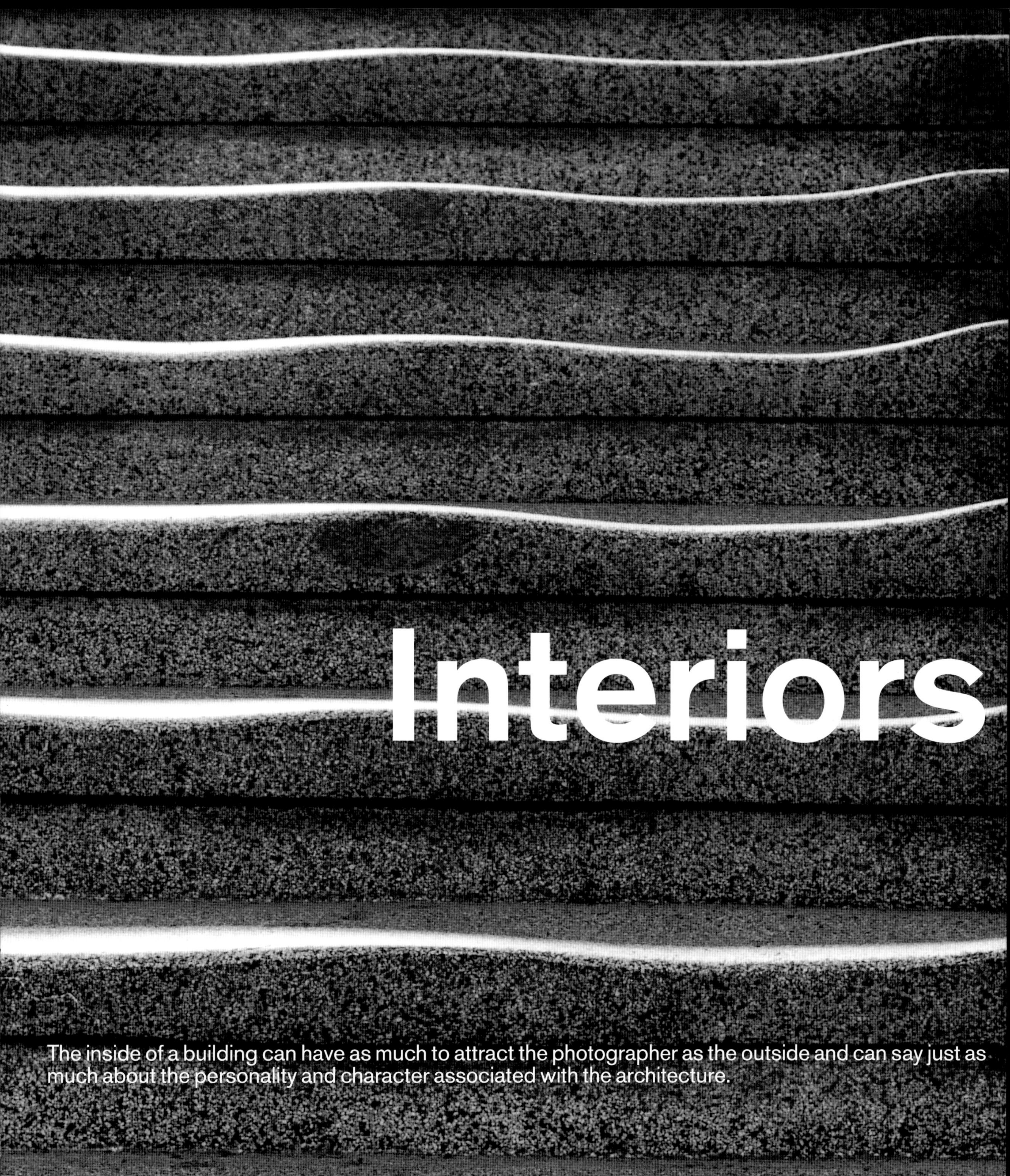

Interiors

The inside of a building can have as much to attract the photographer as the outside and can say just as much about the personality and character associated with the architecture.

Steps at Birmingham Snow Hill Station by Terry Hope
Olympus OM1, 28mm lens, Kodak Tri-x film.
Exposure 1/15sec at f/5.6

"Black and white is excellent at conveying the atmosphere of a scene like this because it adds a sombre edge."

The shattered remains of a derelict building hold a fascination for me and I love to spend time exploring and looking for details that say something about the function that a place once had. There's a mixture of pathos and sadness created by the neglect and a kind of strange beauty that comes from the resistance to decay of certain elements, such as this sturdy set of stairs that once echoed to the pounding of commuters' feet on a regular basis.

I decided that I would set up a shot that looked up at the steps as they stretched away to platform level and I was lucky in that the state of the roof above this point was such that the rain had leaked in and had caused everything to get wet. This had a number of benefits: it meant that the edges of the steps towards the bottom of the flight reflected the light and made up a series of parallel lines that broke up an area that could otherwise just have been dense shadow. It also made sure that there was a patch of highlight at the foot of the stairs that I could use to balance the light beckoning at the top of the picture. Black and white is excellent at conveying the atmosphere of a scene like this because it adds a sombre edge, while colour might pick up on some element such as a red door or a patch of brightly painted wall and would consequently introduce an upbeat feel that was quite inappropriate.

Terry Hope

My Favourite Tip I wasn't trying to achieve an accurate record of this location, rather I was hoping to convey my impression of the place. With this particular scene I decided that a standard lens would fail to show what it really felt like to be down there in the darkness. For a start it would not have allowed me to include anything like enough of the scene around the foot of the stairs and consequently much of the mood would have been lost. It also would have given me a much smaller depth of field and, since I was hand holding the camera, I didn't have the option to stop down and to opt for a slower shutter speed. The final thing that my 28mm lens offered me over the standard was the characteristic perspective of the wide angle, which ensured that the foreground was emphasised in terms of scale against the rest of the stairway. This allowed the stairs themselves to be effectively stretched out and made the patch of daylight at the top appear further away than it actually was. It all enhanced the feel that I was after and added a great deal to the picture.

Technique Exposure was difficult to estimate in these conditions, because the contrast levels between the daylight at the top of the stairs and the shadows in the foreground was impossibly high. All I could do was to aim for a happy medium—I took a reading from a point around midway up the stairs and bracketed from there—and then hoped that I had enough shadow and highlight detail to allow adjustments to be made in the darkroom. Adrian Ensor, who produced this print, held back some of the print exposure in the foreground to make sure the highlight there didn't become too dark and he also gave extra exposure to the brighter areas of the picture, such as the top of the stairs, to add tone there and to prevent it burning out.

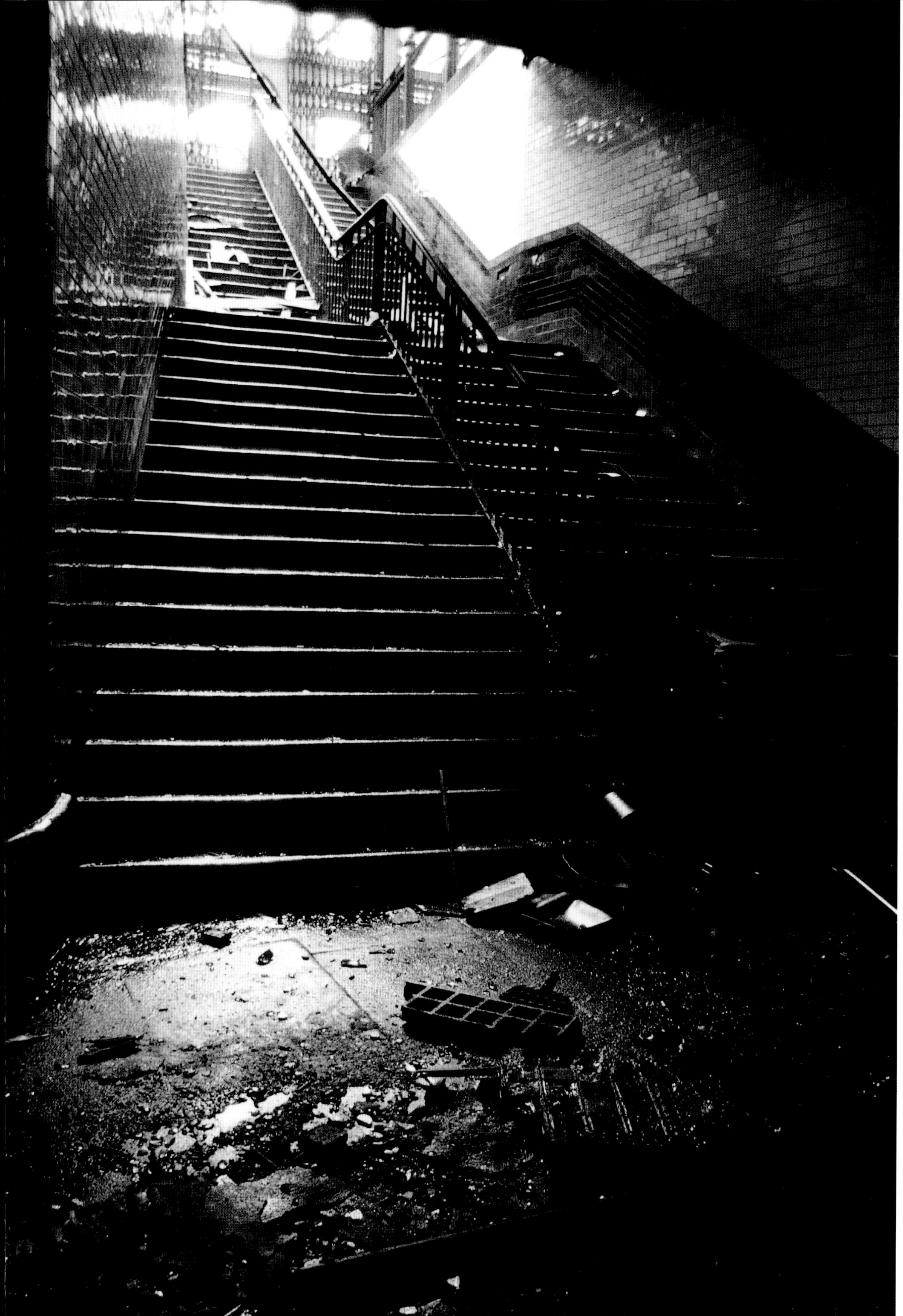

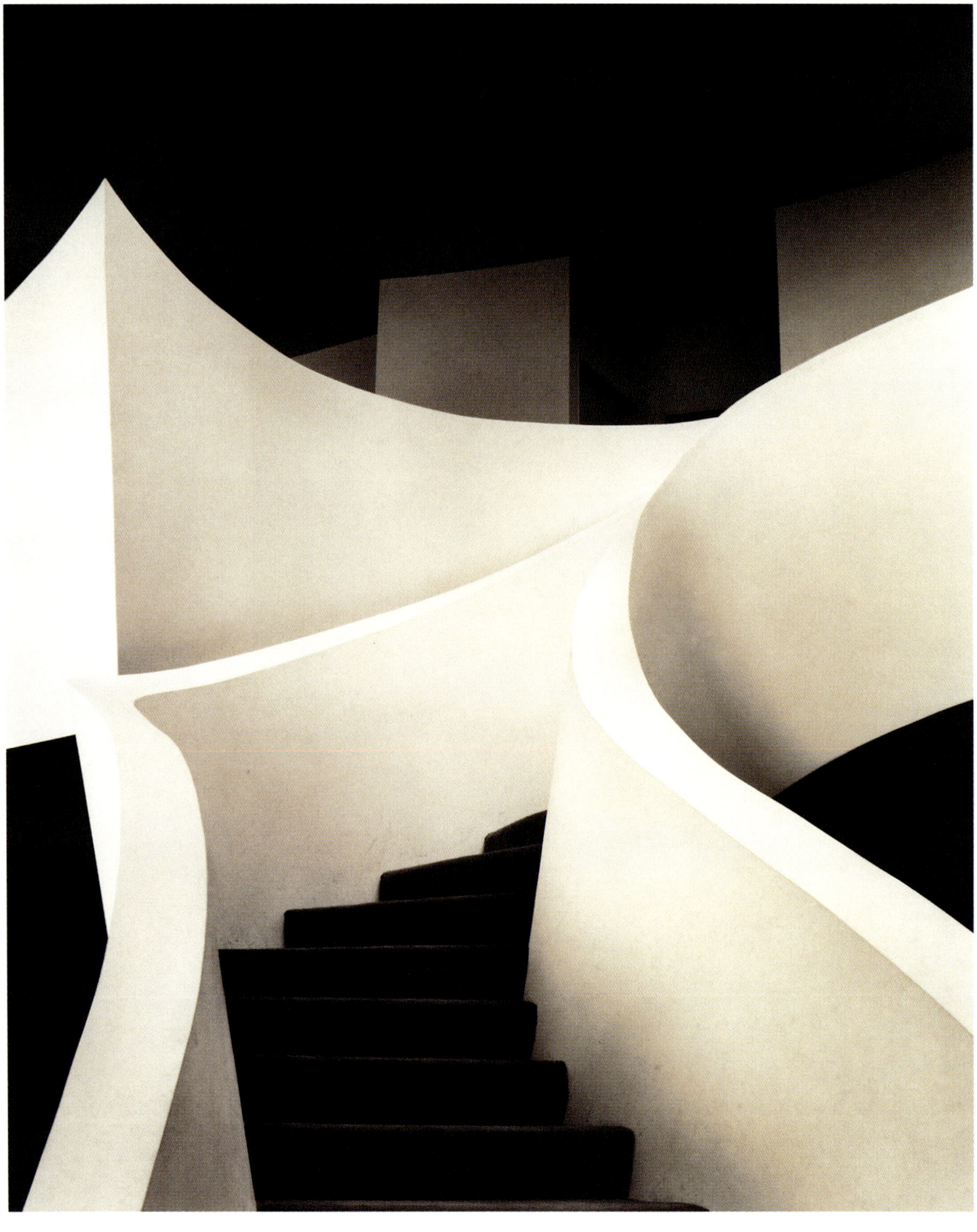

Interior #2 by Anderson & Low
Mamiya 6x7cm, 90mm lens, Ilford FP4 film.

We received a commission to produce a series of images that looked at the sensual elements of modern architecture and one of the locations that we visited was Che House in Australia. As we walked in we were overwhelmed by the sculpturing of the interior. The first thing that you see is that staircase and then you take in the fact that there are no straight walls in this place at all, everything has a curve or a slanting angle. It was this initial feeling that we got when we first arrived that we wanted to put across in our pictures. We wanted to show the character of the place, to make a feature of all the swoops and curves that were there and to put across how it felt to encounter it for the first time.

With interiors, one of the things that we are very concerned to do wherever possible—and it's what we did here—is to use the ambient lighting that is coming in through skylights and windows. It's an important consideration because a good designer will have thought about how a building will react to the light that's entering and will have accommodated that in the plans. If you light the whole place up with artificial sources then you could destroy the ambience that is such a crucial part of a building's character.

Anderson & Low

My Top Tip We're not obsessed with lighting every corner of an interior. It doesn't produce a natural-looking result and, by getting rid of the shadows, you're removing an important element of your picture, since these will contribute as much to your picture as the highlights will. Shadows have a vital role to play because they will add sculpturing and give depth to your picture.

Printing and Processing This picture is all about mid tones and that's what we printed for. The picture was finished by giving it a sepia split tone. The print was placed in a bleach bath for a short period until just the highlights and some of the mid tones were starting to be affected and then it was washed and placed in sepia toner. Because the blacks had not been touched they kept their original tone, as did some of the mid tone areas, while other parts of the picture took on a warm colour. In general there are some browns in the mid-tone but only just, so that the final effect is not overwhelming.

This picture is one of a set that won Anderson & Low the Gold Award in the Association of Photographers Eighteenth Awards

British Museum by Adrian Ensor
Rolleiflex 6x6cm, fixed 75mm lens, Ilford HP5 film.
Exposure 1/250sec at f/16

With the opening of the Great Court at the British Museum in London, an area that, at 6100 square metres in size, is the largest enclosed public space in Europe, I knew that I had to try to present a view that was slightly different. It was tempting to look at the classical architecture and to step back and to show that in its entirety, but I reasoned that there was more to be said and I spent several hours there and returned at different times of the day, to see if there wasn't a train of original thought that I could follow up.

The answer in the end came through the natural daylight that was flooding into the space through the glass roof. As it fell on the walls of the structures in this space it threw the most amazing shadows, created by the pattern of the roof itself. By following the shadow as it changed position throughout the day I could judge when it was going to reach an area that would create a strong image: I concentrated just on this corner of one of the arches and incorporated the door in my composition to add an area of interest.

I love the way that these intricate shadows suggest movement in this most solid of stone structures and also the fact that this is a view that not everyone will recognise. The light has taken this building away from its more usual appearance and added something special and, had I not persevered in my search for a new angle, I would have undoubtedly missed the moment.

Adrian Ensor

By following the shadow as it changed position throughout the day I could judge when it was going to reach an area that would create a strong image

Technique Although taken on a square format, Adrian decided to look closely at his images at the printing stage and he decided that this picture worked better as an upright. Some photographers operate a strict 'no cropping' policy but it can prove inhibiting, especially to those starting to explore architecture for the first time. For those who do want to explore the options at the contact print stage it's a simple matter to produce a couple of L-shaped cards, which can then be used in combination with each other to provide a simple masking tool that will allow various crops to be visually assessed.

Pointer The great thing about natural lighting is that it will change in character throughout the year, which makes it capable of creating a totally different feel in the summer, for example, than in the winter. It makes photography of this kind continually challenging and exciting and it's a compelling reason for a photographer to return many times to a favourite location.

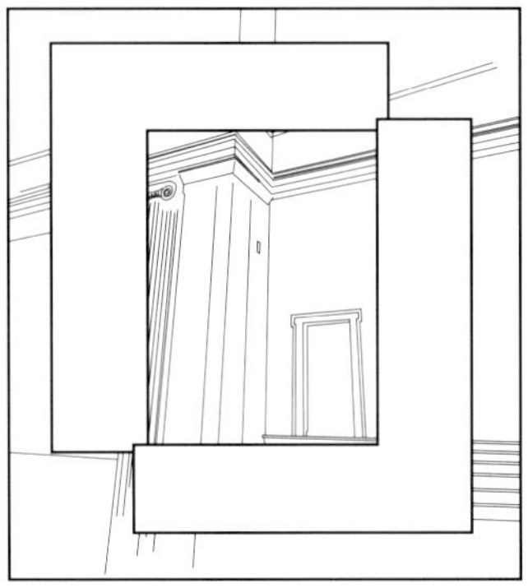

A pair of L-shaped cards used together will help a photographer to see the effect of different crops'

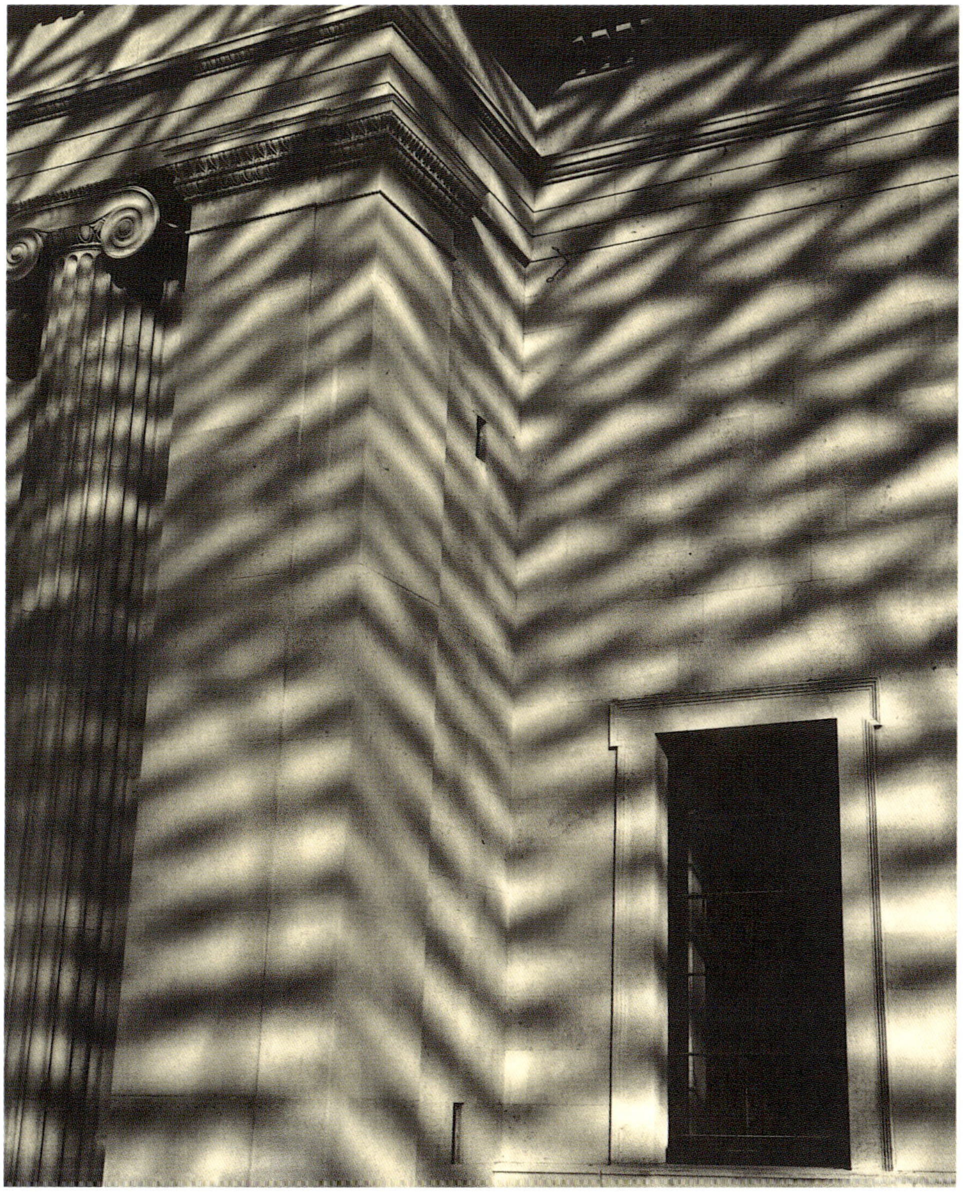

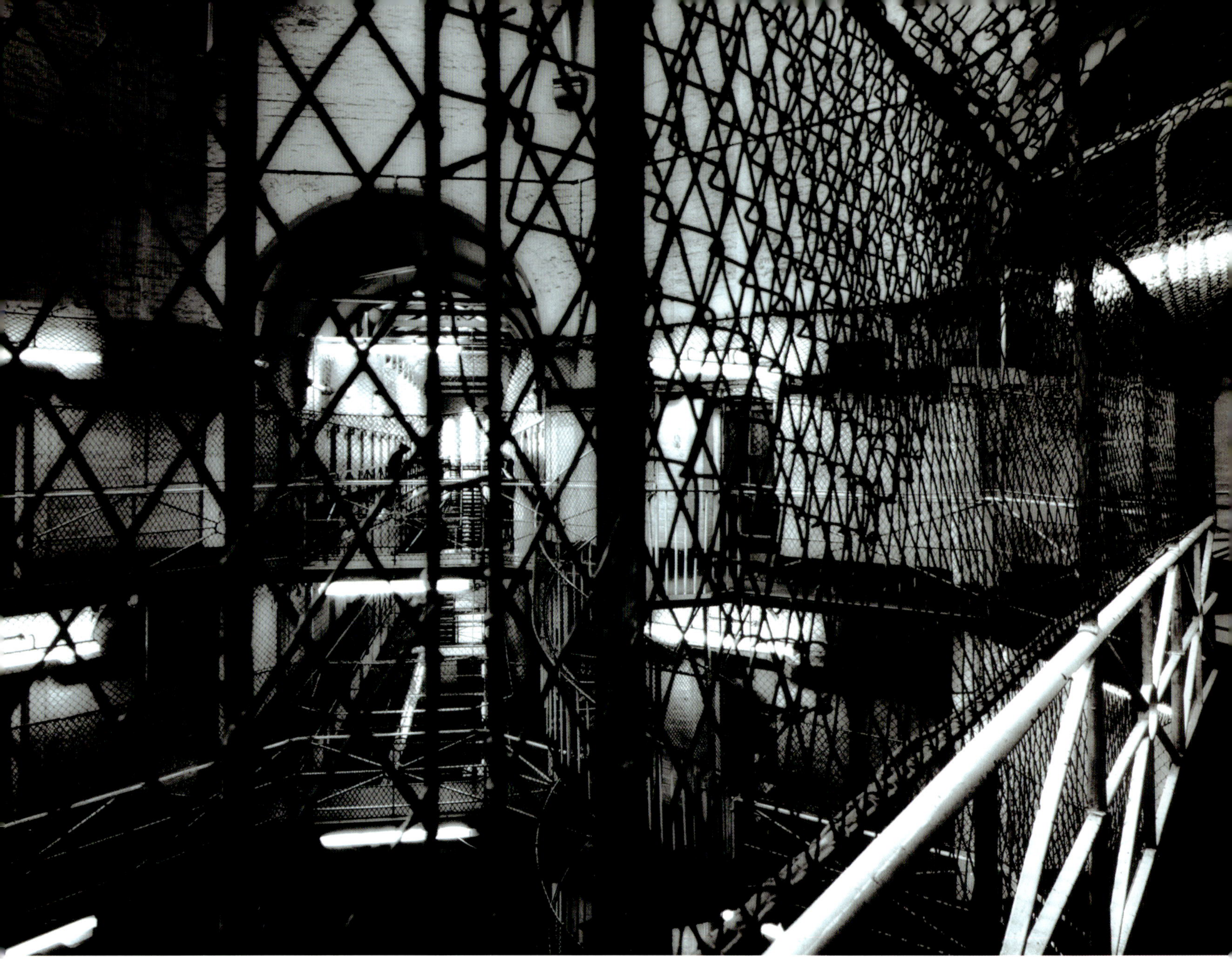

Prison Interior by John Claridge
Deardorff 5x4in camera, 75mm lens, Kodak Tri-X film.
Exposure two seconds at f/11

I was given a commission by a magazine to photograph the way that a management team was operating at a prison and it was a fantastic assignment because, within reason, I had a free rein to go wherever I wanted and to produce the pictures that I felt matched the brief.

You could tell that this was not a nice place to be—I got the feeling that the inmates here were almost liked caged animals—and I wanted to take an overall picture that put this idea across. I set my camera up on one of the main landings and looked across towards a window at the far end, using the wire that bordered this area as my focal point. The light was quite dim, just fluorescent strips, and I realised that the shutter speed was going to be quite slow even with the aperture opened fairly wide. Stopping it right down to achieve the kind of depth of field that would have brought the wire into focus along with the rest of the interior wasn't really an option and so I used camera movements to achieve the same end, introducing a small amount of front tilt and checking the result on the rear ground glass screen until I was sure that I had what I wanted.

John Claridge

Pointer It's often the details that lift a scene and make it something special and here I was lucky in that a warder happened to cross the walkway in the middle distance just as I was about to take the picture. It wasn't planned in any way but it helped to give the picture a subtle lift and added a touch of human interest.

Composition John Claridge has a natural eye for the look of a picture and doesn't consciously set out to compose in any particular way. Here, however, he has instinctively arranged the elements of the photograph to create maximum impact. The window at the far end of the prison is visible through the archway on the left and the camera is looking directly towards it, as though it's a sign that there is still a world outside of this place. Meanwhile the white railings in the bottom right hand corner of the picture, making up the only area of light tone in the frame, create a bold diagonal line that encourages the eye to travel to this part of the picture as well.

The Sea of Steps by Frederick Evans
Platinum print. Technical Details unknown

This is one of the classic architectural studies of the 20th century, taken at the stairway to the Chapter House and Vicar's Close, Wells Cathedral by the celebrated photographer Frederick Evans in 1903. The title he chose for the picture explained much of the symbolism that he was trying to achieve, the steps rippling and building like waves as they sweep towards the light of the doorways above. Look closely and there's more that can be gleaned from the picture: the steps, dating from the 13th century, have been worn down by generations of use and through the archway in particular there's barely a straight line to be seen, emphasising the human presence and the history of the building in an understated but powerful way.

Evans was very much a traditionalist who liked to present his subjects in an uncontrived manner and to make effective use of the volume and perspective that he found in a scene. Taken with a plate camera, this picture would have been carefully set up and composed, the equipment of the time ensuring that nothing could be hurried, something that was often to the benefit of the picture, which would become more considered as a result. The lens was a standard, so that the result was much as the eye would have seen it, and lighting was natural and not tampered with in any way. In short there's little here that takes the image away from reality and yet it's captured a corner of a great building in a way that has brought out the full power of its scale and beauty.

Composition Much of the strength of the picture lies in its classical composition. The camera has been set up to look straight on at the subject so that all the verticals in the frame have remained upright and the archway of the door on the left has been positioned carefully in the frame so that it follows the right angle of that corner precisely. The eye is led by the steps to the doorway and drawn there by the light on the landing beyond. Meanwhile the sweep of the stairs leading away to the right has created a strong diagonal across the centre of the picture, and divides it into areas that have a similar weight. Had this diagonal appeared higher or lower in the image the balance would have been lost and the picture would have lost much of its solidity.

"The standard lens, which has become less popular since zooms have come on to the scene, still has a lot to offer in terms of the natural perspective that it will offer."

Pointer Now that cameras are capable of offering the photographer so much, it's occasionally useful to go back to basics and to see what can be achieved by interfering as little as possible with the scene you're recording. The standard lens, which has become less popular since zooms have come on to the scene, still has a lot to offer in terms of the natural perspective that it will offer while simple cameras featuring just the minimum of gadgets and controls are still capable of producing excellent results and, by requiring more input from the photographer, may well encourage a more careful composition.

Picture The Royal Photographic Society, Bath

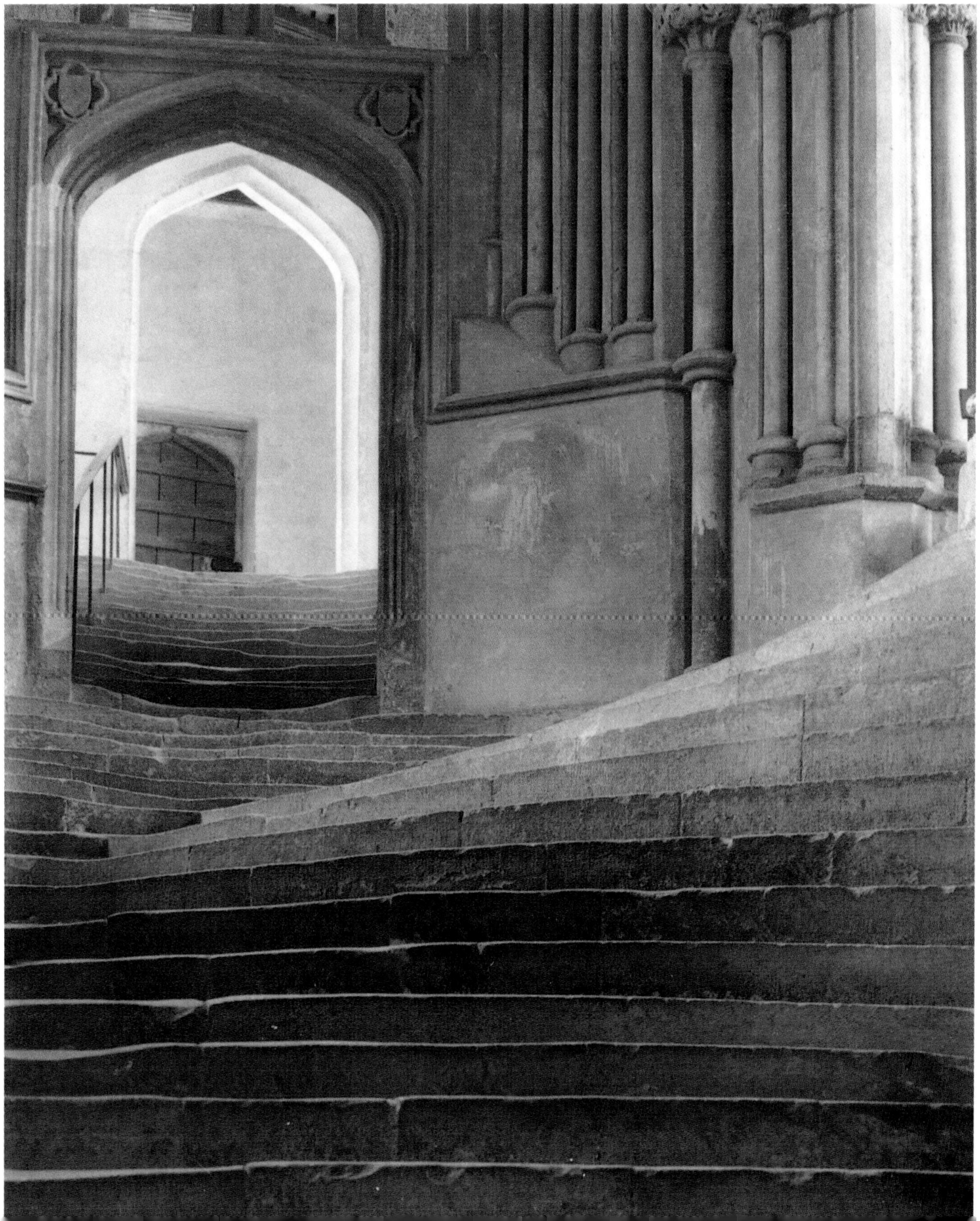

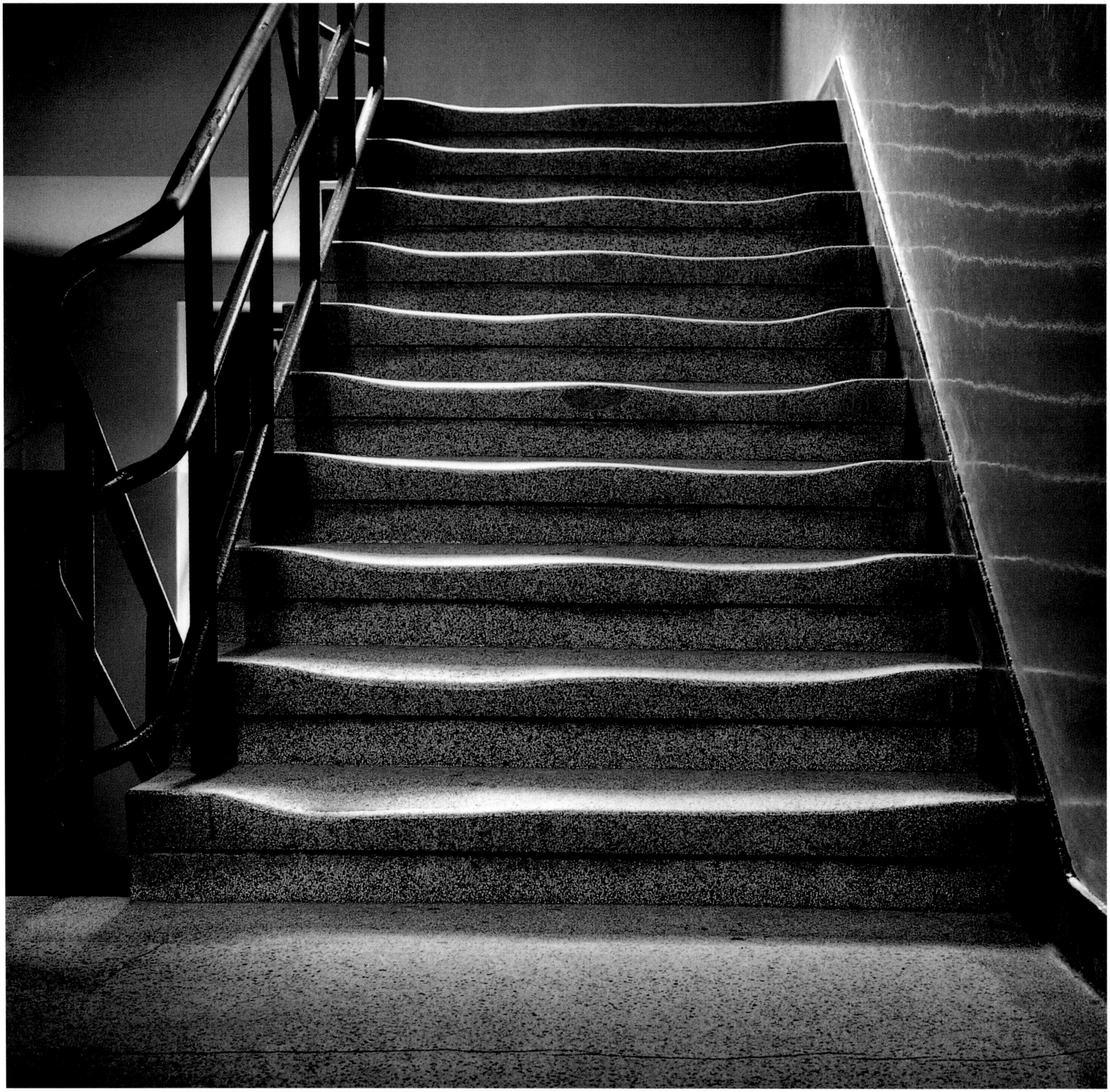

Steps at Auschwitz by Simon Norfolk
Mamiya 6, 75mm lens, 220 Tri-X film ISO 320. Exposure 1 second at f/22

A large part of what I do involves the making of pictures that attempt to comment on something that has happened in the past and often this means that I have to make use of symbolism to bring out the appropriate feeling of absence. Often it's not until people realise where my picture was taken that they understand fully what I'm trying to say and then the message hits home all the harder.

The museum at Auschwitz, in the small Polish town of Oswiecim, contains the physical remains, mostly as ash, of 1.15 million people, which makes it the biggest cemetery in the world. I took this picture in what is now the museum section and when I first saw these worn steps I just thought that it made an extraordinary statement. There's no one in view and yet you look at this picture and just have to ask yourself how many bare feet does it take to wear marks such as these on a stone stairway?

The picture was composed tightly within the square format so that the solidity of the stairs was emphasised and I framed the picture so that I didn't include the window that was situated directly above them. This was throwing light towards the camera, which spilled down and caught the edges of the steps, highlighting them and emphasising the wear that they had suffered. The tungsten light that was used by the museum to illuminate the corridors picked out the foreground and ensured that I achieved some shadow detail there, and I waited until later in the day when the light coming from outside dropped to an appropriate level to enable me to achieve the lighting balance that I wanted in this picture.

Simon Norfolk

Pointer Influences come from all sources and I very much had in mind Frederick Evans' famous picture of the 'Sea of Steps' at Wells Cathedral (see previous page) when I saw this scene. For me it was a chance to make a visual reference to one of the most famous of all architectural pictures and it was just another level on which I felt this image worked.

Technique This particular image was taken unfiltered but I also experimented with other frames where I used a filter to achieve a slightly different effect. Because the light hitting the scene is a mixture of daylight and tungsten (i..e light that either has a blue or an orange bias) it meant that a blue filter lightened the areas that were being lit by daylight—mainly the worn 'crests' of the steps—while darkening down tungsten-lit areas such as the stair risers. An orange filter had the opposite effect and the use of both filters in turn helped me to change the balance between these areas. It's all part of my philosophy, which is to work hard at the taking stage to produce the perfect negative and, once this is achieved, it makes it much easier to get the print that you want.

Detail

You don't have to include an entire building in your picture to say something about its style. Sometimes it's the details that will help you to sum up what it's really all about.

New York Doorway by Ralph Gibson
Leica M2, 90mm lens, Kodak Tri-X.
Exposure not recorded

Location Black and white film is ideally suited to location photography because it allows great play to be made, as Ralph Gibson has here, of the light and shade that surrounds a particular building. Each structure will have its own identity and its character will alter throughout the day and with each change of lighting conditions. Learn to see how it works and make use of it in your photography.

Tone and Texture Shadow is one of the most important ways of adding tone to your pictures. Its shape and position will change continually throughout the day, making it one of the great challenges of photography to utilise it in a positive way. Ralph Gibson is one of the greatest exponents of light and shade of his generation: here he has made the shadow an integral part of his composition and has used its relationship with the lighter tone of the brickwork to build his picture and to give it depth and structure.

If I were really working well I could take a picture of anything, anywhere. I don't rely on an event. The event is my own quality of perception or where I am at any given instant of my life. This doorway was just something that stood out for me: sometimes you can just stand there and you see it all. The scene was lit by bright sunlight and I exposed for the highlights so that I could drop out the shadows.

I follow the sun. I like to feel the sunlight on my eyes and I'm always looking to see how it affects the things around me. I saw this scene from a way back and used a longer lens so that I could compose it in the way that I wanted and didn't have to look straight up at it as I would have done if the lens had been shorter. I'm a great believer in cropping in-camera and I kept the image clean by making sure that I extracted extraneous detail at the shooting stage.

Ralph Gibson

"I saw this scene from a way back and used a longer lens so that I could compose it in the way that I wanted and didn't have to look straight up at it."

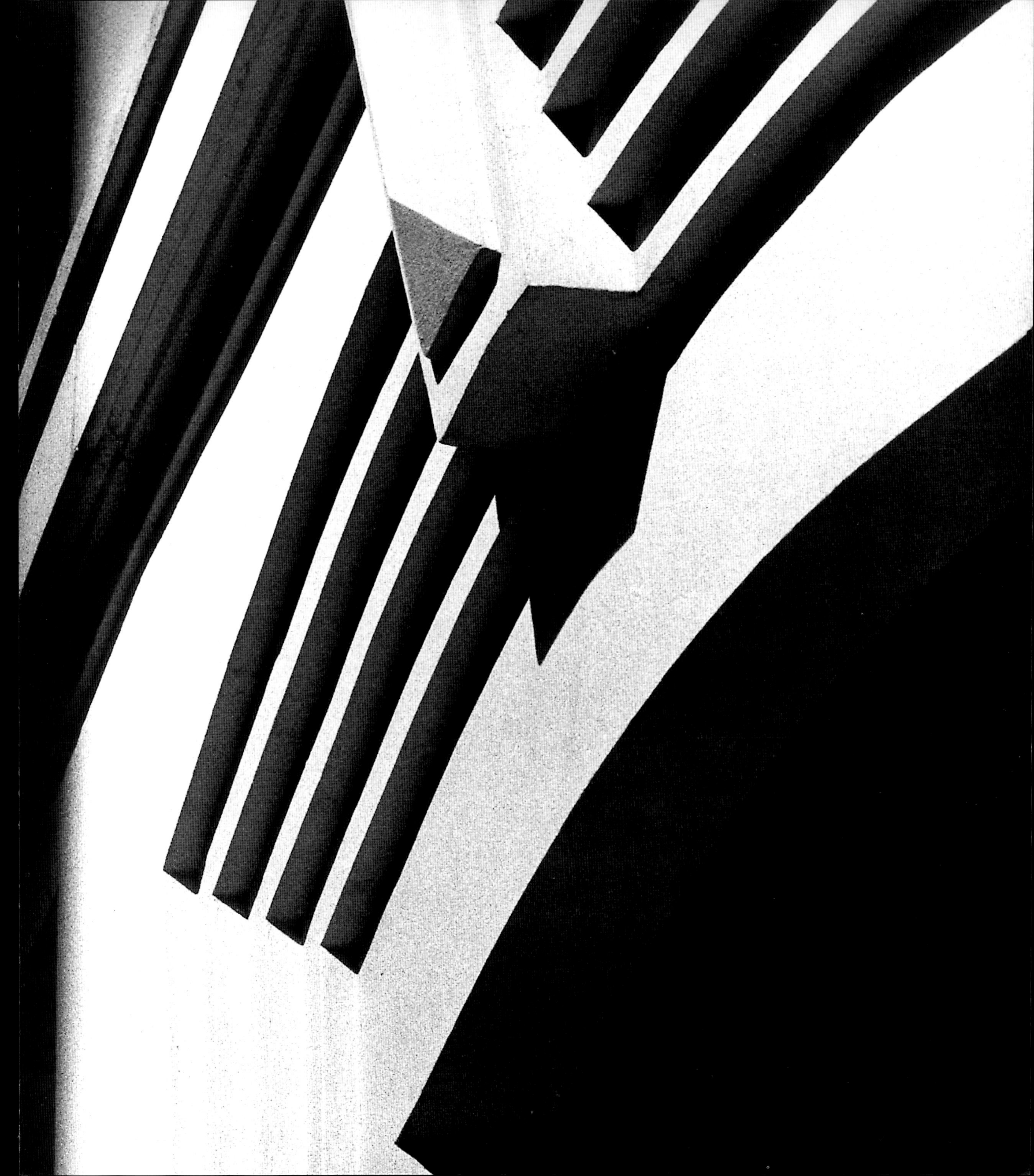

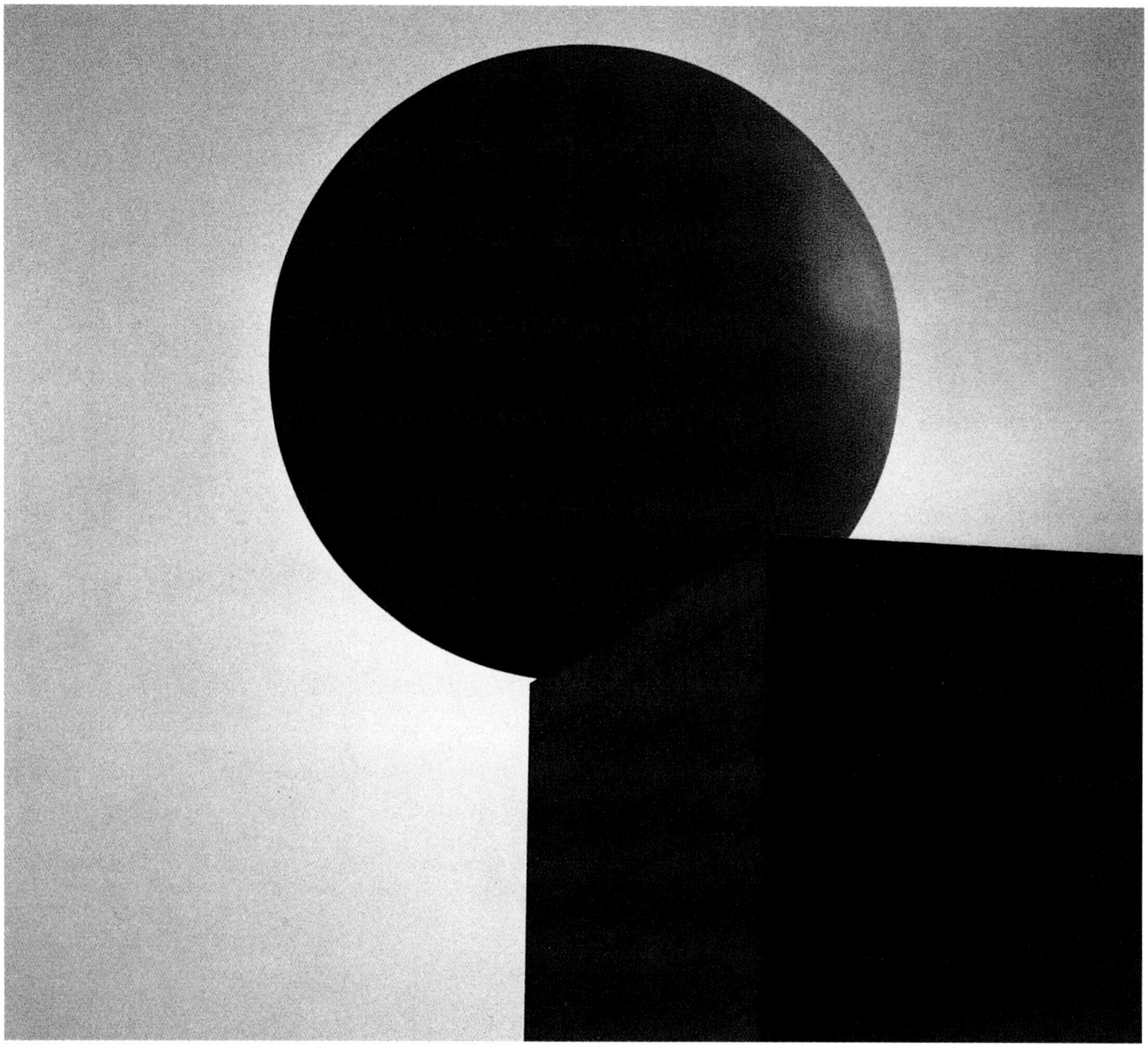

Roofscape, Barcelona by Anderson & Low
35mm camera, 180mm lens, Ilford XP2 film.

A lot of our architectural photography is about conveying the idea of a building by concentrating on its detail and about seeing things that others might overlook, and this picture is a case in point. Although many of those who have seen this photograph think that it's a model that was set up and photographed in the studio, in fact it's an enormous sphere—probably around 20 feet high—that balances on the edge of building next to the old Olympic Village in Barcelona.

The lighting had a crucial role to play in defining the form and shape of this structure and we took this picture in late afternoon when dark tones were dominating and the sky was hazy. One of our intentions when shooting architecture is always to put across the least amount of information necessary to get across the points that we want to make and here everything is so muted that you can barely see the detail in the wall or the highlight on the sphere. Nevertheless it's all there, and it encourages the viewer to spend more time analysing what they are seeing and involves them more in the photograph.

Anderson & Low

Pointer In many ways a building is similar to a person in that it has character and can be portrayed in a host of different ways. A particular viewpoint or lighting effect can change the emphasis of the picture completely and it's up to the photographer to decide what the approach is going to be and then to plan the photograph accordingly, bearing in mind the effect of natural light and the qualities of different lenses.

My Favourite Tip The picture was taken with a 35mm camera, which obviously imposes a rectangular format. At the printing stage, however, it was clear that the photograph worked much better when produced as a square, and so that was how it was treated. We never worry about cropping our work if we think it will improve the final image: we will do whatever is necessary to achieve the end result.

Detail

Column and Sign, Rome by John Claridge
Deardorff 5x4in camera, 240mm lens, Agfa APX 100 film.
Exposure 1/4sec at f/22

I was shooting a commercial job in Rome and the location I was using was just around the corner from this scene. As I passed it something told me that there was something there worth photographing but, at the time, the lighting falling on it was completely flat and there was really nothing out of the ordinary to see. I realised, however, that at a certain time of day it was likely to come to life and so I returned in the early evening as the light was becoming richer and more contrasty and shadows were starting to get longer. Now it was a different story and this apparently aimless collection of shapes and textures had come to life.

I used a long lens to allow me to frame tightly and I simply picked out a section of the scene that I felt worked well as a composition. The feel I was after was one that was very abstract and yet I wanted everything to hold together within the frame and to feel balanced and comfortable.

The light was perfect. It created strong shadows that added terrific modelling to the scene and it turned the window in the top part of the picture into almost a void of dark tone. It also skimmed the surface of the wall around the window and revealed the textures there that helped to add interest to what otherwise could have been quite a bland area of the picture.

John Claridge

Technique I wanted to enhance the graphic feel of this picture still more and so I calculated the exposure and then underexposed by one stop. This allowed the shadows to darken down still further and it ensured that, even though the light hitting the scene was seriously bright, the textures in the highlight areas were fully revealed.

Pointer Little areas of architectural detail can work very well if you're looking to achieve abstract images and black and white is the ideal medium with which to capture these. This particular image would not have worked in colour because of the direction sign in the centre of the picture. The splash of vivid hue that this would have introduced would have been too distracting and it would have taken the eye there instead of allowing it to see the scene as a complete entity.

"I used a long lens to allow me to frame tightly and I simply picked out a section of the scene that I felt worked well as a composition."

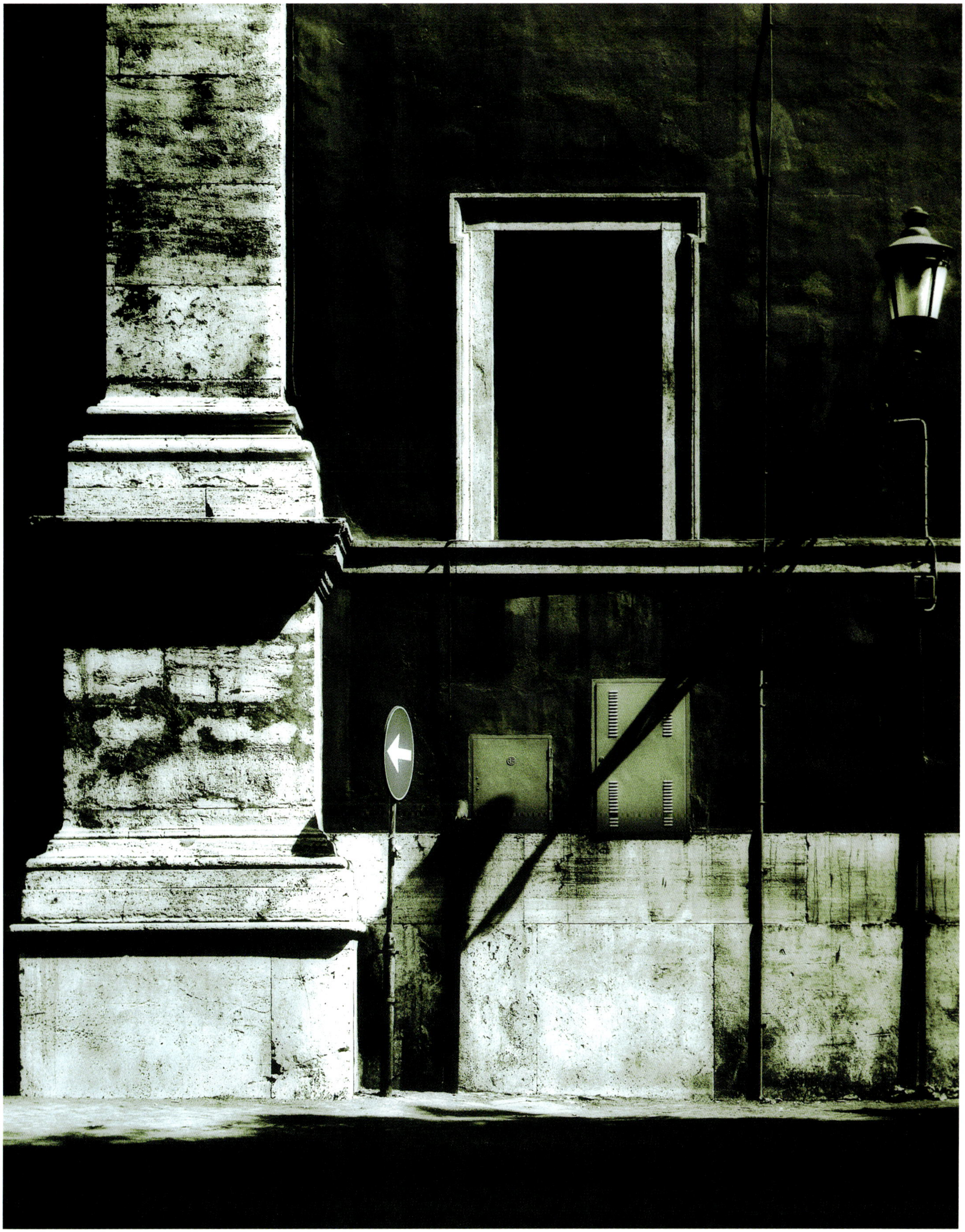

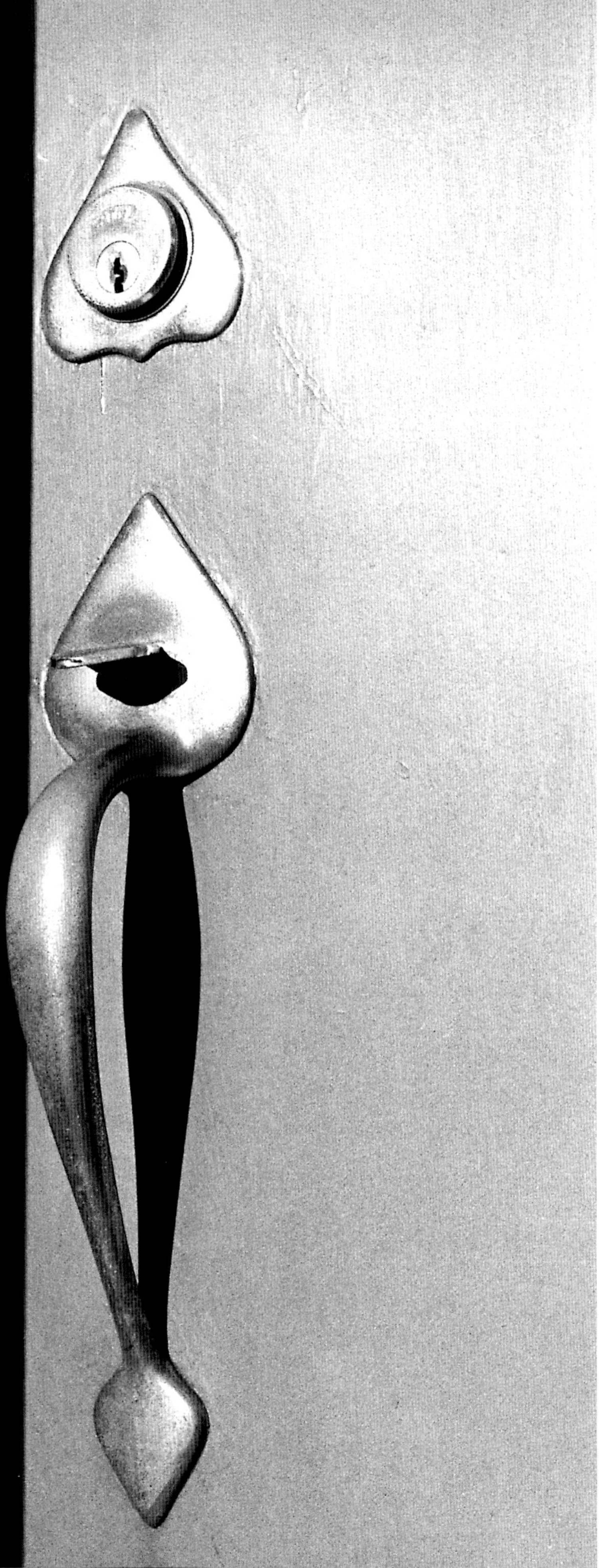

Detail

Door Handle by Ralph Gibson
Leica M2, 50mm Dual Range Summicron lens, Kodak Tri-X film.
Exposure not recorded

"One of the things about working up close is that the pictures compositionally will always be either one hundred per cent successful or one hundred per cent unsuccessful."

This image is one from my Quadrant series, in which I set myself the task of photographing everything from a distance of three feet. As well as giving continuity and a theme to the pictures it meant that I knew where to look. I didn't know what my next picture would be, but I knew where it would be. This door handle and lock was such a simple thing that would have been very easy to walk past and that was what attracted me to it. Things take on a presence if you look at them long enough and if you look closely enough.

One of the things about working up close is that the pictures compositionally will always be either one hundred per cent successful or one hundred per cent unsuccessful. There's no middle line. You don't just crop a little off here and you don't get little things happening in the background that are good or bad for the picture. It's the way it works: the pictures are very up-front and they are either a total success or a total failure.

Ralph Gibson

Pointer Setting a personal project is an excellent way of giving shape and meaning to your pictures and it can be something that is as unusual and challenging as Ralph Gibson's three-feet rule. Suddenly there's no danger of wandering into a situation and snapping away without thinking: every picture has to be worked on and the chance is there to develop important visual skills as seemingly mundane subjects are turned, as here, into striking pictures.

Tone and Texture This picture, which is compositionally simple to start with, has had still more of its distractions stripped away through the absence of colour. Now reduced essentially to two contrasting slabs of tone, Ralph Gibson has been able to concentrate on the form and structure within the scene and to emphasise to a startling degree the importance of this seemingly trivial item of door furniture.

Detail

Sign of the Times by Terry Hope
Olympus OM1, 50mm lens, Tri-X film.
Exposure 1/60sec at f/8

I've always found decaying buildings to be far more interesting to photograph than those that are pristine, because there is so much more to work with. The general debris and signs of neglect that can be found in a place that has been abandoned can be used to great effect and, by honing in on particular details, it's possible to make a comment about the building in a wider sense and to capture something of the atmosphere that can be found there.

This particular location was a major railway station that once served the heart of Manchester and I spent a day there, photographing its remains and looking for interesting angles that would serve to say something about its more glorious past. In a shattered office upstairs I found what I had been looking for: on the floor was a poster that had obviously at one time been used in the station bookshop. I don't know how it had found its way upstairs but, with its references to prosperity combined with the political overtones associated with the British Labour Party, it somehow seemed to speak volumes about the state that this building now found itself in.

I positioned it at an angle close to a window so that its creases were highlighted by the light that was coming through and used a wide angle lens to accentuate the scale of the poster and to highlight its importance in the picture.

Terry Hope

Printing and Processing Because of the contrast levels involved, this was quite a difficult scene to meter and I decided to bracket the exposure so that I had a variety of negatives to work from. The one that was the most successful recorded some of the detail in the foreground while also registering the buildings through the window. At the printing stage Adrian Ensor balanced the picture by holding back the exposure in the bottom half of the picture and giving extra exposure to the buildings seen through the window in the top half.

Pointer Don't be afraid to exert an influence in the picture if you think your intervention will improve the composition and the strength of the message you are giving. Here the picture was made much more powerful by the placement of the sign and yet the scene still has a natural and uncontrived feel to it.

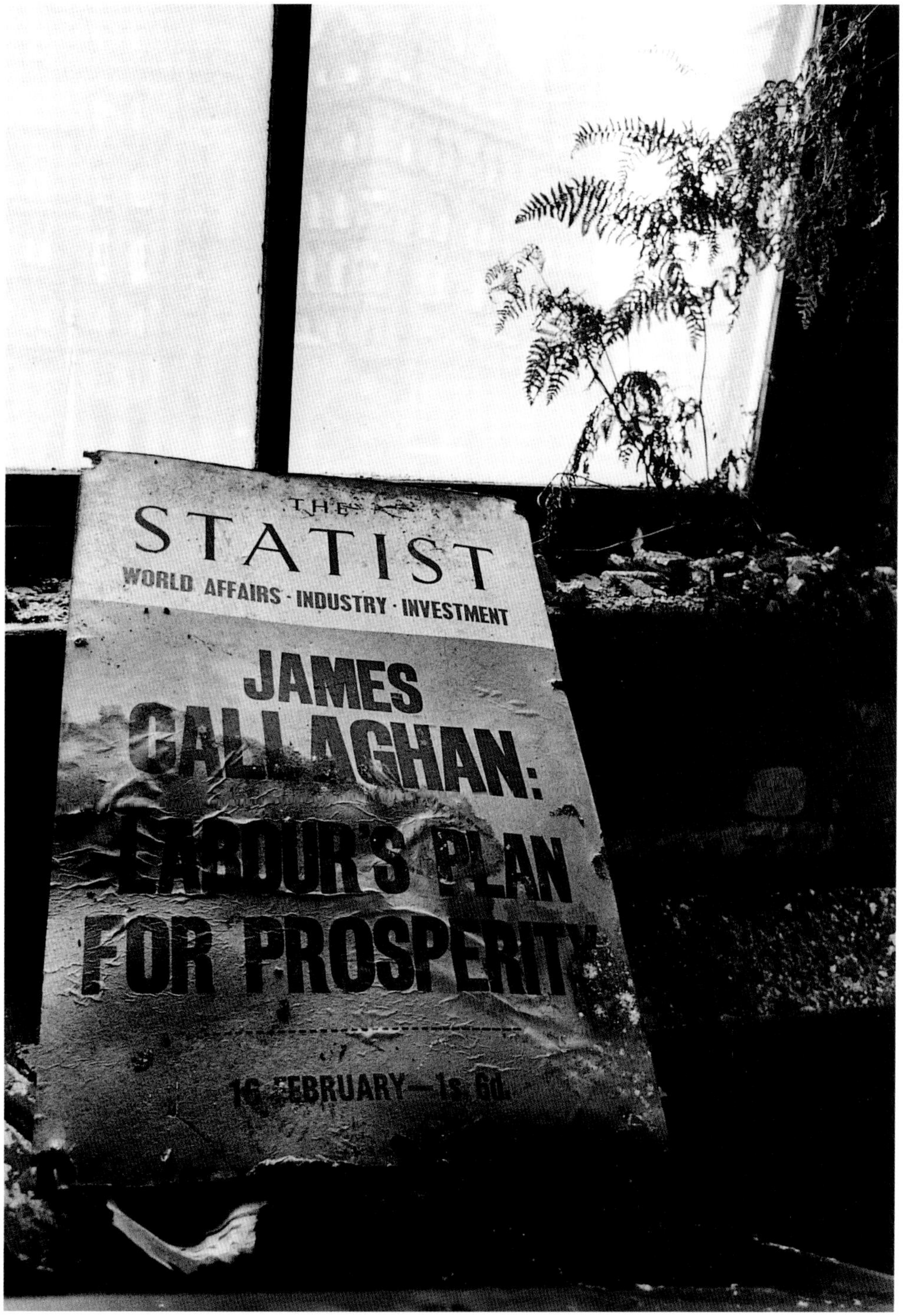
THE
STATIST
WORLD AFFAIRS · INDUSTRY · INVESTMENT
JAMES
CALLAGHAN:
FOR PROSPERITY
16 FEBRUARY—1s. 6d.

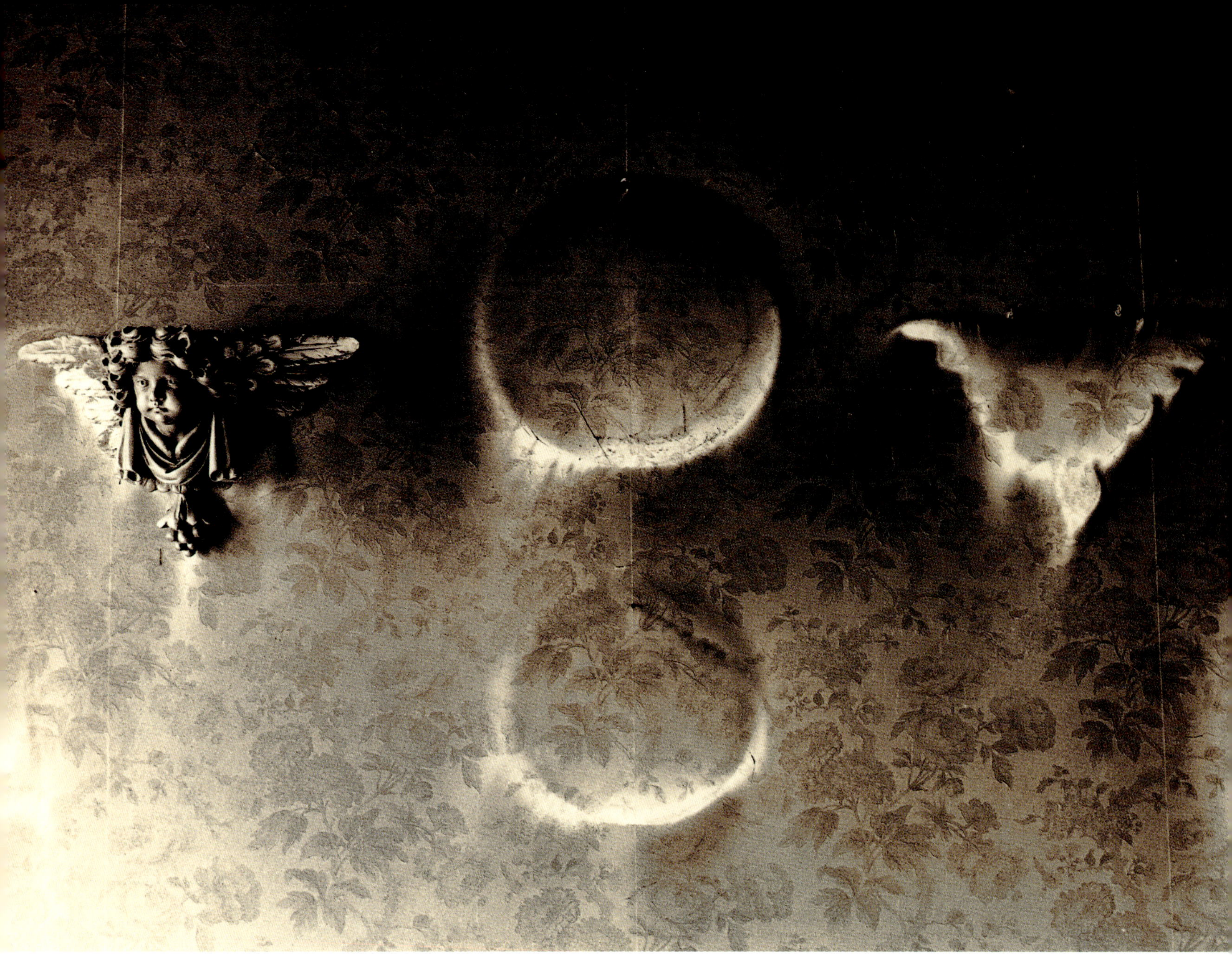

I got the chance to photograph the scene of devastation in a friend's fire-damaged flat before the repair work had started and it was an opportunity to take some unusual and moody pictures. I wanted to put across something of the sense of loss that I felt when I entered the place and I thought that the best way to do this would be to concentrate on details.

When I found this cherub I knew this was what I had been looking for. Only this one had survived in situ on the wall but there was a clear mark where the other one had once been and I liked this idea of things that were no longer in position leaving their mark to prove they once existed. I also felt that this solitary figure on the wall made a point about ordinary and personal things, things perhaps that were treasured possessions, being lost to the flames. It was quite a poignant image.

I wanted to keep things as natural as possible and so decided to work just by the light that was coming through the window to the left of the picture. This created quite strong shadows across the cherub that was left, but I thought that this worked well and I also liked the way that the light fell away across the wall, allowing the right hand side to be much darker than the left. It gives a natural feel and I would much rather have that than try to balance it up in some way.

Gavin Kingcombe

Burned Cherubs by Gavin Kingcombe
Mamiya 6x7cm, 90mm lens, Kodak Tri-X film.
Exposure four seconds at f/11

Technique To ensure that he achieved the depth of field that he wanted, Gavin set an aperture of f/11 and then used a shutter speed of four seconds to compensate for the low lighting that was to be found in the room. Shooting at these speeds can present problems with camera shake and there are ways of minimising the effect: a sturdy tripod is obviously a must and a cable release that will screw into the shutter to allow the camera to be fired remotely will also help enormously. Many SLRs also feature a button that will flip the mirror up prior to the picture being taken. Compose the image in the viewfinder and then activate the mirror. If you now wait for a second or so for vibration to stop and then press the cable release only the shutter will fire, minimising the risk of camera shudder.

Composition Symmetry can be a very strong element of composition and here the power of the picture lies in the fact that that it is perfectly balanced. Gavin has emphasised the fact that the cherub was once one of a pair by lining his camera up so that it looks directly on to this section of wall with equal spacing around all the elements.

"I wanted to put across something of the sense of loss that I felt when I entered the place."

Sculpture of Beckett's Murder, Toddington Manor by Simon Marsden
Nikkormat FT2, 50mm lens, Kodak Tri-X film.
Exposure 1/125sec at f/8

I was producing pictures for my book '**Phantoms of the Isles**' that rounded up a number of ghost stories from around the United Kingdom and this involved me looking for images that were appropriately spooky at each of the locations that I visited.

Many of the photographs that I took were produced on infrared film and were overall views of the building that was said to be haunted but there was also a need for pictures that could sum up certain aspects of the tale that I was trying to tell. Often a well observed detail can put across a great deal more than a grand panorama can and it was up to me to source some of these as well.

On this occasion I was visiting Toddington Manor in Gloucestershire, which had connections in the long distant past to the murder of Thomas à Beckett in Canterbury Cathedral in 1170. In short there is a story that the ancestors of the family that built this fantastically gothic house in 1820 had been involved in the killing and the guilt that this has inflicted is reflected in the fact that there are statues depicting the event to be found above the main doors of the building.

The house is now neglected and the statues—which stand alongside horrifying figures and grotesque gargoyles—are now largely covered in intricate spiders' webs, which I found especially appealing since they helped me to achieve the right sense of horror. I moved in close on the battered face of the statue that depicted Thomas à Beckett himself and shot hand held using just the light that was available.

Simon Marsden

My Top Tip I'm always looking to extract the atmosphere of a place and the camera equipment that I use is, in many ways, secondary to everything else. I'm using the same camera now—a Nikkormat FT2—that I've had for 33 years and illustrated several books using just this plus a 50mm and 24mm lens. I've now supplemented the camera with a further five FT2 bodies so that I've got the back-up that I never had before and I'm now working on my eighth book, so I think I can say that I've found my preferred way of working! I'm so used to the camera and the way that it works that I can use it almost without thinking and I love this kind of freedom.
It means that I can concentrate on the pictures I'm taking without having to worry about the technicalities.

Pointer Simon Marsden is one of the most successful photographers of haunted sites in the world and he's proved that there is no need to build up a bag full of high tech camera gear before powerful and compelling architectural studies can be taken. His eye for a picture is his secret and that's something that even someone with the most basic camera gear can work on developing. A good exercise is to shoot some film using a single use camera, basically just a film and a lens. If you can still come back with some strong images from that, then you know that you've got the ability to become a good photographer.

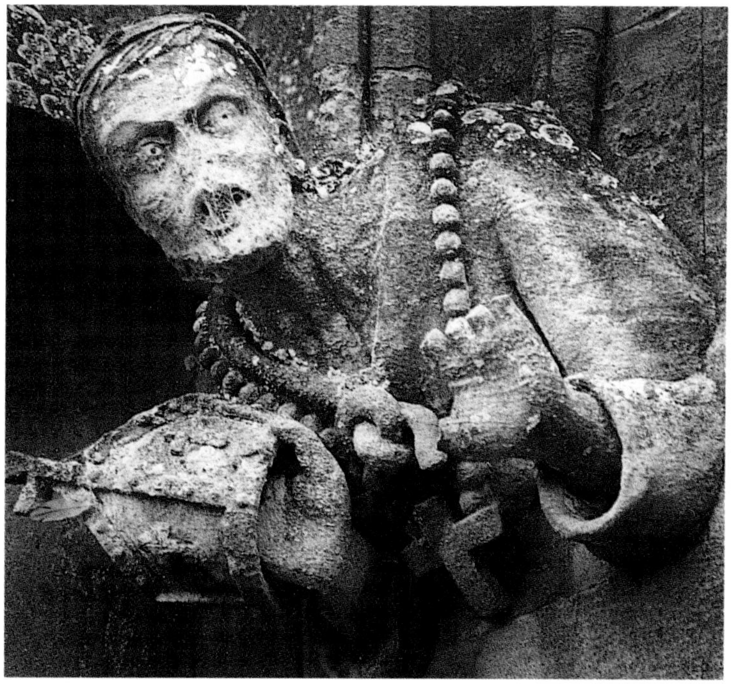

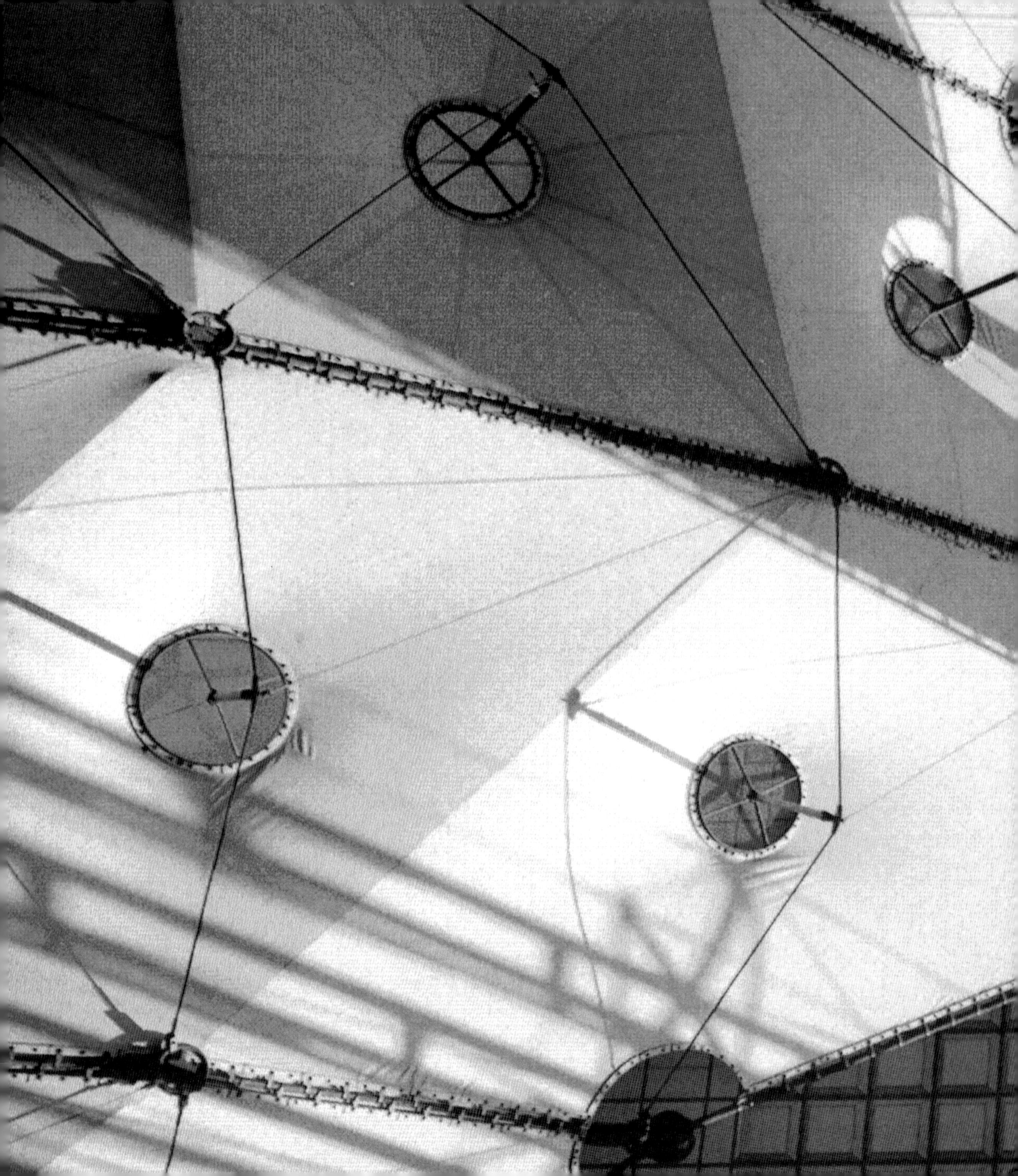

Gallery

It's time for a treat. Sit back and enjoy this collection of wonderful pictures, from a selection of great architectural photographers.

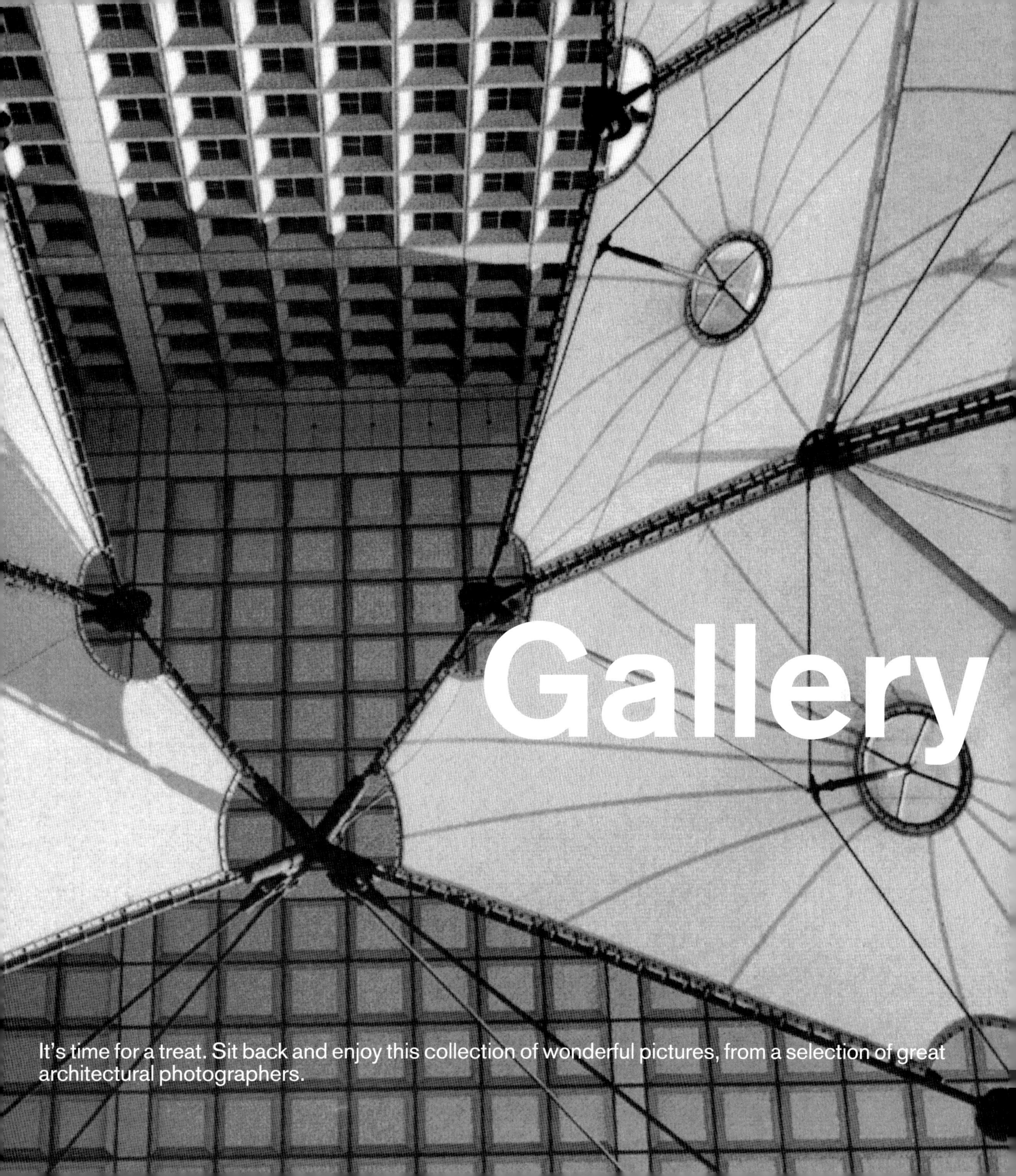

Chrysler Building by Tom Baril
Linhof 5x4in camera, 135mm lens, Polaroid Type 55 film.
Exposure 1/15sec at f/22

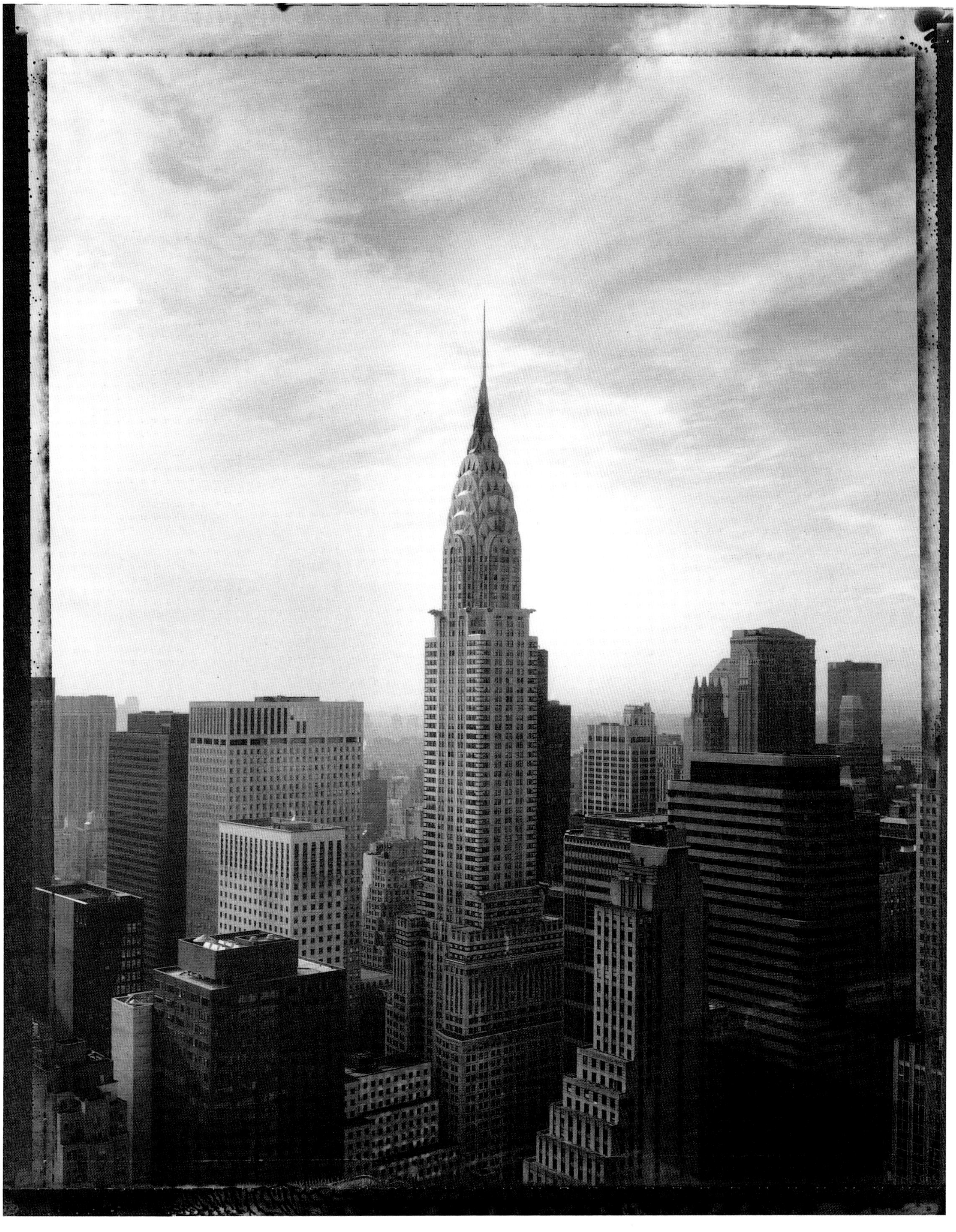

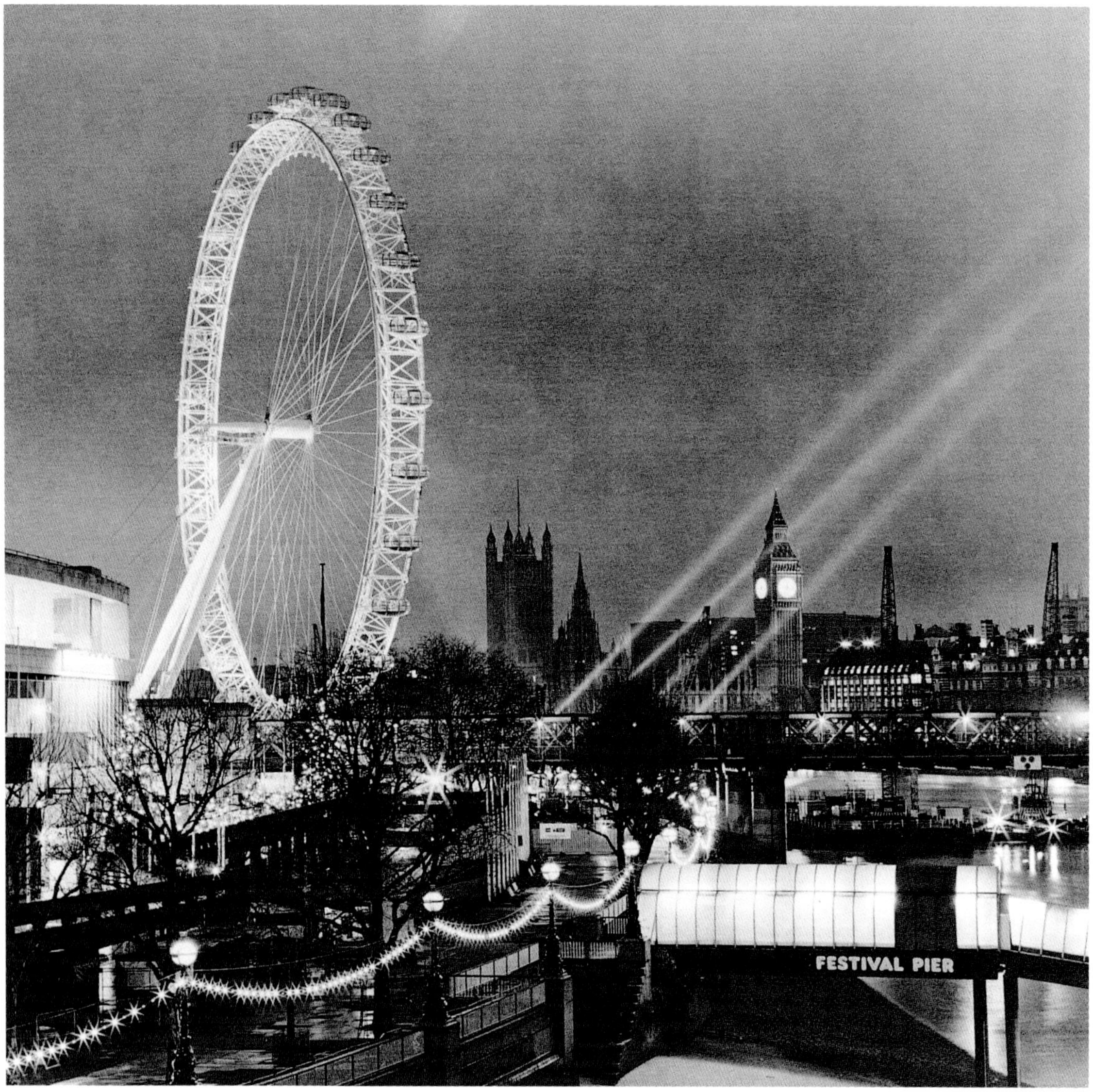
FESTIVAL PIER

London's Millennium Wheel by Anderson & Low
Mamiya 6x7cm camera, 110mm lens, Kodak T-Max 400.

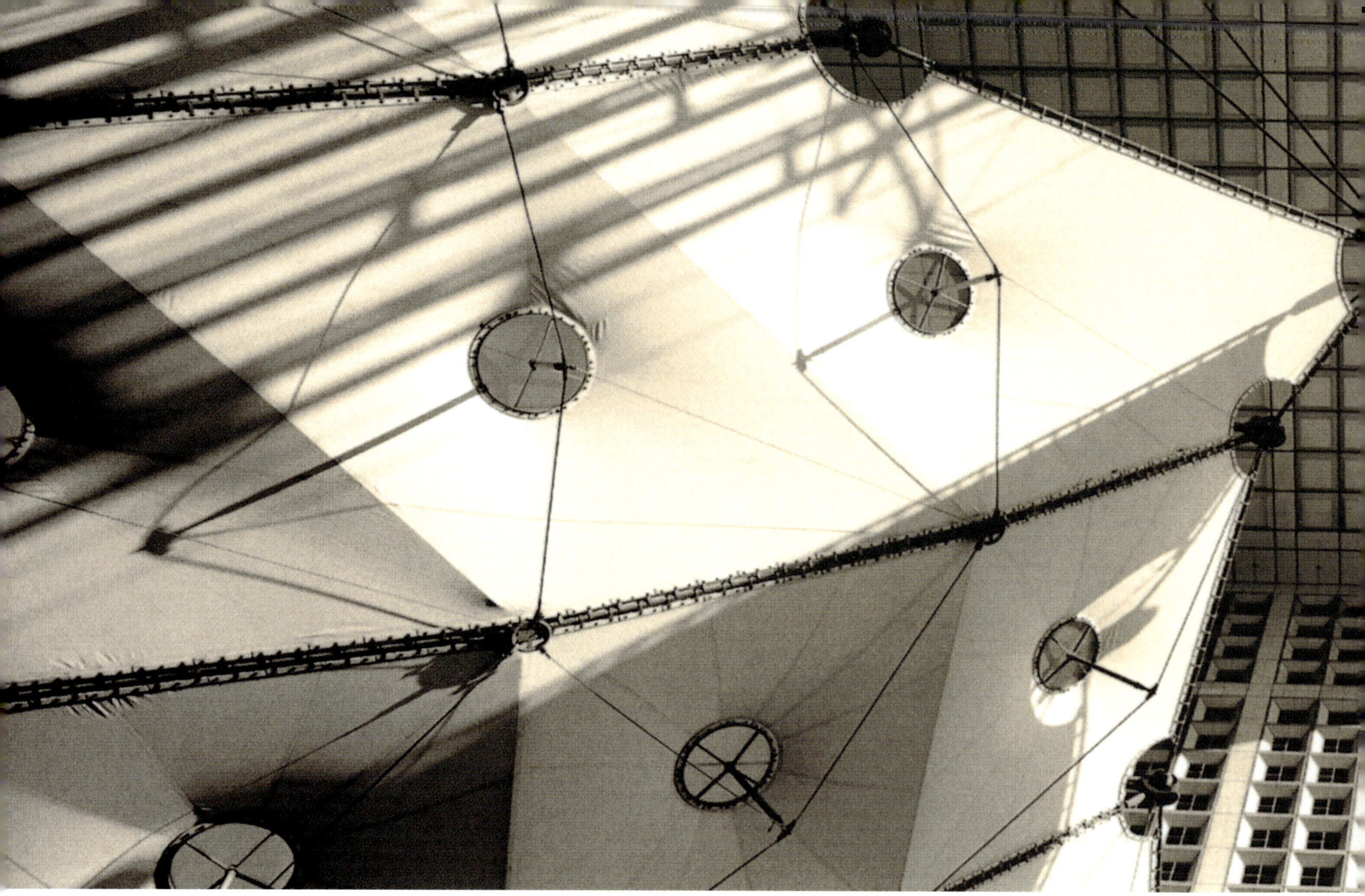

La Defence, Paris by Barry Cawston
Fujifilm 6x17cm camera, 90mm lens, Kodak T-Max 100 film.
Exposure 1/15sec at f/22

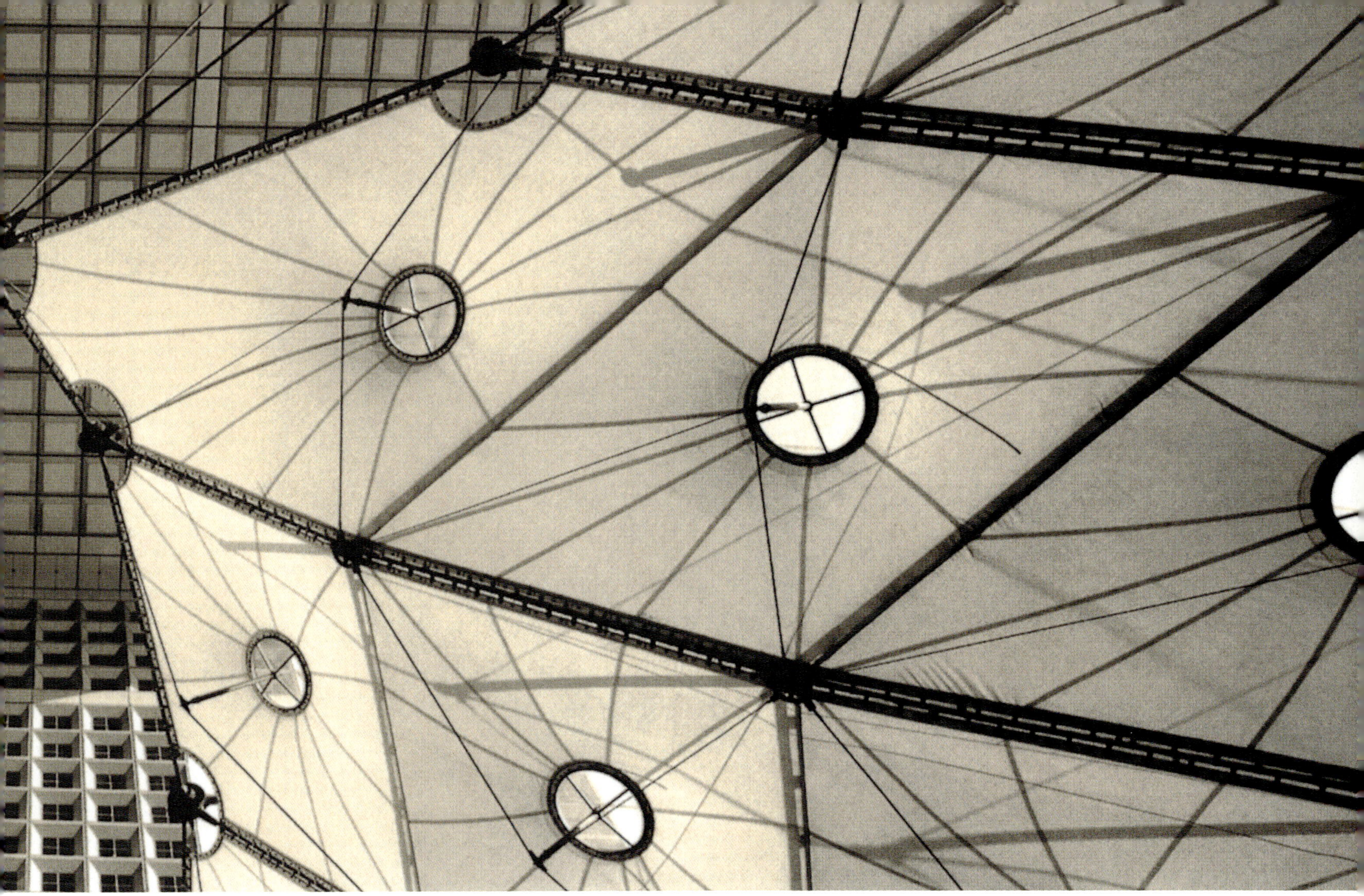

Sag Harbour, New York by Ralph Gibson
Leicaflex, 180mm lens, Kodak Tri-X film.
Exposure not recorded

The Flatiron—Evening by Edward Steichen
Three Colour Half-tone reproduction in Camera Work, 1906

Picture: The Royal Photographic Society, Bath

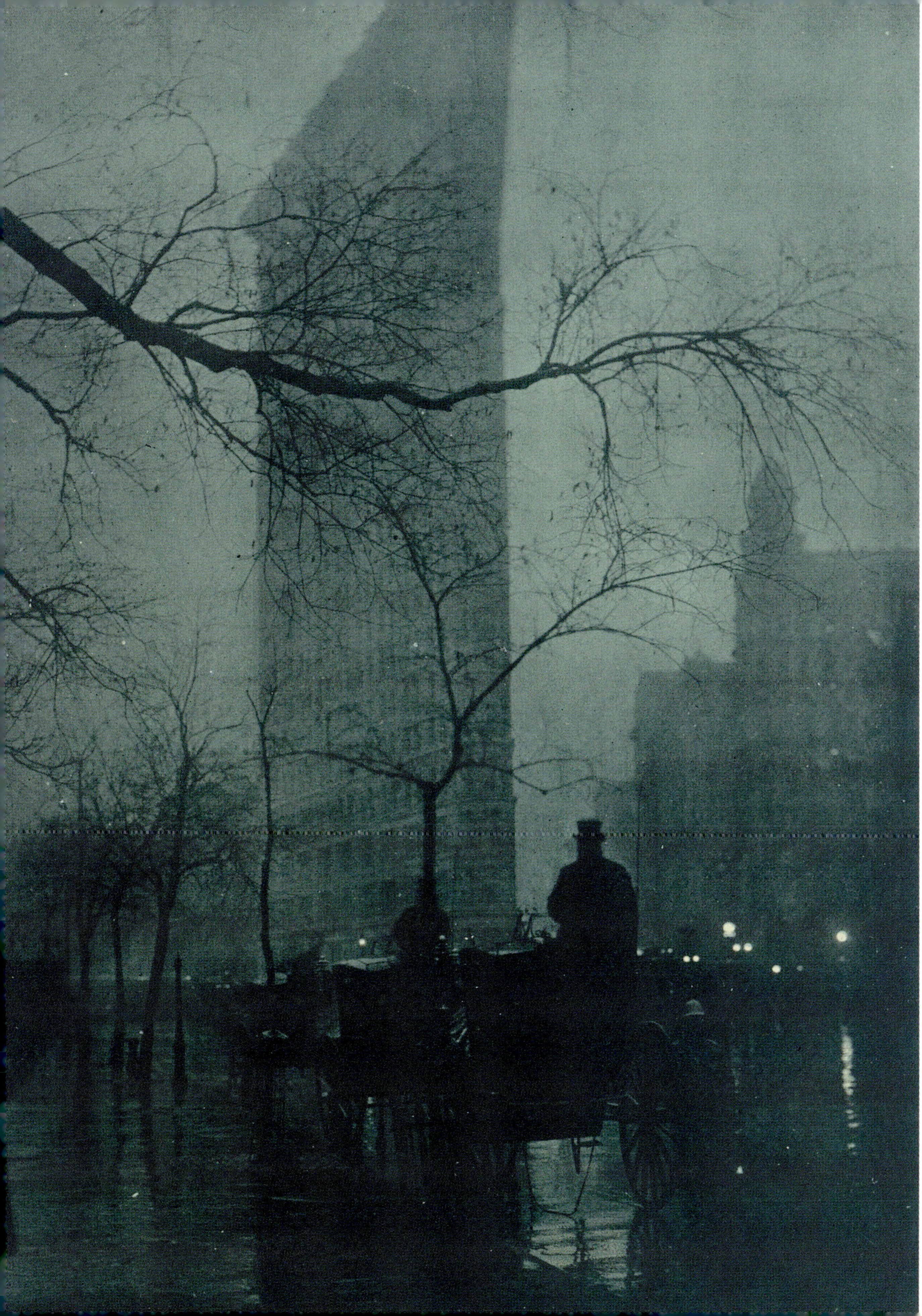

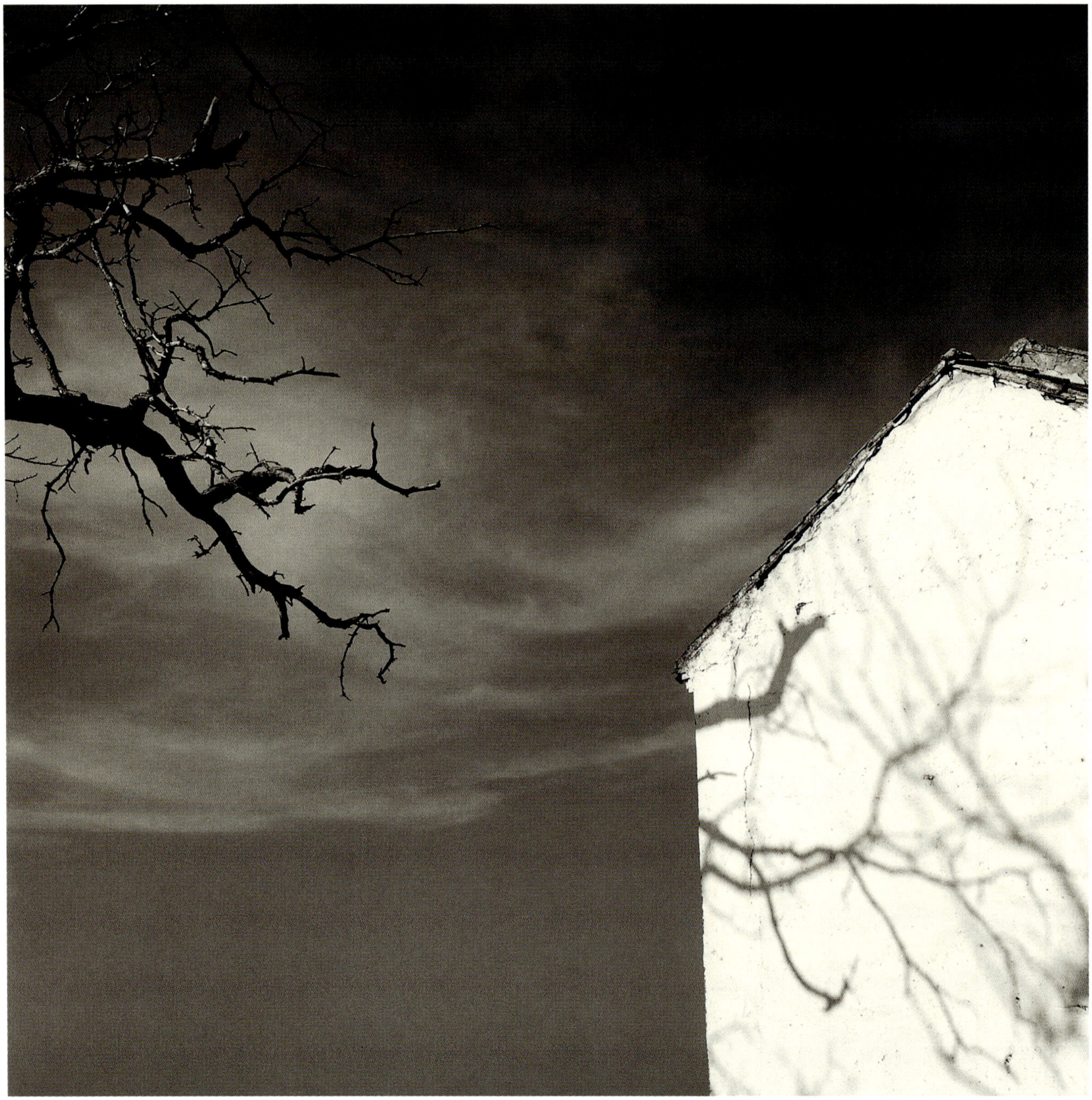

The House of Federico Garcia Lorca by Adrian Ensor
Rolleiflex 6x6cm camera, fixed 75mm lens, Ilford HP5 Plus film.
Exposure 1/125sec at f/16

Untitled III by Ron Bambridge
Wista 5x4in camera with 6x7cm roll film back, 90mm lens, Ilford HP5 film.
Exposure 1/125sec at f/16

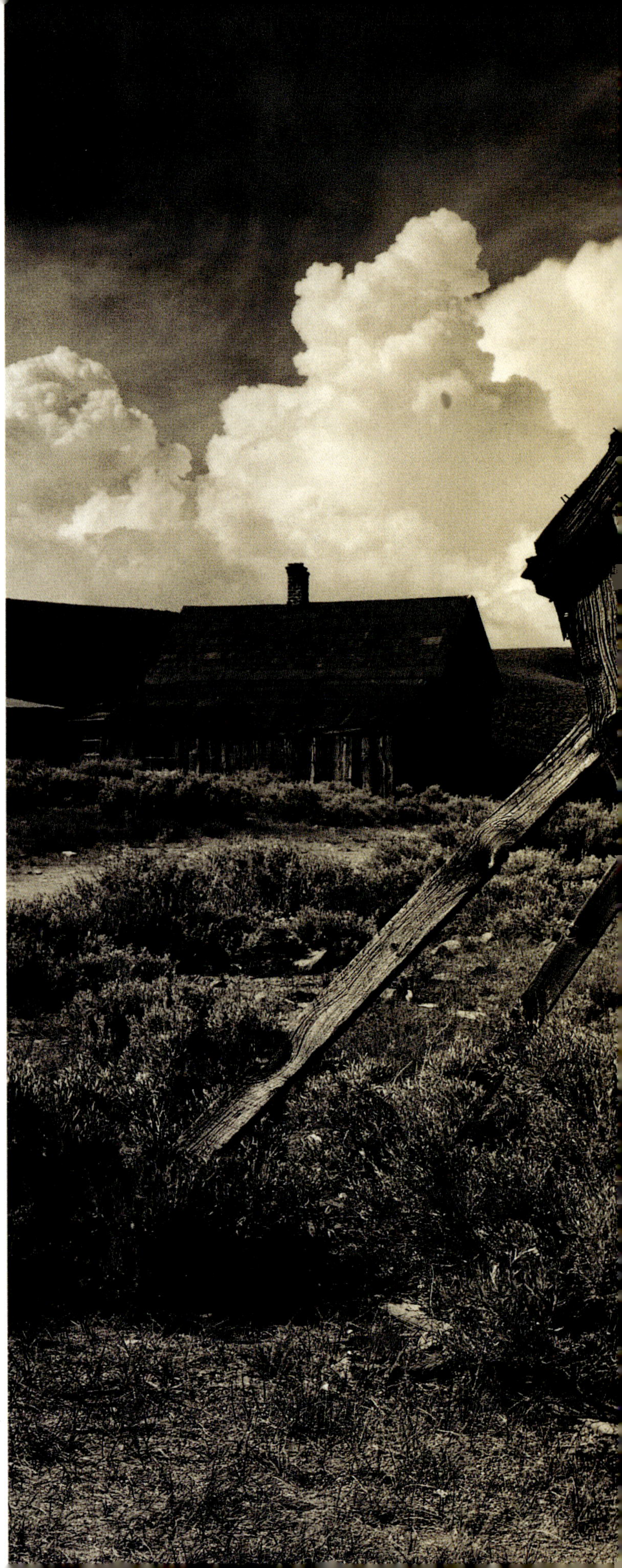

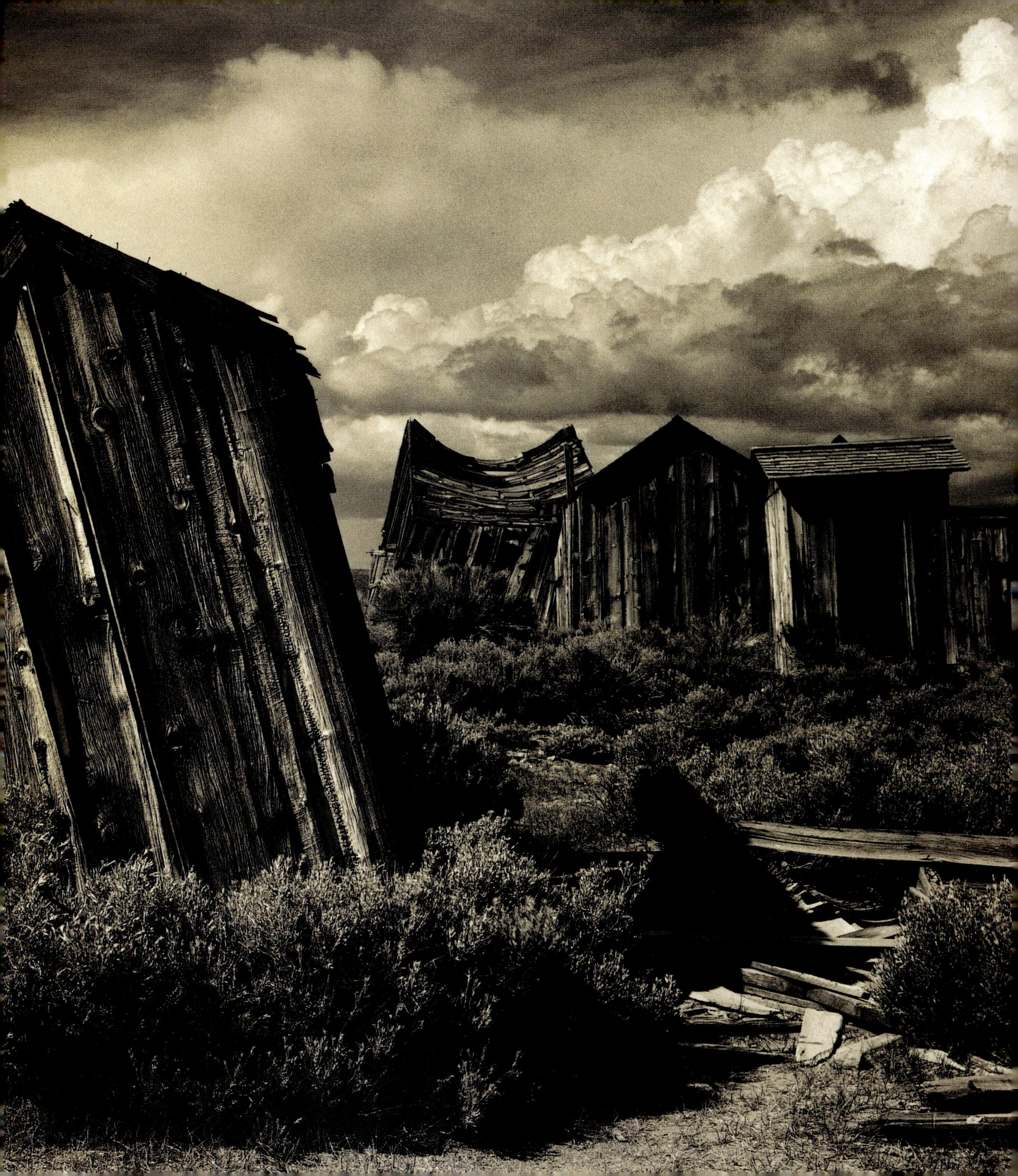

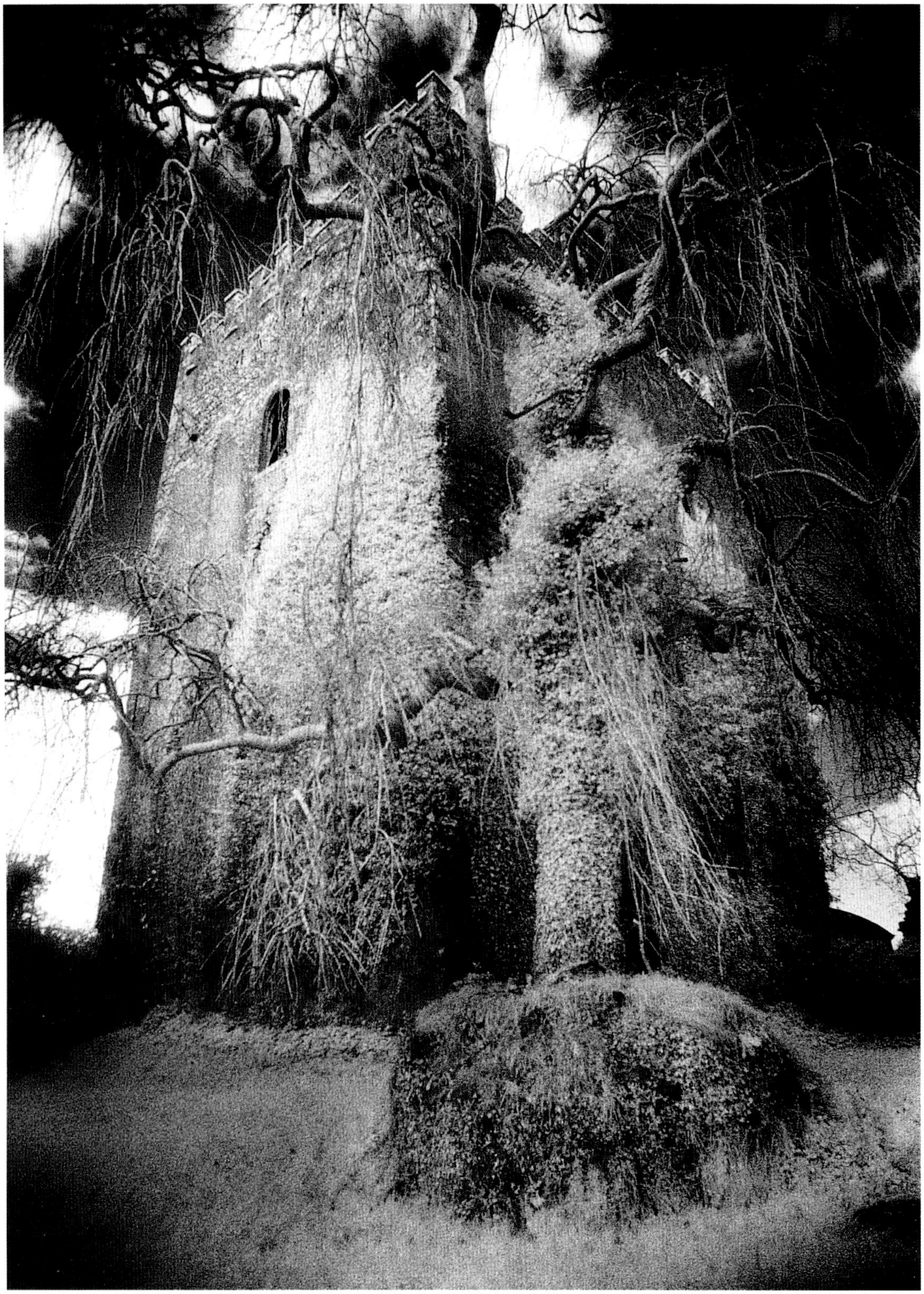

Ballaghmore Castle, Co Tipperary, Eire by Simon Marsden
Nikkormat FT2, 50mm lens, Kodak High Speed Infrared film. Polarising and 25A red filters used.
Exposure 1/250sec at f/5.6

Tone, Texture

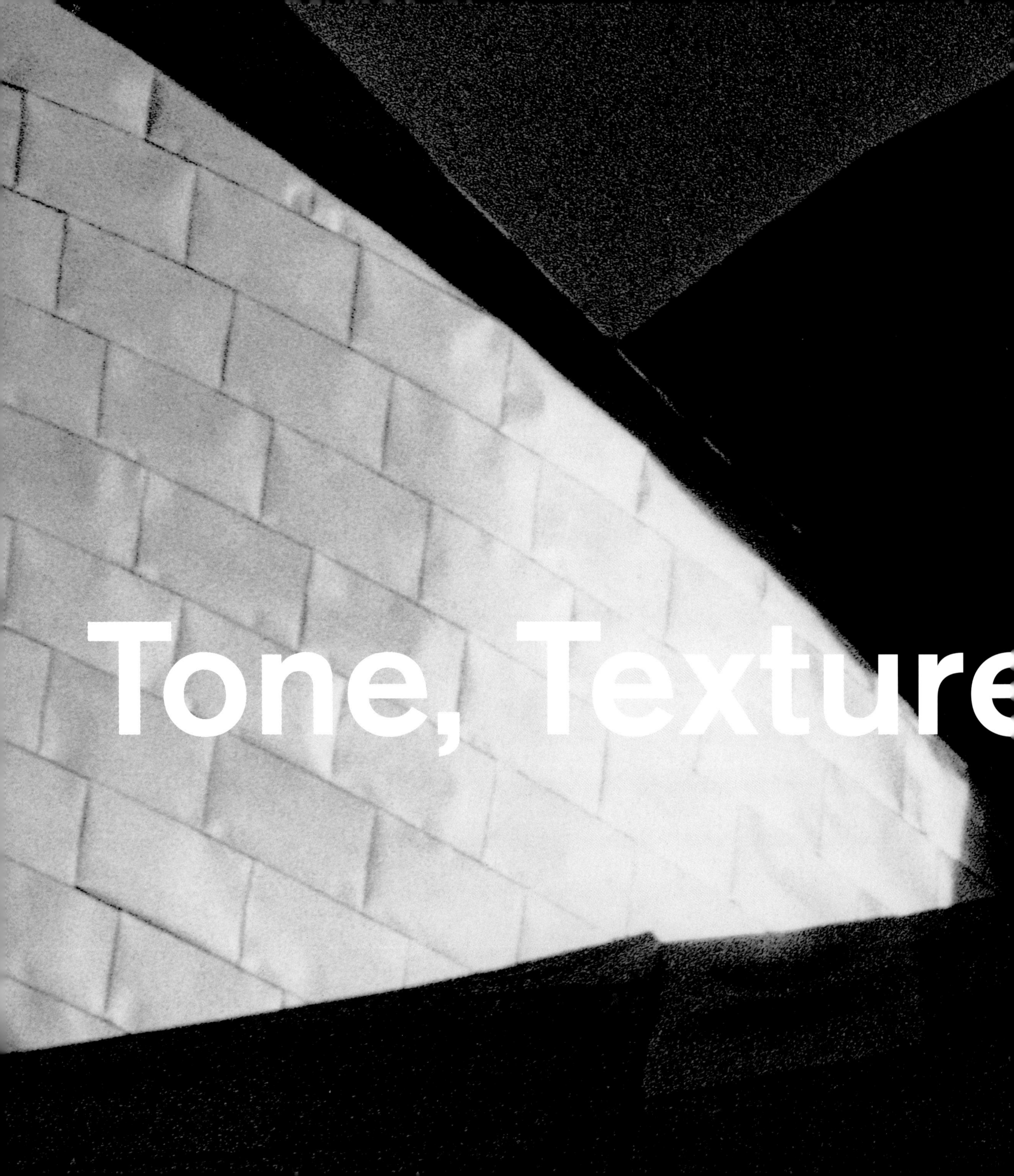

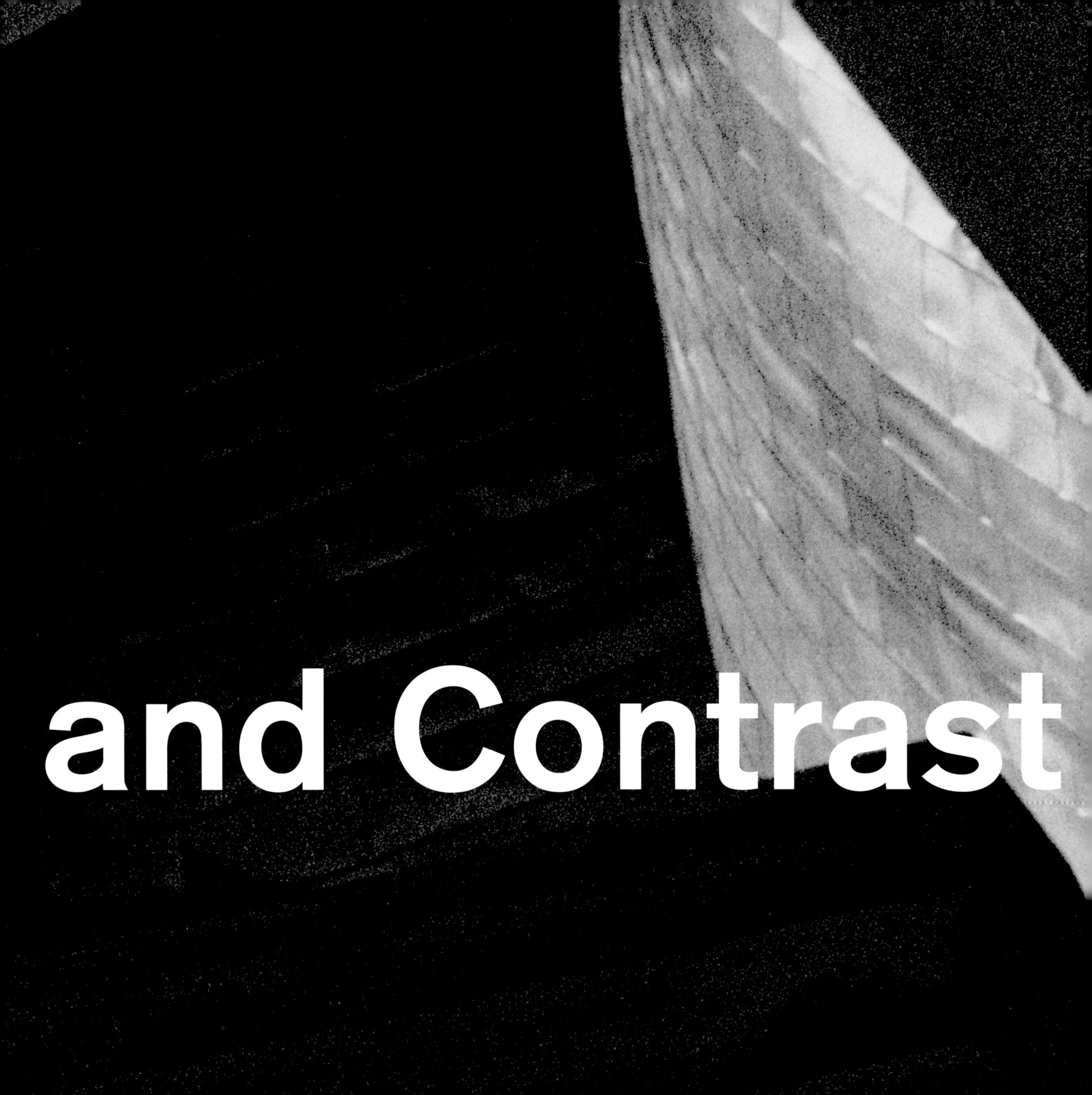

and Contrast

The great architectural photographer learns to appreciate and to use the light that's given, to reveal something special about the scene that's being pictured.

Tone, Texture and Contrast

Melbourne City Link Gateway by Anderson & Low
35mm camera, 180mm lens, Kodak T-Max 100.
Exposure not recorded

"The picture is the most important thing, not the way in which it was achieved."

The Melbourne City Link Gateway in Australia is a huge bright yellow structure that juts out over six lanes of motorway and it has no function whatsoever other than to serve as a piece of art in an architectural form. It's probable that a lot of motorists don't even really study it, but at night it's transformed into something quite spectacular, being lit in such a way that it appears to turn itself inside-out like an M.C. Escher drawing.

We decided to concentrate just on the structure itself and to remove any reference to other elements that would have revealed its true scale. In black and white the distractions that colour would have presented are also removed and the tones serve to reveal the shape and the texture of this construction. This has reduced the picture right down to its barest elements, but for us it still works as a powerful image, one that is all about form and the presence provided by a very simple but powerful object.

Anderson & Low

Printing and Processing The background to this structure is the black of the night sky and, by altering the exposure and the print contrast levels, we had the ability to determine how dense this would ultimately be. Extra exposure at the taking stage would have revealed more of the detail in the background but we wanted to keep things simple and so underexposed slightly instead and used a hard grade of paper, ensuring that the sky achieved a rich and impenetrable tone.

Pointer We don't standardise on any one piece of kit but prefer to work with a range of cameras and lenses, making decisions in each individual case about what we will use and how we will approach a specific picture. Every situation is different and we judge each on its merits, shooting on a mixture of medium format and 35mm and working with a full range of lenses, printing papers and toners to achieve the effect that we want. The picture is as important as the way in which it was achieved.

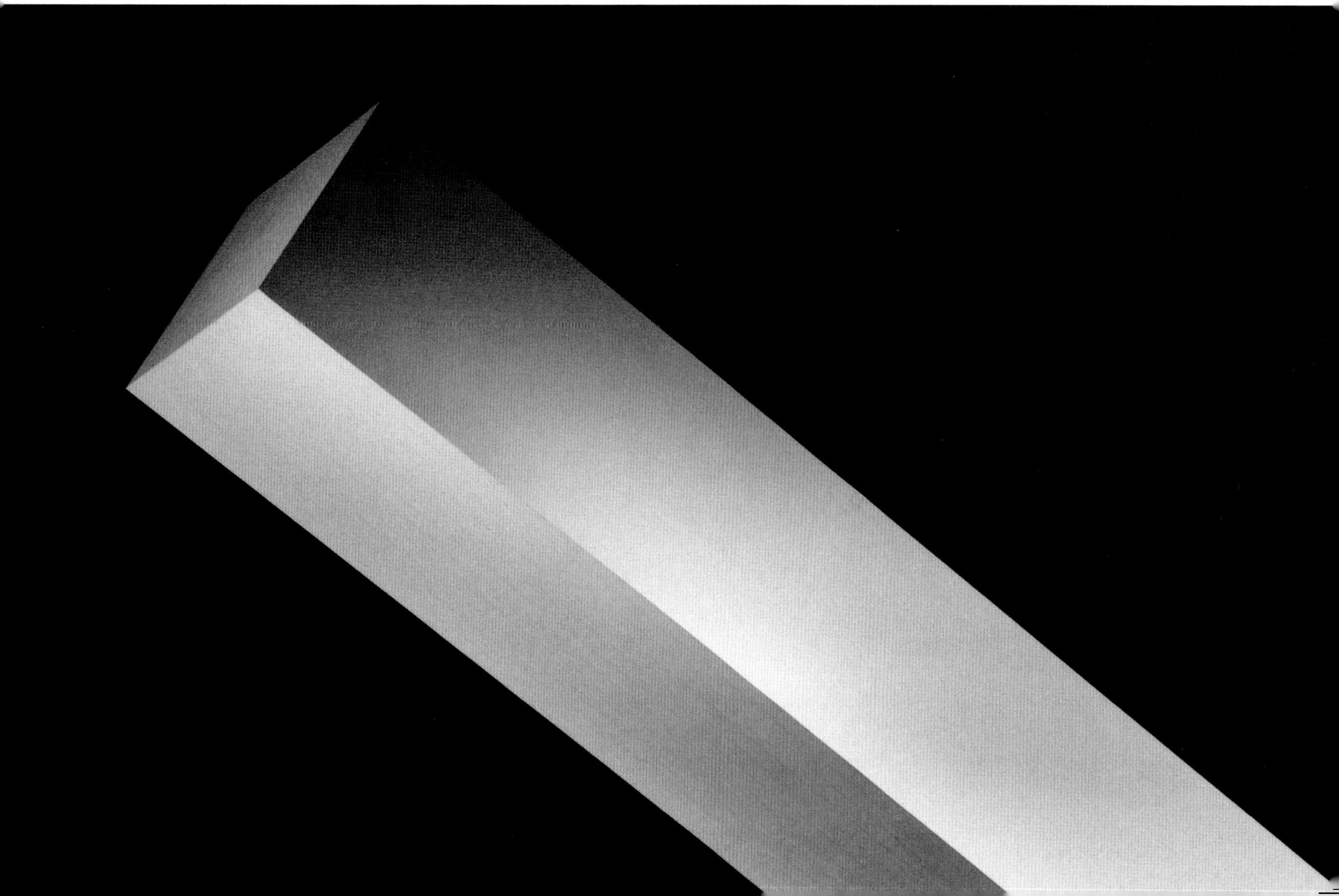

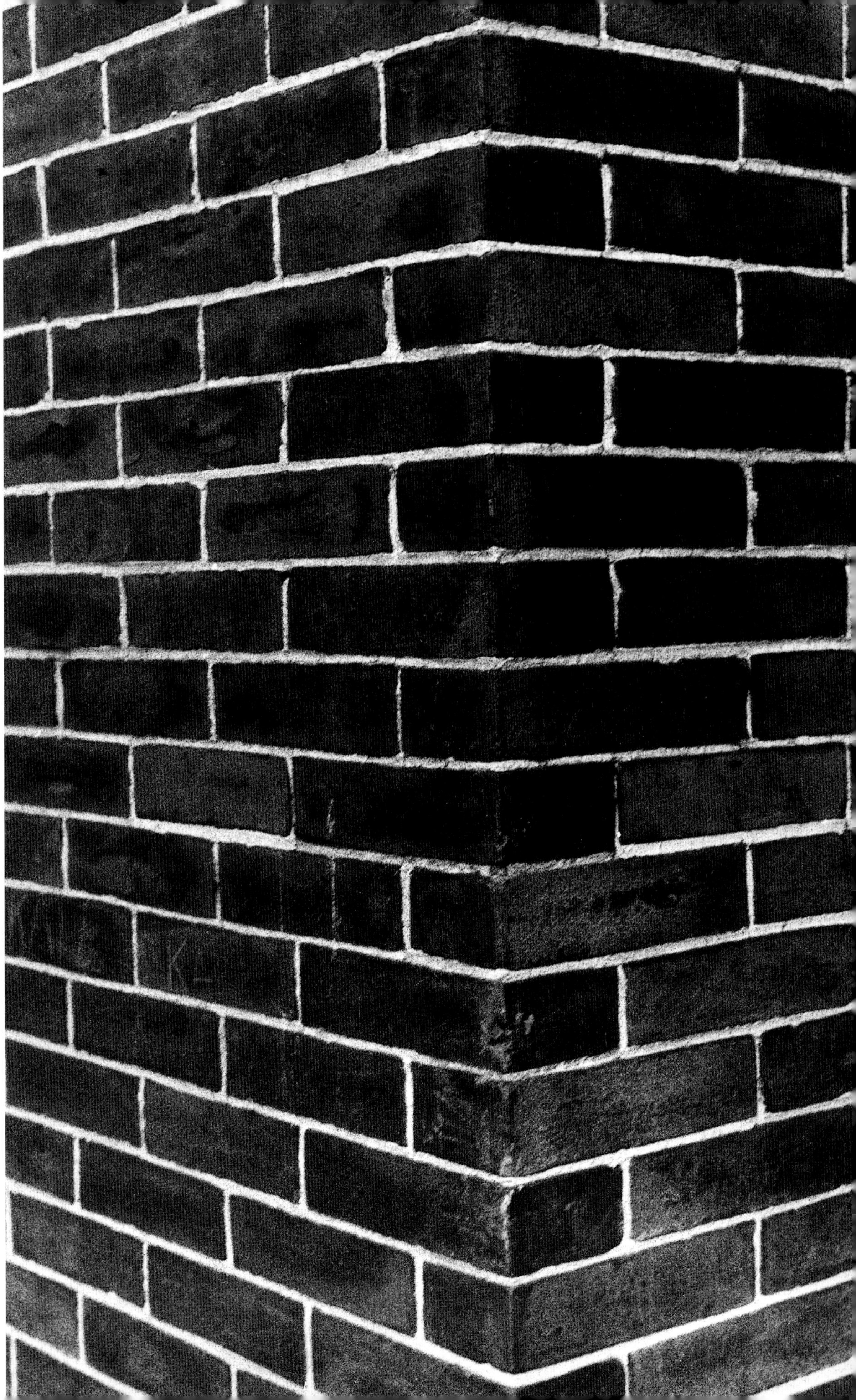

"Every photograph is a lighting event and through experience you acquire the ability to read the light that you encounter so that you can use it to your advantage."

Tone, Texture and Contrast

Brick Wall by Ralph Gibson
Leica M2, 90mm lens, Kodak Tri-X film.
Exposure not recorded

This picture has a kind of an optical effect to it in that, if you look hard enough, it doesn't stop moving. You can't tell which part of the wall is in front of the other. It was something that I noticed very clearly at the time: I was walking past and I saw something happen and so I retraced my steps and moved very slowly until I got that axis of the two panels of bricks, the vertical panel on the left against the large vertical panel on the right. And as I stood there concentrating I saw that this would cause a certain visual intensity but it was a question of which focal length to use: I knew immediately that I had to flatten the whole thing out a little by using a 90mm.

The picture is divided almost exactly down the middle by the vertical line where the bricks meet, as it had to be for the visual effect to work. Photographic composition is entirely a question of volume, proportion, focal length and distance to subject. Get that right and you can photograph anything.

Ralph Gibson

Location When you're on location, lighting is always perfect-–it's the photographer's interpretation of it that is sometimes lacking. Every photograph is a lighting event and through experience you acquire the ability to read the light that you encounter so that you can use it to your advantage.

Pointer It's a fallacy to imagine that you have to start with a dramatic subject in order to make a memorable architectural study. As great photographers like Ralph Gibson have proved endlessly, there is potential in the most everyday of subjects but it takes a trained eye to see how this can be realised. Learn to read the way the light affects a scene, make a feature of shadows and textures and don't be afraid to move in close or to introduce an extreme in-camera crop to extract only the most telling elements of your subject.

Tone, Texture and Contrast

Square in Tuscany by John Claridge
Deardorff 5x4in camera, 75mm lens, Kodak Tri-X film.
Exposure 1 second at f/22

I took this picture from a vantage point at the top of an old bell tower and I'm sure that no-one had been up there for years because it was completely dark, covered in cobwebs and, as my assistant found out when he ventured up there with the camera, it was also full of pigeons!

My reason for being there was to shoot a commercial picture for a car company but I knew that I had to take a picture for myself on black and white film, particularly as I could see that the potential was there for a picture late in the day that would reveal all the textures hidden away in these ancient terracotta roofs.

As dusk starts to fall the light changes very quickly and we could see it moving around this scene, causing the shadows to lengthen and to become deeper. Eventually there was a point when the front of the church to the left of the picture was in complete shade and I knew that the contrast in the scene was close to its height. I took the picture looking almost directly towards the sun, taking care to angle the lens so that it didn't catch any flare.

I was right on the edge of the tower and didn't have the option to use any camera movements to increase the depth of field and so I stopped the lens down to f/22 and settled for a long exposure. Because there was no movement within the scene I knew this wouldn't cause me any problems.

John Claridge

Printing and Processing I wanted to emphasise the shadows and consequently the texture in this picture and so I printed for the highlight detail and allowed everything else to go dark. It gave me a much more moody and atmospheric effect, which I thought suited the subject perfectly.

Pointer By stripping away the colour from a scene, black and white makes it easier for the photographer to pare a subject down to its most basic elements and to concentrate on form, tone and texture. In this case the traditional terracotta colouring of these Tuscan roofs would have created a distraction and diluted the effect that John Claridge was aiming for.

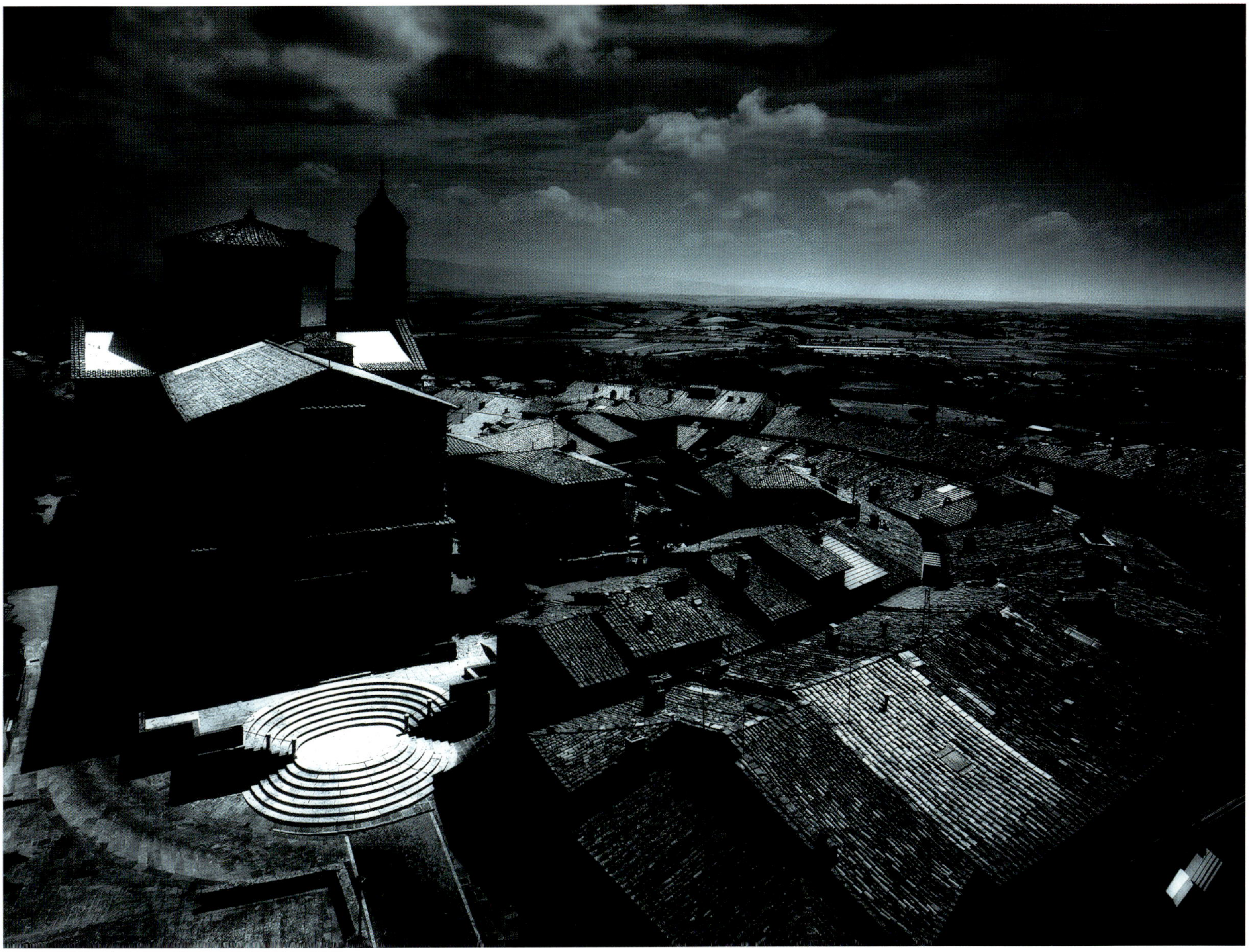

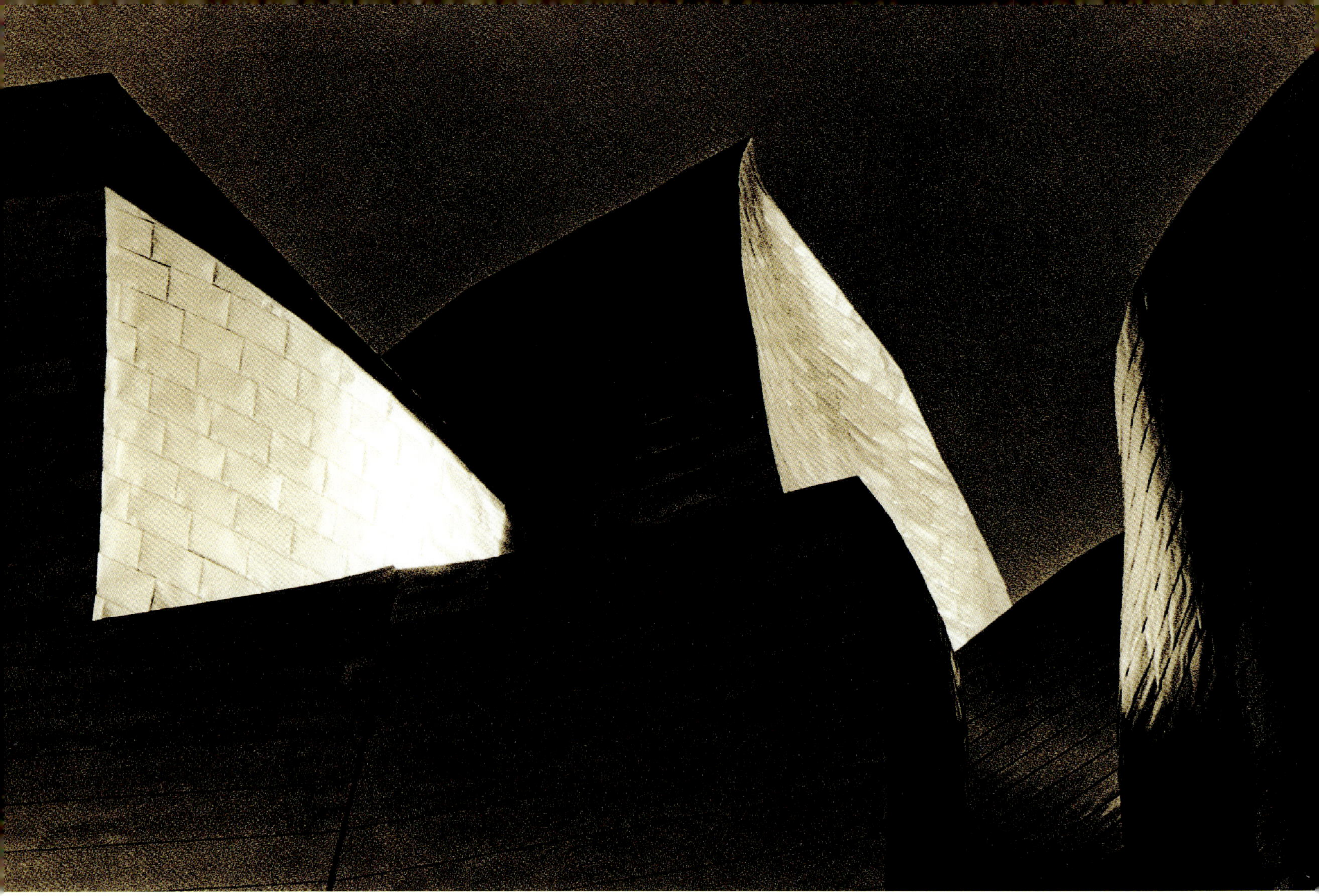

Guggenheim Museum by Adrian Ensor
Nikkormat 35mm SLR, 110mm lens, Kodak Tri-X film.
Exposure 1/125sec at f/16

The Guggenheim Museum in Bilbao, Spain, is one of the world's most amazing structures and I found it to be a particularly rewarding personal project. It has been designed to contain extremes of light and shade and, allied to the reflections that are also visible around the building, it means that, if you're taking a black and white approach, there's always the chance of producing something interesting based around tones and textures.

Using a long lens I decided to walk around the structure and to look for tiny areas that I could pull out that would provide the basis for an abstract image. I found that, as I started to take pictures, I gradually was paring down the results that I was achieving until I reached a point where there was nothing about the picture that was related to a conventional architectural study. Instead I had honed in on sections where deep shadows were juxtaposed with bright highlight, creating areas of contrast that you would never normally find on a more traditional building.

I've always been attracted to shapes and the way that shapes can be used in architectural photography and, by taking this approach to its extreme, I felt that I had achieved something unusual that had still managed to reveal some of the character of this extraordinary building.

Adrian Ensor

"Using a long lens I decided to walk around the structure and to look for tiny areas that I could pull out that would provide the basis for an abstract image."

Printing and Processing Jeff Conn, a printer who worked at my darkroom, took my rather thin negatives of the Guggenheim Museum and made them into lith prints, making the exposure on to Oriental Seagull paper and then developing this in a life-expired lith developer. Because the developer was less than fresh it gave the print a wonderful deep pink colouration and added grain to the sky, while the fact that the negative was slightly underexposed increased the contrast in the scene still further and enhanced its graphic qualities. I finished the picture by toning it in thiocarbamide, which gave the print an almost golden glow.

Details Sometimes focusing on just a small area best reveals the character of a building. In the same way that a human subject can be shown in a variety of different ways on film, so can a structure, and it's up to the photographer to decide what they want to say and then to search for the best way to visually put that across. By narrowing his view to just this tiny section of the roof, Adrian has commented on the unconventional nature of the Guggenheim and has also revealed something about its texture and design. More importantly, however, he's put across something of the atmosphere of the place and what it felt like to be around it and this is the kind of emotional response that helps to make an architectural study something removed from a mere record.

Tone, Texture and Contrast

Untitled II by Ron Bambridge
Wista 5x4in camera, 6x7cm roll film back, 75mm lens, Ilford HP5 film.
Exposure 1/15sec at f/11

Visiting the ghost town of Bodie in California I was struck by the way that the wooden buildings there, which had been abandoned by the former residents and left to the elements, had become weathered over the years and had acquired the most wonderful textures. This particular detail, created by the fact that someone had opened the door and wedged it with a small rock, caught my eye and I decided that it would make an interesting picture, especially as the light was throwing shadows across the door, highlighting its battle scars and creating a contrast against the torn remnants of wallpaper that could just be made out in the background.

I used a lens that was slightly wide in terms of the 6x7cm back that I was using to enable me to move back as far as I could from the subject in what was quite a restricted space and I framed the picture so that the door filled around half the frame and was nicely counterbalanced by the darker tone of the shadows to the left. Because the light was reaching the door indirectly its effect was quite soft and so it revealed detail without creating extreme contrast and that allowed me to set an exposure that pulled up just enough detail in its surroundings to place it into context.

Ron Bambridge

Printing and Processing To add the finishing touch to the image, Ron decided to have it toned in thiocarbamide. This is a two-bath toner: the initial stage is a bleach bath that reduces the density of the tones and this is followed by a wash and an immersion in a toning solution to bring back the intensity of the image and to add colour. Thiocarbamide has become a favourite with many photographers because it is so versatile: any number of variations to the mixture of the components in the toning solution will introduce a different final colour to the print, allowing the final result to range from purple brown through to yellow brown (see Printing and Processing section).

Pointer A sturdy tripod is an invaluable aid to the photographer looking to photograph texture, since the effectiveness of the final image depends on it being bitingly sharp. There is a further advantage in that composition can be adjusted precisely and will then remain exactly the same for a series of pictures if required. By slowing down the pace at which a photographer can work, the use of a tripod also ensures that more time is spent thinking about the detail of a picture and that can help to improve the overall strength of the final image.

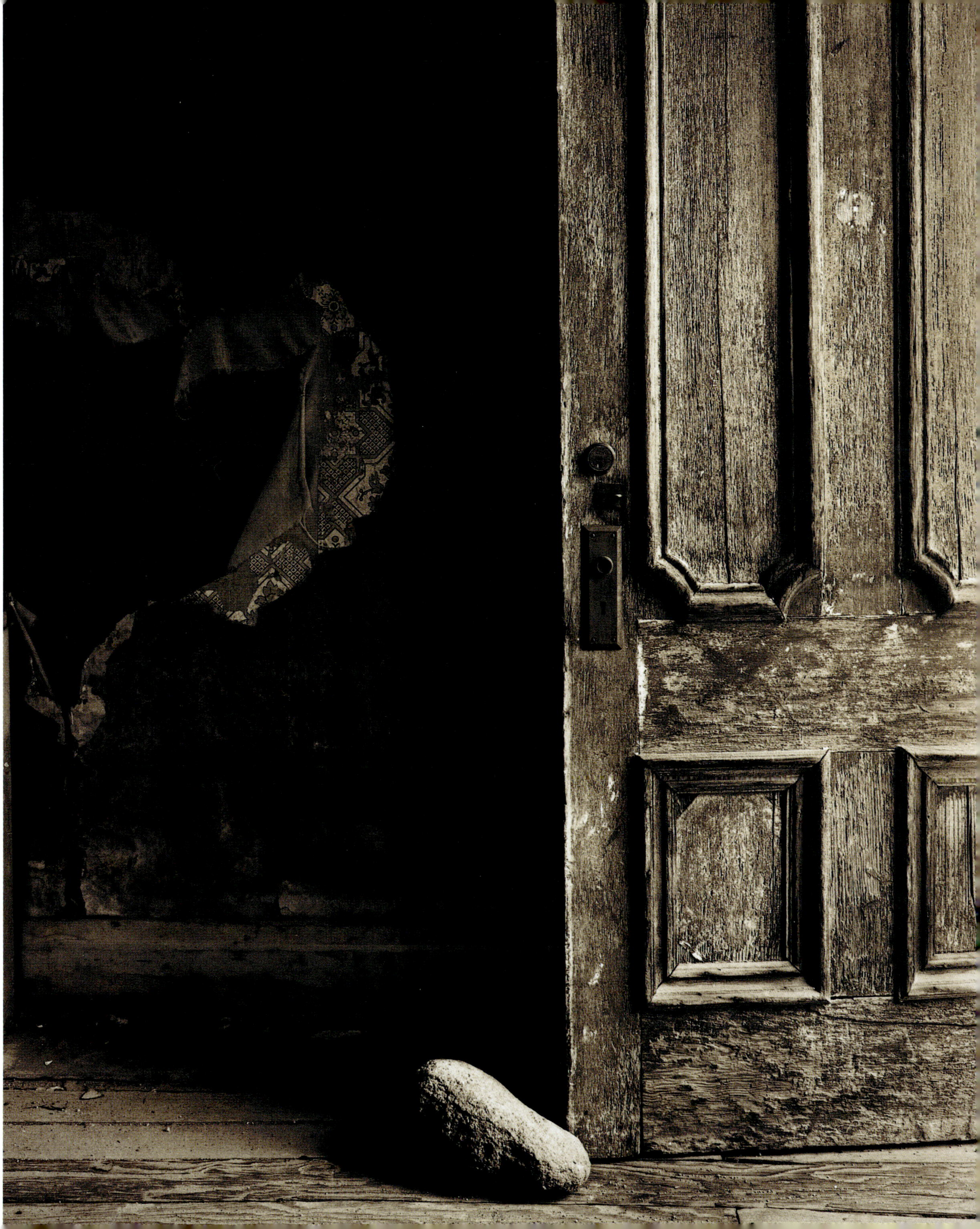

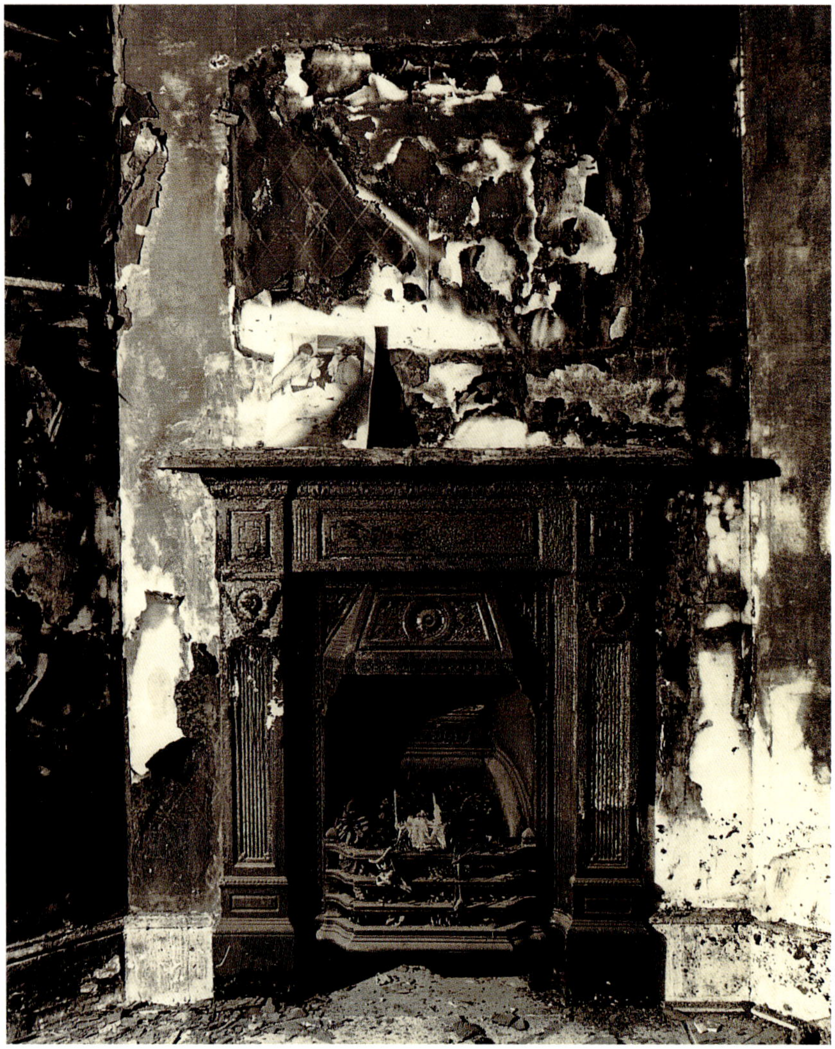

Tone, Texture and Contrast

Fire damaged room by Gavin Kingcombe
Mamiya 6x7cm, 65mm lens, Kodak Tri-X film.
Exposure one second at f/11

A friend of mine who is a photographer's agent had experienced a terrible fire that had destroyed most of her flat. Maybe it was something to do with her association with photographers but, when she told me about this, she suggested that I might like to pay a visit before the rebuilding work commenced because she could see that it had potential to make an interesting series of pictures. I appreciated her bravery and realised that she was absolutely right: most of the place had suffered enormous damage and the fire had created amazing texture and areas of intricate detail that were perfect subjects for black and white photography.

I came across this fireplace in one of the rooms and the heat of the fire had blistered its paintwork and peeled back the paper from the walls around it. The room was in almost complete darkness and so I knew that I was going to have to use an artificial source of light. In a normal situation I would have set up my softbox and worked with that, but here the need was to accentuate the textures in the room and I realised that a single directional light would work better. There were workmen already on site starting to make repairs and so I borrowed one of the 500W tungsten lights that they were working by and pointed this directly at the area I wanted to photograph. The illumination this provided was very harsh and contrasty and emphasised the texture in a way that the more gentle light of the softbox could not have matched.

Gavin Kingcombe

My Favourite Tip Calculating the exposure in a situation such as this was always going to be a little tricky and so I took a test Polaroid to make sure that the result I was going to achieve would be exactly what I wanted. I used black and white Polaroid film in this situation because I knew that this would give me the clearest indication of the way that the tones would register.

I stick with black and white Polaroid even when working in colour. This is because I believe that, by removing the colour from the equation, the photographer is given a clearer indication of the contrast and exposure levels that will be achieved in the picture. As a bonus, the black and white Polaroid film develops quicker than the colour version and this speeds everything up.

Pointer Learn to improvise so that you can make use of situations that you encounter. Lighting in particular doesn't need to be too formal: unlike colour film that will need to be balanced to the colour temperature of the kinds of source being used, black and white has the ability to cope with lighting of all types.

"Most of the place had suffered enormous damage and the fire had created amazing texture and areas of intricate detail."

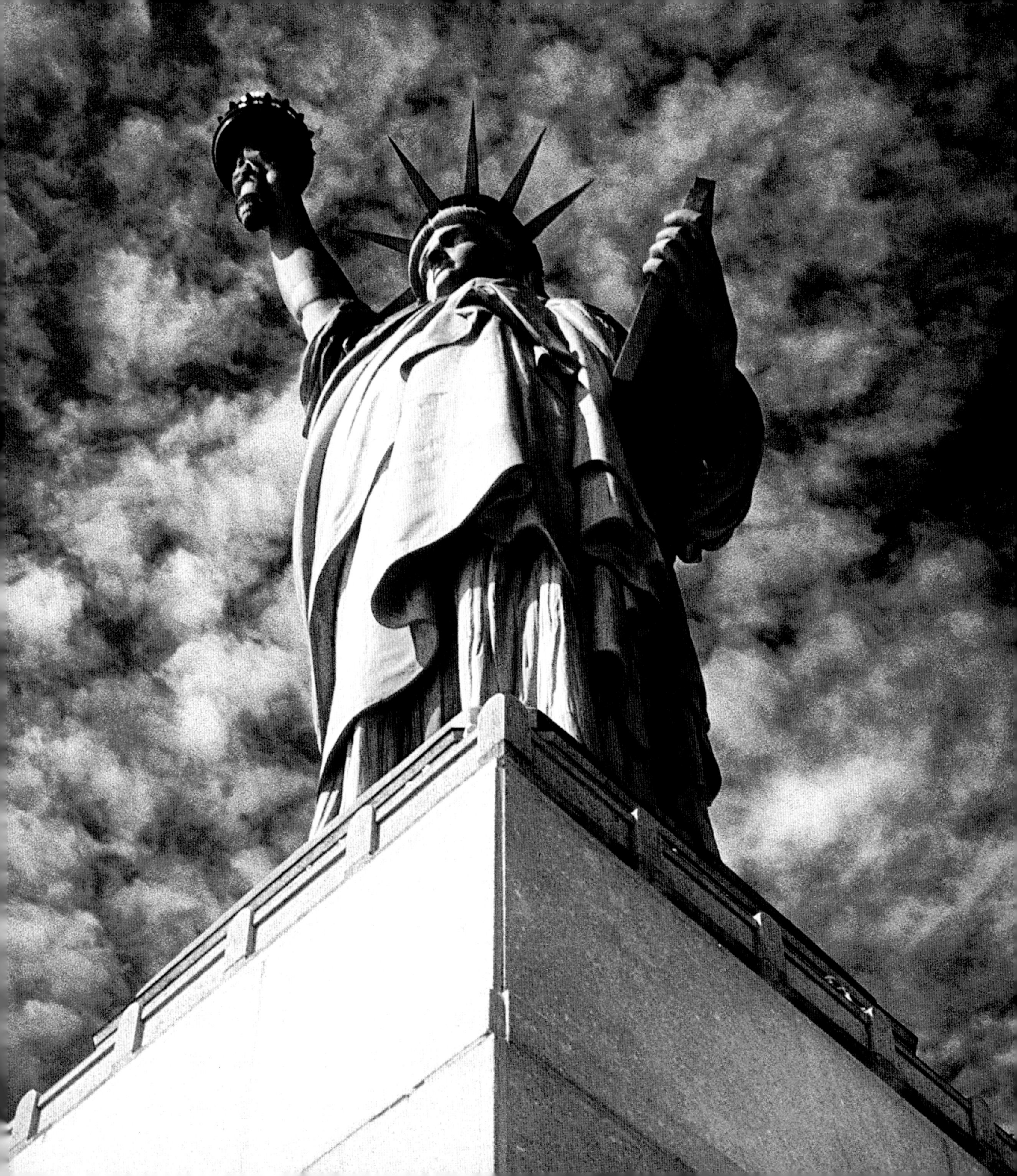

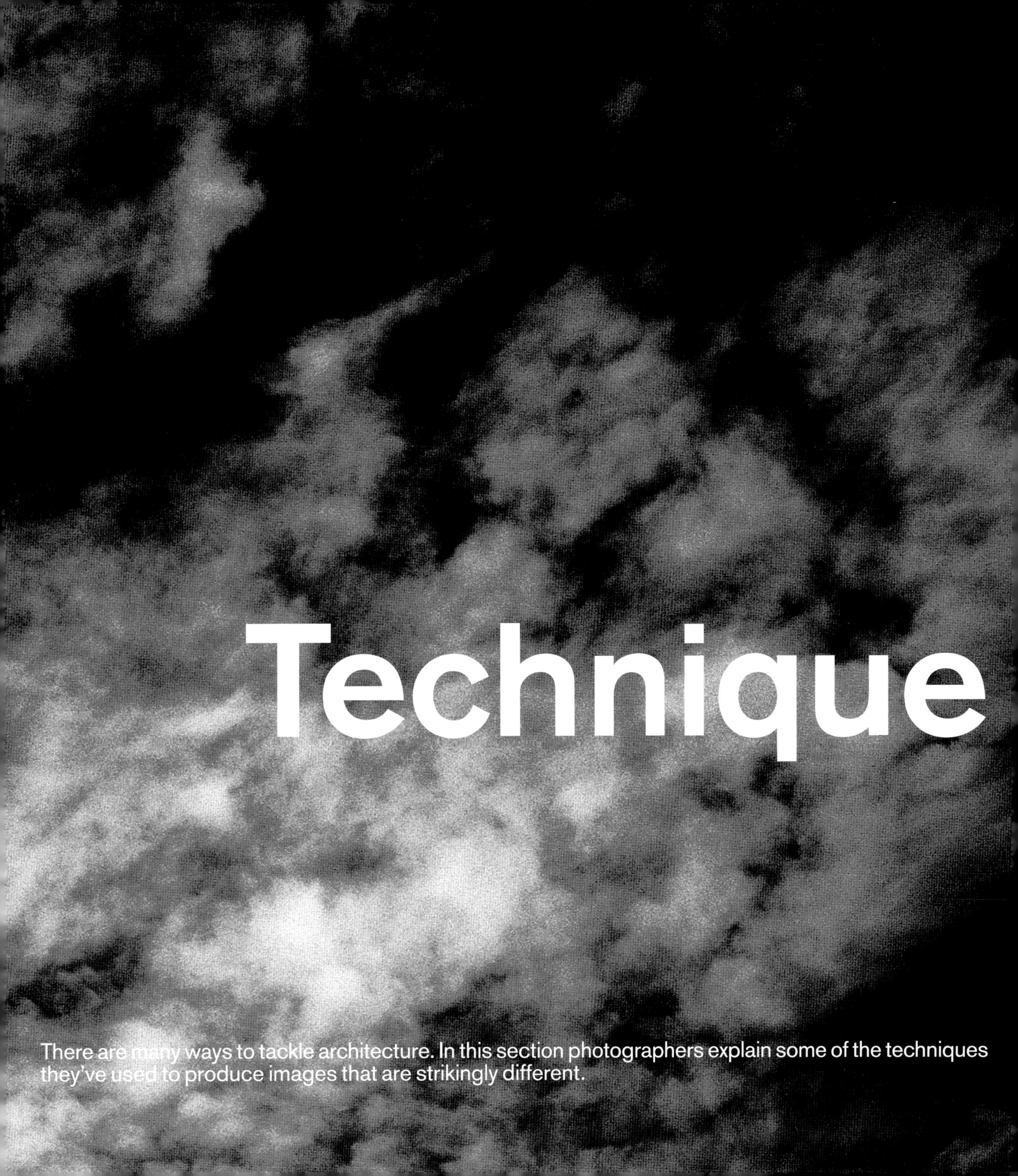

Technique

There are many ways to tackle architecture. In this section photographers explain some of the techniques they've used to produce images that are strikingly different.

Technique

Empire State Building by Tom Baril
Linhof 5x4in camera, 300mm lens, Kodak Tri-X film.
Exposure 5 seconds at f/8

The weather in New York was terrible and it had been raining for a couple of days, which was preventing me from carrying out a shoot that I had been planning to do at the Empire State Building. This was a difficult assignment in any case because this building has been photographed a million times before and it's a struggle to find something new to say about it.

When the rain stopped I decided to venture out and to see if there was the opportunity for a picture. The cloud cover was still low and, as it started to clear from around the top of the Empire State, the lights up there started to show through and I realised that this was quite an interesting effect.

I set my camera up looking at the building and used a long lens to allow me to frame just the top part of it. Then, to heighten the atmosphere that was already being created by the clouds, I decided to work with the narrowest depth of focus that was possible so that just one tiny part of the tower was sharp. By using my maximum aperture I kept depth of field to a minimum and then I used camera movements to reduce down the plane of focus still further.

With the camera pointing upwards at around 45 degrees the film plane on the camera was adjusted so that it was virtually parallel to the building while the lens panel was also swung in that direction, though not to quite the same degree because I needed to keep the top of the building in the frame.

I was able to monitor the result by looking through the ground glass screen on the back of the camera and the effect that I achieved gave me a new look at a familiar building.

Tom Baril

Pointer The controlled, independent movement of lens or film plane that is possible with a large format camera allows the photographer to influence the kind of picture that is achieved. There is a whole range of movements possible and each will have a specific effect. One of the most common for architectural photographers is rising front, the vertical movement of the lens parallel to the film plane. By raising the lens, say, 1cm, the image produced is also raised by 1cm and this can be extremely useful if the photographer wants to include the top of a tall building in a photograph without tilting the camera back and introducing distortion.

Swing back (horizontal or vertical axis) involves the pivoting of the film plane around an imaginary horizontal or vertical axis drawn across the face of the film at right angles through the lens axis. This enables the film to be swung out or into the plane of sharp focus for a subject and can help to dramatically increase—or indeed decrease—the depth of field in a picture.

Details Trying to include an entire building in a picture can sometimes reduce the potential for a strong picture. Choosing to feature just one element—as Tom Baril has here—can be a much more successful approach, allowing character and atmosphere to be built up while still presenting an image that is a recognisable portrait of a well known structure.

Courtesy of Bonni Benrubi Gallery, New York.

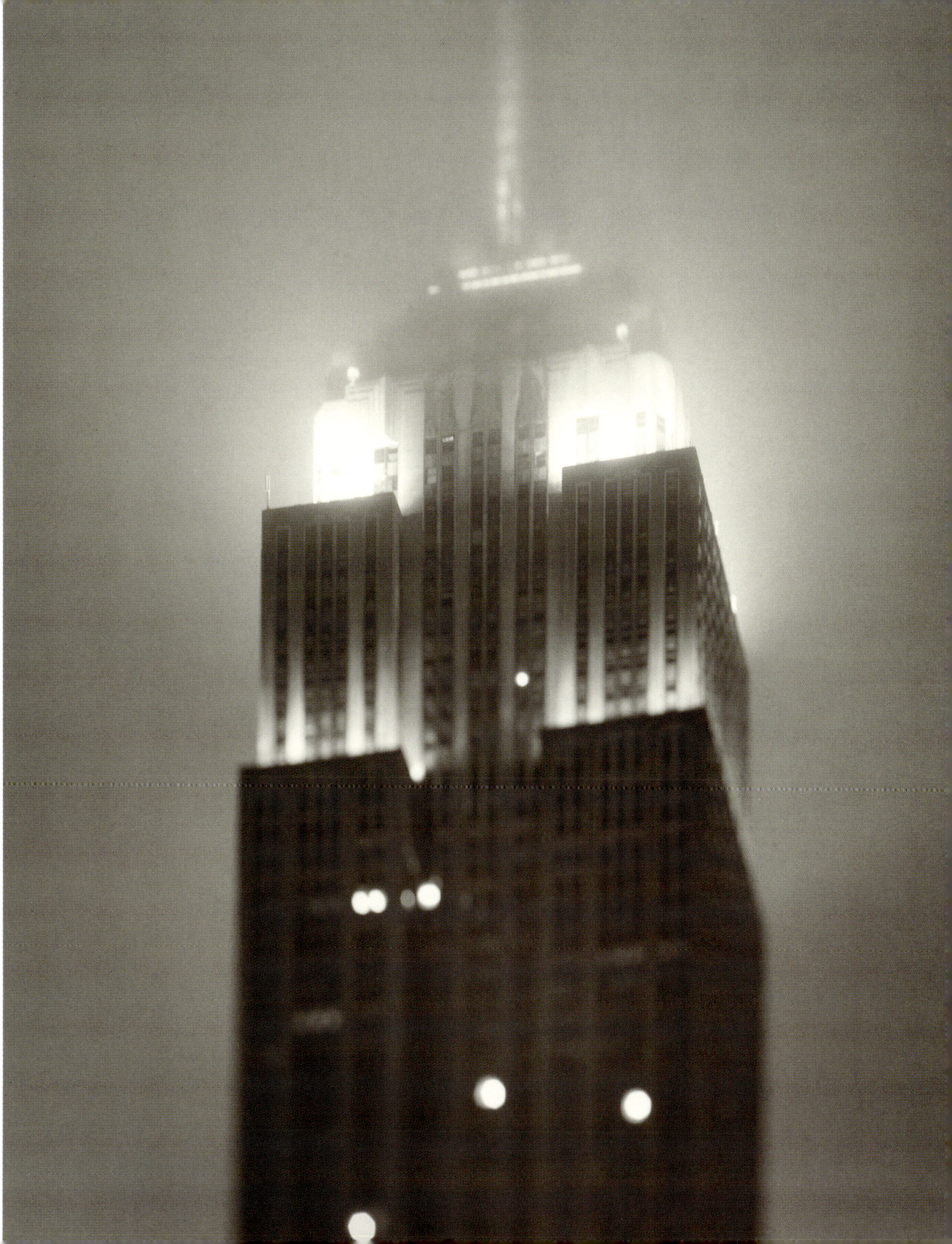

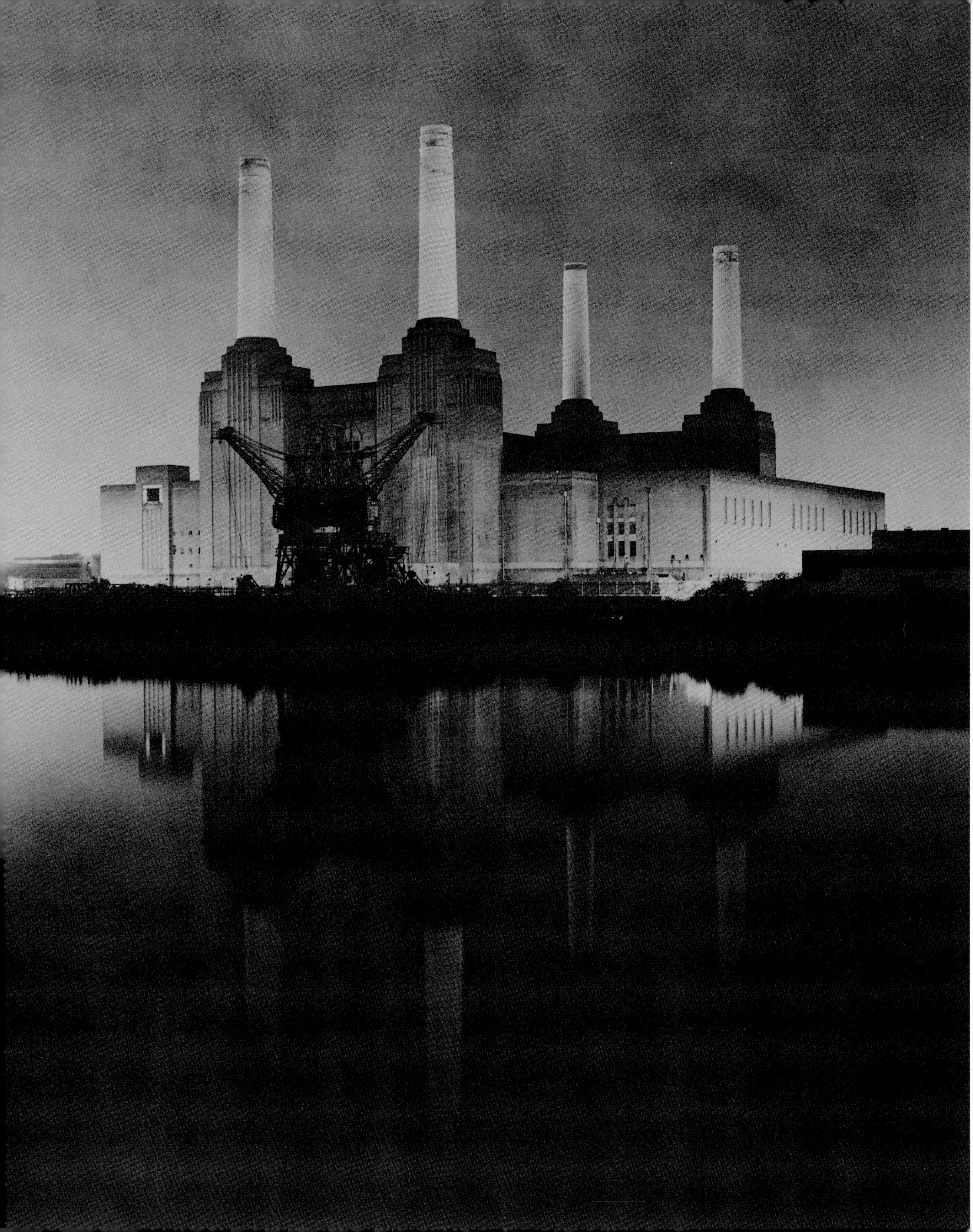

Battersea Power Station by Anderson & Low
6x7cm camera, 110mm lens, Kodak T-Max 100 film

Pointer Photographing architecture at night can lead to some extraordinarily powerful results and can allow the photographer to show a completely different aspect of even the most popular landmark buildings. The main requirement is a heavy-duty tripod that is capable of keeping steady for several seconds if required. Any hint of camera shake can ruin the effect and will show up immediately in the way that highlights, such as street lamps, will have moved. Work with a cable release and flip the mirror up if using a SLR prior to taking the picture so that this action doesn't disturb the camera at the taking stage.

This was taken at 3 am and it just seemed to be the right time to photograph this great building. Any piece of architecture will change in character depending on the time that you shoot and somehow the peace and tranquillity that descends in the dead of night seemed appropriate for such a beautiful building, that is currently so shockingly neglected and abused by developers. We wanted to convey the sense of wonder that comes over us when we look at this building and to echo the work of painters, such as Monet, Turner and Whistler, who have depicted the Thames and its surroundings over the years. Part of what we're doing is to record our impressions of places before they change or are lost forever. Battersea Power Station is virtually on the point of collapse and, even if it's saved, it may be gentrified or bastardised in some way in the process of redevelopment and it will utterly lose its character.

We wanted to capture some of this on film before it was too late. The picture was set up so that it was composed in a very symmetrical way and the reflection in the water of the Thames that echoes the shape of the building helps to reinforce this feel. By shooting at night we ensured that the time exposure combined with the movement of the water smoothed out this area of the picture and the whole mood of the picture is quiet and sombre, in keeping with the subject matter.

Anderson & Low

It's not usually necessary to use a fast film when shooting architecture at night because there will be no movement to capture and so exposures can be as long as necessary. When taking an exposure reading try to direct the meter towards an area of average contrast: don't include a highlight in the view since this may well indicate serious underexposure. To be safe try to bracket a little either side of the exposure indicated but veer more towards overexposure because this is likely to be a more accurate reflection of what is required.

Printing and Processing The picture was printed by Anderson & Low on conventional bromide paper but then processed in lith developer to create an effect similar to a charcoal drawing. When fresh, the lith developer produces a result that is extremely contrasty and features a pink tone but when the developer starts to become exhausted the results are actually much more interesting, although it may take some time for the print to reach the required density.

"By shooting at night we ensured that the time exposure combined with the movement of the water smoothed out this area of the picture."

You visualise something in your mind that you want to achieve and then you have to set about producing that on film. In this particular case I was visiting one of the disused slate quarries in Wales and, looking around, I was taken by all these remnants of a bygone age that were scattered around. This was a lost culture, something had disappeared and there were just a few traces left behind to show that it had ever existed. I felt that I should try to put something on film that summed up my feelings about this.

Finding this old set of wheels lying in a fast running stream I decided to set up a picture that would feature them as a dramatic foreground, albeit one that would still be in context with the rest of the image. I decided to emphasise the scale of the wheels within this scene by using the widest lens that I had for my large format camera—a lens so wide that special bellows have to be fitted to the camera to prevent vignetting around the edges of the picture—and then I set up my camera just a matter of inches away from them and composed my picture so that the remains of the quarry formed the background.

The water itself, had it been sharp, would have been full of detail and would have become a distraction within the picture and so I decided to let it become a blur that would simply add to the atmosphere of the picture. The use of a slow ISO 50 film ensured that, on this dull day, a lengthy exposure would be required and I set the aperture to f/45 so that the shutter speed became several seconds in length, easily enough to allow the water to take on a misty almost ethereal feel.

John Claridge

Technique

Wagon wheels by John Claridge
Deardorff 5x4in camera, 65mm lens, Agfa APX 50 film.
Exposure 5 seconds at f/45

Printing and Processing This was not an easy picture to print, because the brightness of the foreground was such that it required an enormous amount of burning in to prevent it acquiring too much importance within the picture. I also wanted the piles of slate on each side of the water to have a brooding feel and so these were printed down just a touch. Because these were dark areas to begin with, however, and they weren't reflecting a lot of light back, there wasn't much that needed to be done, although I did need to take care that enough detail remained in the base of the slate on the left of the picture to put this area into context.

Pointer Each lens will have its own qualities and will impose its own feel on a picture and so it's up to the photographer to select the one that will suit a particular subject. The wide angle will emphasise the scale of subjects close to the camera and will increase their importance within the picture, while also maximising the depth of field that is achievable. A long lens, however, will give distant subjects the appearance of being closer together than they actually are and so can allow a photographer to build a relationship between elements of a scene that won't be apparent with the naked eye.

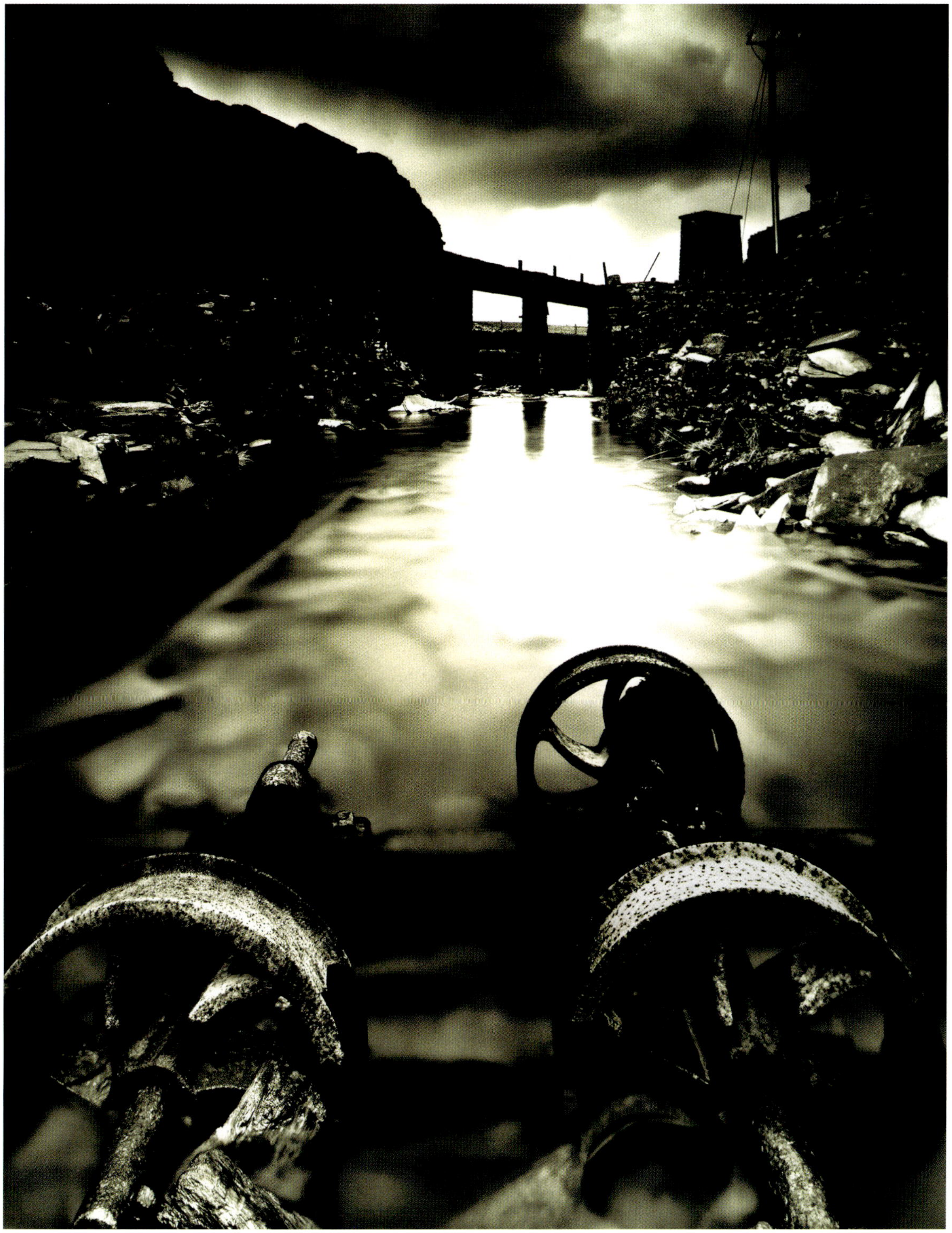

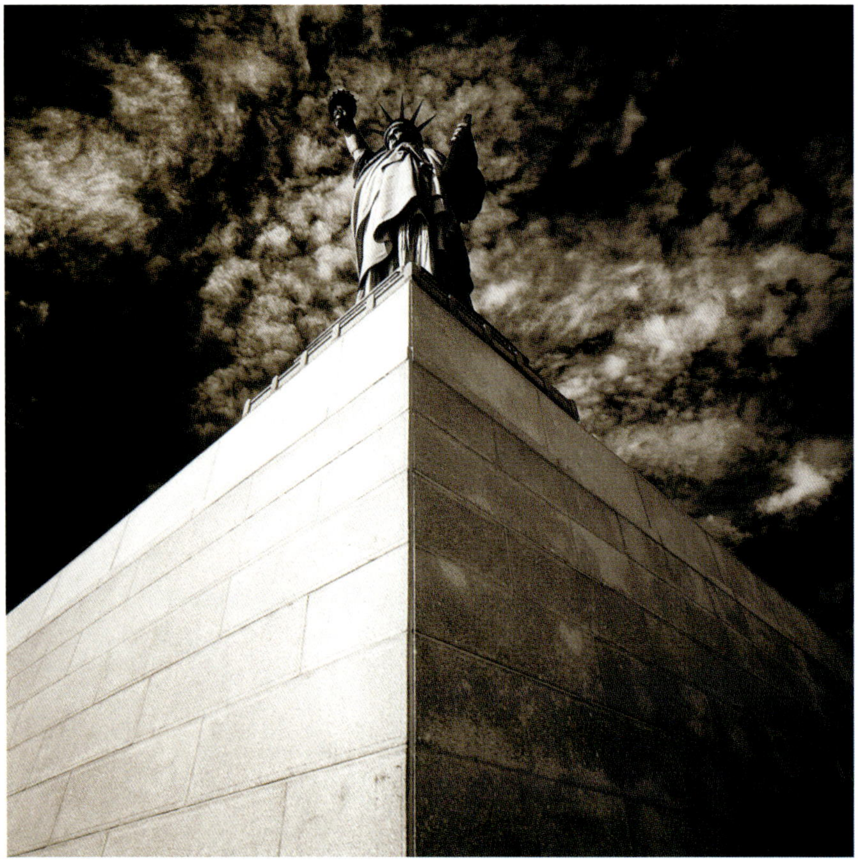

Technique

Statue of Liberty by Manuela Höfer
Hasselblad 903SWC 6x6cm camera with fixed 38mm superwide lens, Konica Infrared 750 film. Exposure not recorded

"The clouds on this particular day were fantastic and this encouraged me to look for a picture that would build on this feature."

I was visiting the Statue of Liberty and wanted to come away with a picture that was strikingly different to those that are usually taken by visitors. The specialist camera that I had with me offered an extremely wide field of view and so I thought that I would try to make use of the distorted perspective that this would give and combine this with the unusual tones that would result from the use of an infrared film in combination with a Wratten #25 red filter.

Initially I thought that I would travel to the top of the statue to see what I could find to photograph from there. This day, however, the queues were too long and so I decided to walk around the base and to see if I could find something from that viewpoint instead. The clouds on this particular day were fantastic and this encouraged me to look for a picture that would build on this feature, particularly since I knew that the infrared material I was using would darken down the blue in the sky which would serve to highlight the clouds still further.

Eventually I found what I was after by lying flat on the ground and angling the camera so that it looked directly up at the statue with the sky serving as a background. By working from a position that was so close to the plinth that the statue stands on I emphasised its size and strength in the picture—its structure picked out all the more by the lighting which divided this up into slabs of light and shade—and gave the statue itself a dominating appearance that I felt was appropriate for something that is seen by so many as a symbol of America.

Manuela Höfer

Pointer Black and white infrared film is sensitive to wavelengths that the human eye can't see and will reproduce a scene as a surreal mixture of tones that can be highly effective. The film will need to be used in conjunction with a red filter to filter out all the blue light and to make sure that only red (or indeed infrared) light reaches this film. There are a primarily three to choose from:

— Wratten #87 opaque red. This filter will cut out all the visible light and only allow infrared light to reach the film and using this filter produces the most dramatic effects.

— Wratten #89B opaque red. This is similar to the #87 but is not totally opaque so that, on a bright day, it is possible to see through the lens.

— Wratten #25 red. This is by the easiest filter to use because it's possible to see through the filter and to compose in the normal way. The results, while not as dramatic as those obtained with a #87, are still very pronounced.

Those wishing to use infrared materials will find that there are several unusual conditions that need to be observed. Firstly the film usually needs to be loaded and unloaded from the camera in darkroom conditions, because light will be able to penetrate the film cassette and will fog the film. Film such as Kodak's high speed infrared material also has no nominal ISO rating and so photographers will need to experiment with exposure/development to ascertain the 'correct' exposure index (ISO rating) for their way of working. Infrared also focuses at a slightly different point to the visible spectrum and so you'll either need to set a small f-stop to increase the depth of field or adjust the focus to the red mark which is usually provided on the barrel of interchangeable lenses.

Composition Building on the symmetry within the scene increased the feeling of strength in this picture. The striking juxtaposition of light and shade on the plinth has given Manuela the chance to use this as a focal point and she's positioned the line where these two areas meet directly in the centre of the picture, allowing it then to take the eye up through the picture to the statue itself.

Buckingham Palace by Thomas Kellner
Pentax ME Super, 135mm lens, Kodak T-400 CN film.
Exposure around 1/125sec at f/8

I was determined to find an original way of tackling architectural photography, something that would show well known buildings in an unusual manner and which would allow me to make some kind of personal comment about them.

My inspiration came from studying the work of impressionist and cubist painters such as Robert Delauney and I decided that I would try to 'deconstruct' the buildings on film, to photograph them in component form and to piece them together in the way that I wanted through the medium of a contact print. My aim is to visit landmark buildings in capital cities all around Europe, places that are photographed all the time by tourists, and to make the point that these are places of mass photography where people really waste film. I want to say that this is an over-photographed building: don't waste more time or materials on it.

The parameters I set myself at the start of the project were that I would only put together one black and white and one colour contact picture of each building and that I would photograph in strict frame order, a fact that would be reflected in the continuity of the frame numbers. I also decided that there would be no faking: I would not take a second roll of film and substitute pictures, so I had to get everything right in the one take.

With the picture of Buckingham Palace I first worked out what time of day I had to be there to achieve the lighting that I wanted— I also need to keep exposure consistent throughout the sequence so that the contact print has even density — and then I set up my camera on a tripod a suitable distance from the building. I needed to produce a rough sketch of the scene before I started to work out what needed to be included in each frame and I also needed to plan things so that I could complete the image within the 36 frames on my film. By allowing seven frames to cover the width I knew that I could make the image five frames deep and I then worked my way down from the top, building up the picture as I went.

I planned this image so that the bottom layer of pictures was fixed but all the other layers had movement within them as I tilted the camera at angles to create the distorted effect that I wanted. If I get anything wrong as I'm working with a 36-exposure deconstruction then I need to start the whole process again: I have produced pictures made up from anything up to 36 rolls of films – huge images made up from a total of 1296 exposures – and with those I can simply re-shoot one film within the sequence if I realise at the time that I've made a mistake.

Thomas Kellner

Pointer This particular image is rectangular and roughly to the format of a single 35mm negative but the beauty of the contact print method is that it's possible to make a picture to any format that you like. If a building had a thin upright shape, for example, the contact print could have been five frames across and seven strips deep to accommodate this.

My Favourite Tip I shoot my pictures on Kodak's T-400 CN film, which is a chromogenic material. This makes things easier for me by allowing me to get it developed through the C-41 process at the same time as my colour material.

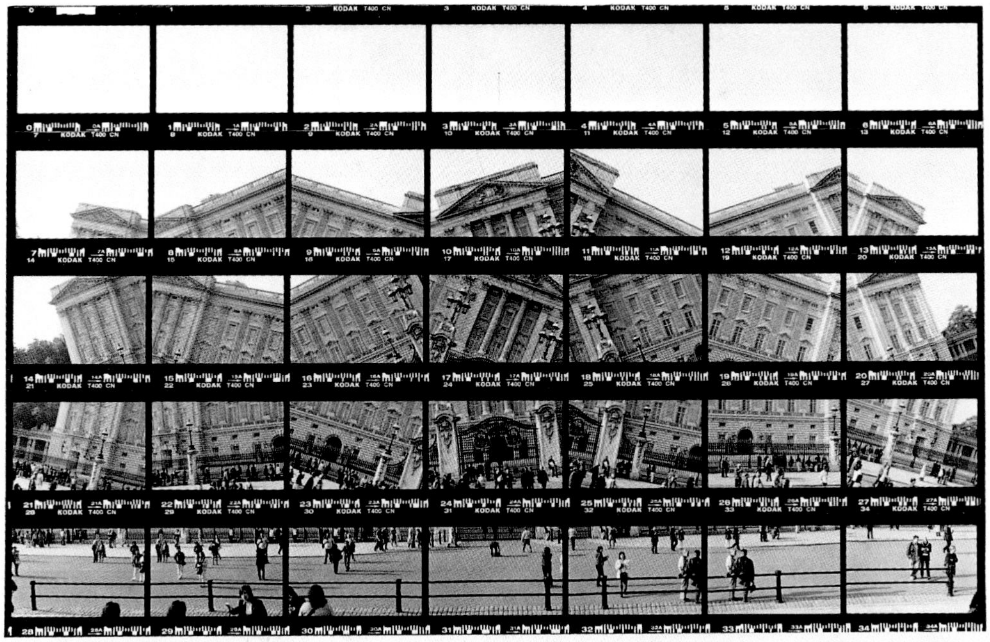
KODAK T400 CN

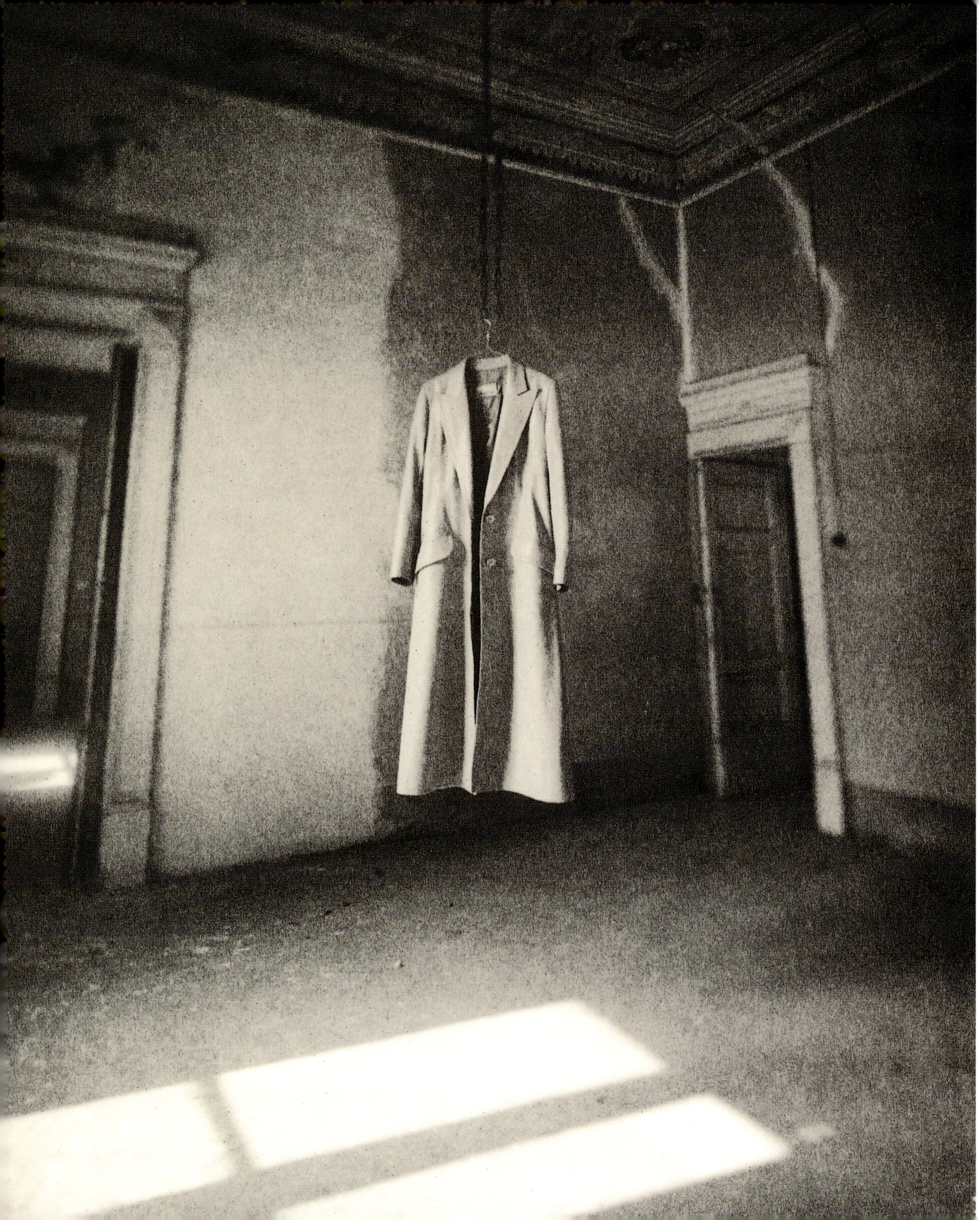

Technique

Hanging Coat by Barry Cawston
Wista 5x4in camera, 75mm lens, Ilford FP4 film.
Exposure one second at f/45

I had been given a commission to photograph a ruined building near Naples in Italy that was being converted into a centre for an arts trust and, while I was there, I was asked if I would take a photograph of a coat that someone had brought with them. To start with I worked in colour but then I realised that black and white would suit the subject better and I switched to FP4. The look I was after was one that was a bit odd and dreamlike and I decided to achieve this by using a wide angle lens to set the walls and doorways at an angle and then I set the focus so that it was extremely narrow and concentrated in a very tight diagonal band that extended through the middle of the picture, taking in the coat and little else.

I was able to achieve this by using the movements that were featured on my 5x4in camera. The design of the camera is such that the front lens panel and the rear film back are connected by flexible bellows and have the ability to rise and twist in a variety of directions. By using these singly or in combination with each other it's possible to influence the appearance of the picture or the depth of field within it. Here I twisted the front element to the left and the rear film back to the right to control tightly the line of focus within the picture, checking the result on my ground glass viewing screen on the rear of the camera to ensure that I had the look that I wanted.

The result is a picture where the coat almost appears to be hovering in quite a ghostly fashion, suspended from a chain that once, I imagine, served as support for a chandelier.

Barry Cawston

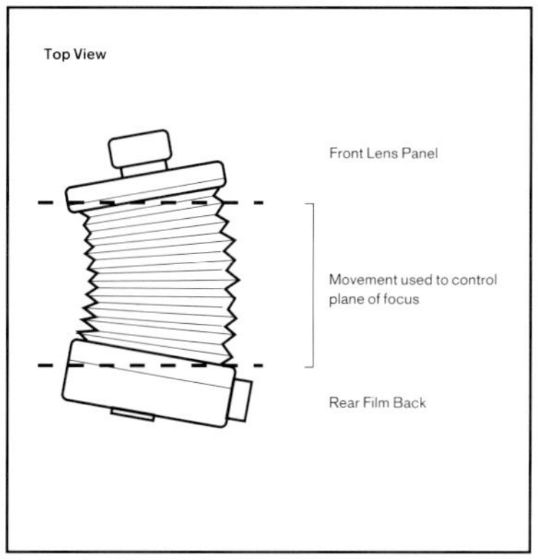

Printing and Processing This picture was printed on standard bromide paper but put through lith developer to add grain and tone and to achieve a look that was in keeping with the mystical feel of the photograph. The older and more exhausted that the developer becomes the more extreme the appearance of the prints that result and this one was made when the developer had already had something like 15 prints through it, and it had lost much of its potency. The result of this was that the print needed a lot of exposure from the enlarger—in this case around two minutes with the aperture fully open—and it then required around fifteen minutes in the developer before it came through to the point that I wanted. This ensured that the grain in the picture was increased significantly while contrast levels were knocked back. I love this way of working because it's virtually impossible to produce two prints that are exactly the same and it adds a unique quality to the final result.

Pointer I love using natural light in an indoor setting and had noticed how, at a certain time of day, the shape of the window was projected on to the floor in this room. That was what I wanted to use in my picture and I timed my shoot to coincide with the time when I knew this effect would happen.

Printing a

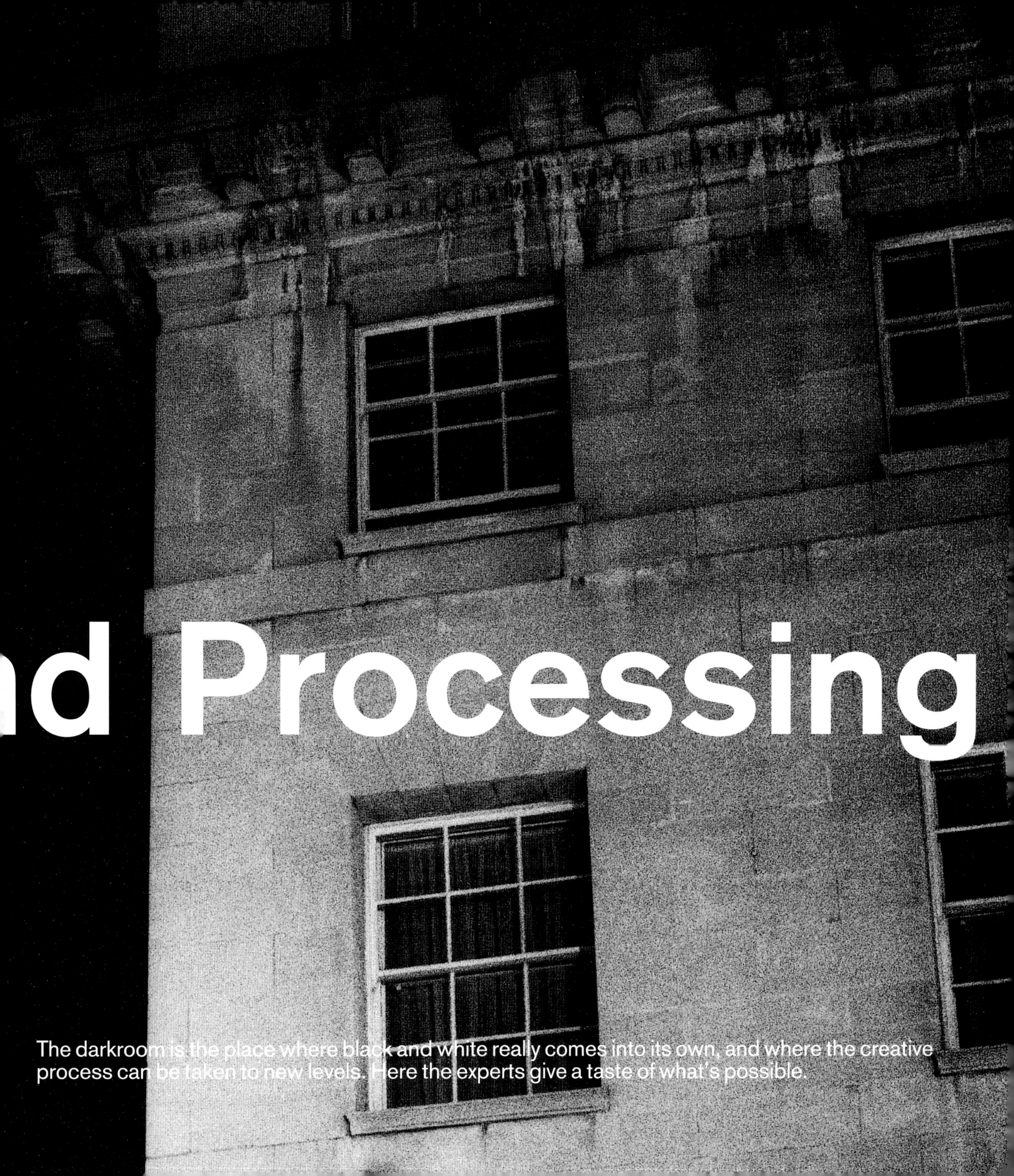

nd Processing

The darkroom is the place where black and white really comes into its own, and where the creative process can be taken to new levels. Here the experts give a taste of what's possible.

Statue in Portland Square by Adrian Ensor
Rolleiflex 6x6cm with fixed 75mm lens, Ilford HP5 + film.
Exposure 30 seconds at f/22

This is one from a series that I have been producing that feature statues at night. This is the time when I think that many of them take on a very special quality: they always look more impressive when the street lights are on and when some of the clutter that inevitably surrounds them has been lost in the darkness and there is the chance, as here, to play around with the way that they're lit and the shadows that they create.

I came across this particular shadow in Portland Place, which is just around the corner from where I have my darkroom. When passing one night I noticed this incredible scene, which has been created by the statue's proximity to a street light. Not only was the shadow of the horse's head being thrown on to the side of a building but the rest of it was picked up on the adjacent house, making up the complete form, albeit in two parts.

My approach to statues is simple: it's not what the statue represents that's important, it's what I can make of it and I approach them all with the idea in mind that I will try to do something unusual and thought provoking. Many of them have become so much a part of the street furniture that people hardly see them any more but I think that with an original approach they can make the basis for some wonderful pictures.

Adrian Ensor

Technique With a lengthy time exposure, it's extremely important to keep the camera completely steady so that there's no chance of camera shake. A heavy-duty tripod is a must and this should be positioned somewhere where it won't be close to passing traffic or rattled by wind. It's too risky to fire the shutter by hand because this is very likely to cause the camera to shudder so invest in a cable release that will allow you to fire the camera remotely. With a camera such as the Rolleiflex, which is a twin lens reflex, there is no danger of camera shake being caused by the shutter firing. With a single lens reflex, however, the action of the mirror flipping up can create vibration so, if your camera allows it, flip the mirror up prior to taking the picture to avoid this problem.

Printing and Processing
I processed this negative in Microphen, which I find gives me a little extra in terms of film speed, around one stop, and the print was then produced on Agfa Classic warmtone paper. I decided to tone it in thiocarbamide but instead of using my normal bleach, which is made up from potassium ferricyanide and potassium bromide, I used just the ferricyanide. I discovered the effectiveness of this when an assistant once forgot to put the second ingredient in and I find that it gives me a blue black in conjunction with warm mid-tones and I liked the effect. The thiocarbamide toner is very versatile and can be mixed in a variety of ways to give a different toning effect. Depending on the relative strengths of its components it can produce a final print that ranges from purple brown to yellow brown in colour.

Formula
Toner Bleach
Potassium Ferricycanide 100g, Potassium Bromide 100g
Add water to make one litre of stock solution.

Thiocarbamide Toner
Solution A—Water (40 deg c) 750ml, Thiocarbamide 100g
Add water to make one litre

Solution B—Water 750ml, Sodium Hydroxide 100g
Add water to Sodium Hydroxide—not the other way round—to make one litre.

Process
Bleaching—For fully toned prints, dilute one part of bleach to at least nine parts of water, then immerse the print and agitate evenly until it turns a pale straw colour. For partially toned or split toned prints, increase the dilution and remove the print before all the silver has been bleached. Wash thoroughly to remove all yellow bleach stains.

Toning
Solutions A & B can be mixed in the following ratios to give varying shades of brown.

Sol A	Sol B	Water	Colour
10ml	50ml	460ml	Purple Brown
20ml	40ml	460ml	Cold Brown
30ml	30ml	460ml	Mid Brown
40ml	20ml	460ml	Warm sepia Brown
50ml	10ml	460ml	Yellow Brown

Immerse bleached print into toner, agitate until print returns to its original density, remove and wash thoroughly. Take care not to breath in the chemicals during the bleaching and toning processes. Work in a well-ventilated room and wear a mask, and always handle prints with tongs or wear rubber gloves to prevent the skin coming into contact with the chemicals.

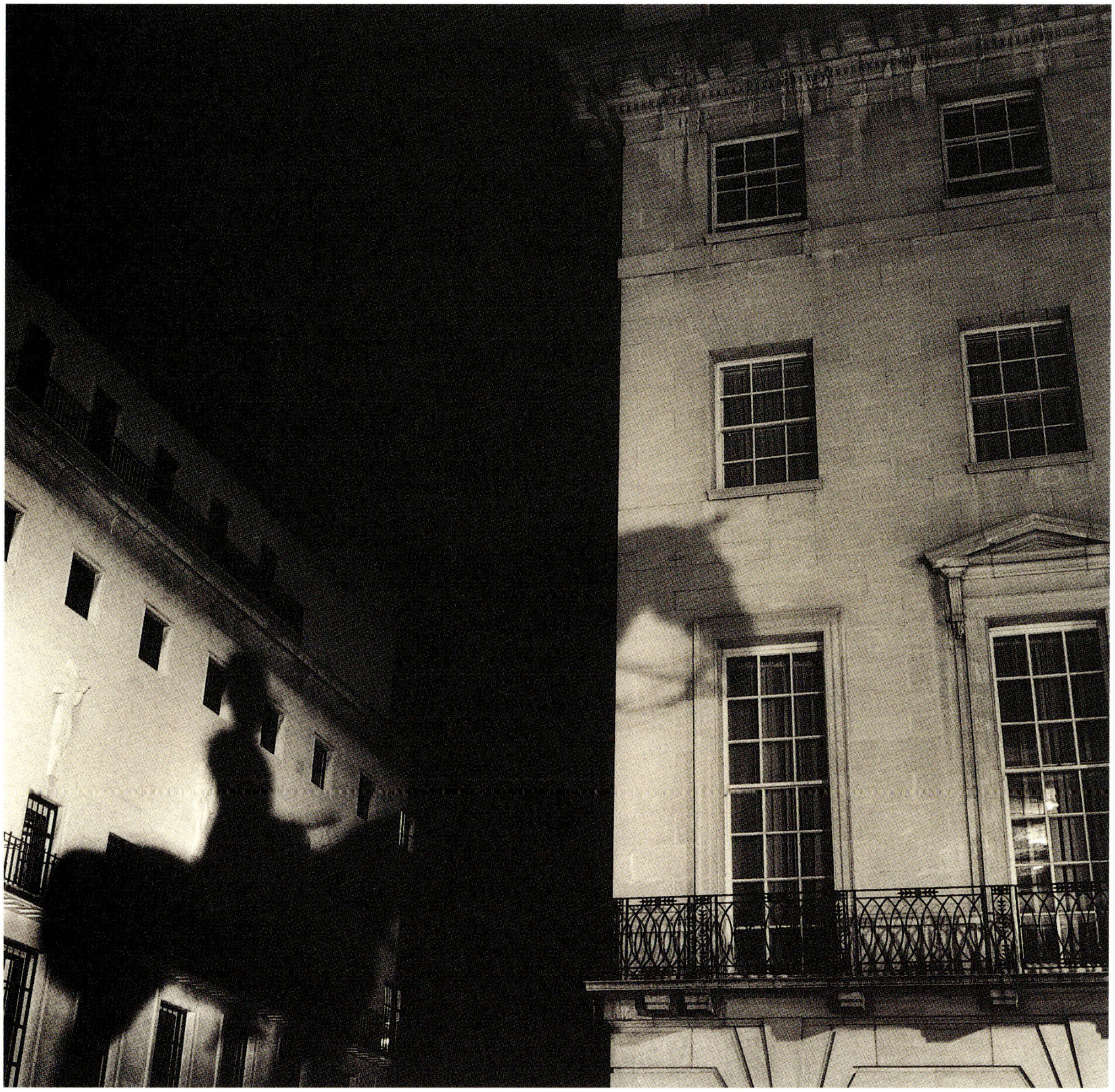

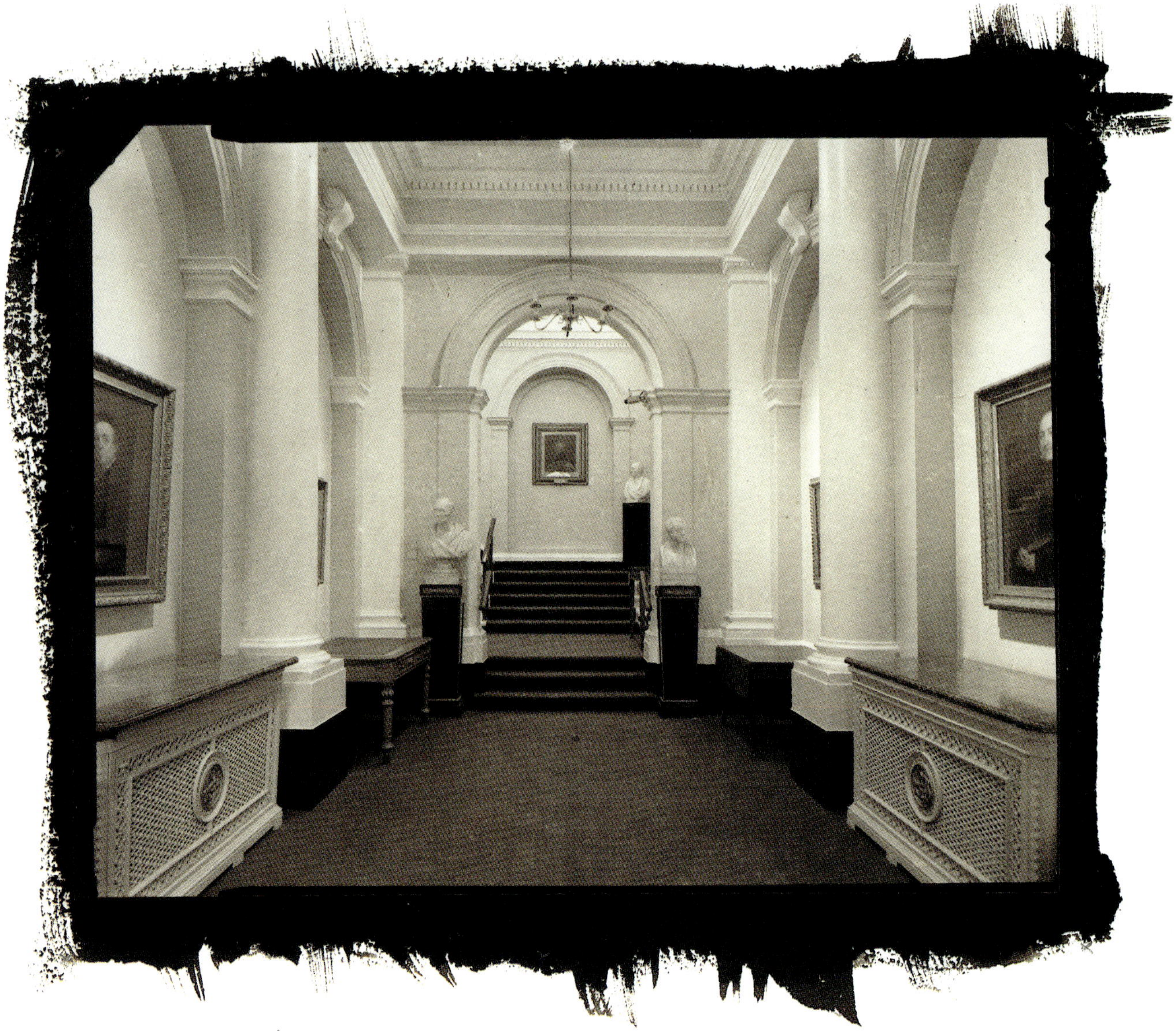

Printing and Processing

Interior of Burlington House by Randall Webb
Wista 5x4in camera, 70mm lens, Kodak T-Max 400 film.
Exposure two seconds at f/22

This is an image that I produced for the Geological Society, one of the learned societies that are based in Burlington House in London's Piccadilly, also the home, of course, of the Royal Academy of Art. I used a wide lens on my 5x4in camera to ensure that I was able to pull in as much of the interior as possible given that I was working in a very confined space and I took the picture using only available light, hence the length of the exposure that needed to be given.

After giving the negative normal development, I decided to make a Palladium print to give to the Society. This is a very similar process to Platinum except that it is far less expensive to produce. Both processes are highly regarded by leading professionals not only for their permanence but also for the delicate range of tones that they are capable of rendering. In addition they are the only old processes where the contrast of the print can be varied, as with Multigrade, by changing the ratios of the various chemicals used to coat the paper.

Randall Webb

Printing and Processing The ideal negative for a Palladium print should contain slightly higher contrasts than required for printing on grade 2 but, more importantly, the negative should contain a wide range of tones from light to dark.

The paper itself is prepared by taking a sheet of good quality drawing paper—I used Fabriano Roma Michaelangelo, which is hand made—and this is coated with a solution of water, palladium chloride, ferric oxalate and potassium chlorate. When dry the paper is exposed with a negative in a contact printing frame in sunlight or under a UV lamp. It is then developed in potassium citrate, cleared in diluted phosphoric acid and washed in clean water.

The traditional method of clearing the print was to use a bath of very dilute hydrochloric acid or spirits of salts. This method has been largely abandoned as it tends to reduce the permanence of the paper.

Technique Coating the paper is relatively simple, but will need practice. To brush the emulsion on, as I did here, take your sheet of paper and attach it to a flat piece of hardboard with a strip of masking tape along each edge to hold it flat. Now take the negative and place it on the paper and very lightly mark where you want its position to fall. Now take the saucer containing the emulsion, and dip into it with a flat paint brush (the best are flat wooden handled 'hake' brushes from any good art supplier) about one inch wide, taking care not to overcharge the brush. Then brush the emulsion onto the paper within the area where the negative will fall, taking care to be gentle to avoid abrading the paper's surface. The paper should absorb the liquid to the extent that, when you look across the surface of the paper, no pools of liquid remain. At this stage you can carry the liquid across your markings to give a small margin of brushed emulsion with a ragged edge. When exposed this will give you the brushed edge that is characteristic of so many old process prints.

Printing and Processing

Brooklyn Bridge by Tom Baril
Linhof 5x4in camera, 215mm lens, Kodak Tri-X film.
Exposure 1 second at f/45

"I wanted to produce an image of the Brooklyn Bridge that was strikingly different and I decided that I would concentrate purely on a detail."

I wanted to produce an image of the Brooklyn Bridge that was strikingly different and I decided that I would concentrate purely on a detail. I wanted to say something about the structure but I wasn't interested in trying to show the whole thing. In the end I decided that I would focus on the cables that hold this bridge together and I picked out this point where they reached an anchorage, because I thought that this provided a dramatic focal point.

Angling my camera up at the bridge, I used a long lens to allow me to include just this small section of the structure and I composed carefully so that the tower was framed between two sections of cable.

Tom Baril

Print and Processing Wishing to emphasise this viewpoint still further I decided to enhance the picture at the darkroom stage by holding back the area where the anchorage was occurring and darkening down its surroundings. My basic exposure on to Kodak Ektalure paper was 20 seconds at f/11 and then I took a dodging tool and held back the centre section of the picture while giving a further three basic exposures to the rest of the print, i.e. 3x 20 seconds at f/11. In addition to this extra exposure I softened the image by exposing it through a piece of diffusing glass that I keep in a slide mount. This had the effect of taking some of the detail out of the bridge around the area that I was interested in and it concentrated the attention still further on the point that I wanted to emphasise.

Technique Dodging and burning are the terms given to the technique of adding or holding back exposure from selected areas of the print to control the density. Here Tom Baril has altered the emphasis in his picture and drawn attention to the area that he wants the viewer to concentrate on. Another use might be to even out the contrast levels in a picture that is impossible to print with one exposure. A picture that has particularly bright highlights, for example, might call for some extra exposure—burning—to be given just to those areas. A useful tool to make would be a sheet of thick card with a hole roughly torn in the middle. Positioning this to allow the exposure to reach just selected areas adds density to just those points, although it's crucial to keep the card moving at all time to avoid the edges of the hole becoming obvious. Dodging is used when the aim is to prevent exposure reaching selected areas and the tool that could be used here is a piece of card attached to the end of a thin strip of wire. This can be moved around the area where density might otherwise build up too strongly and, again, continual movement is crucial to avoid its use becoming obvious.

Courtesy of Bonni Benrubi Gallery, New York.

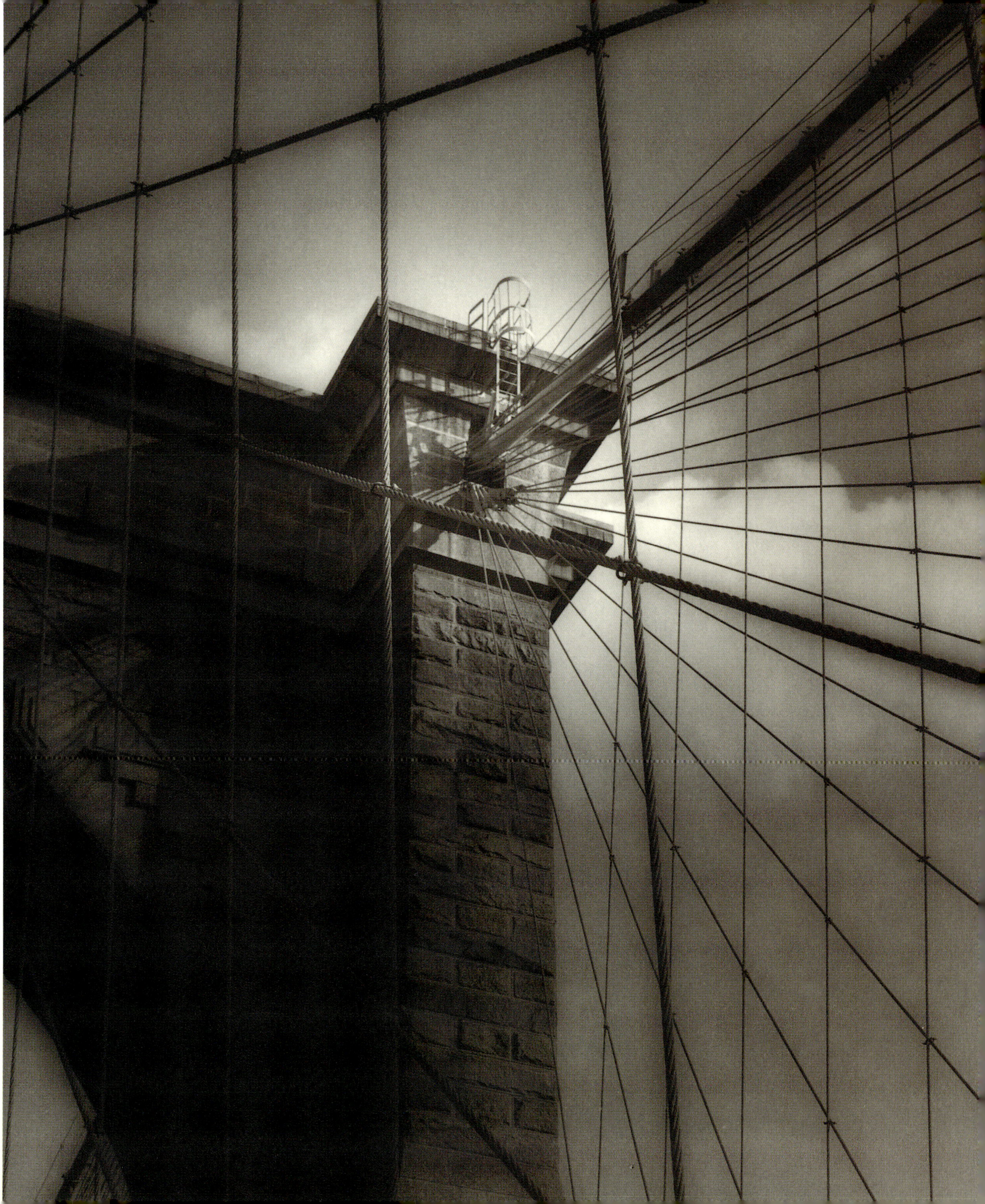

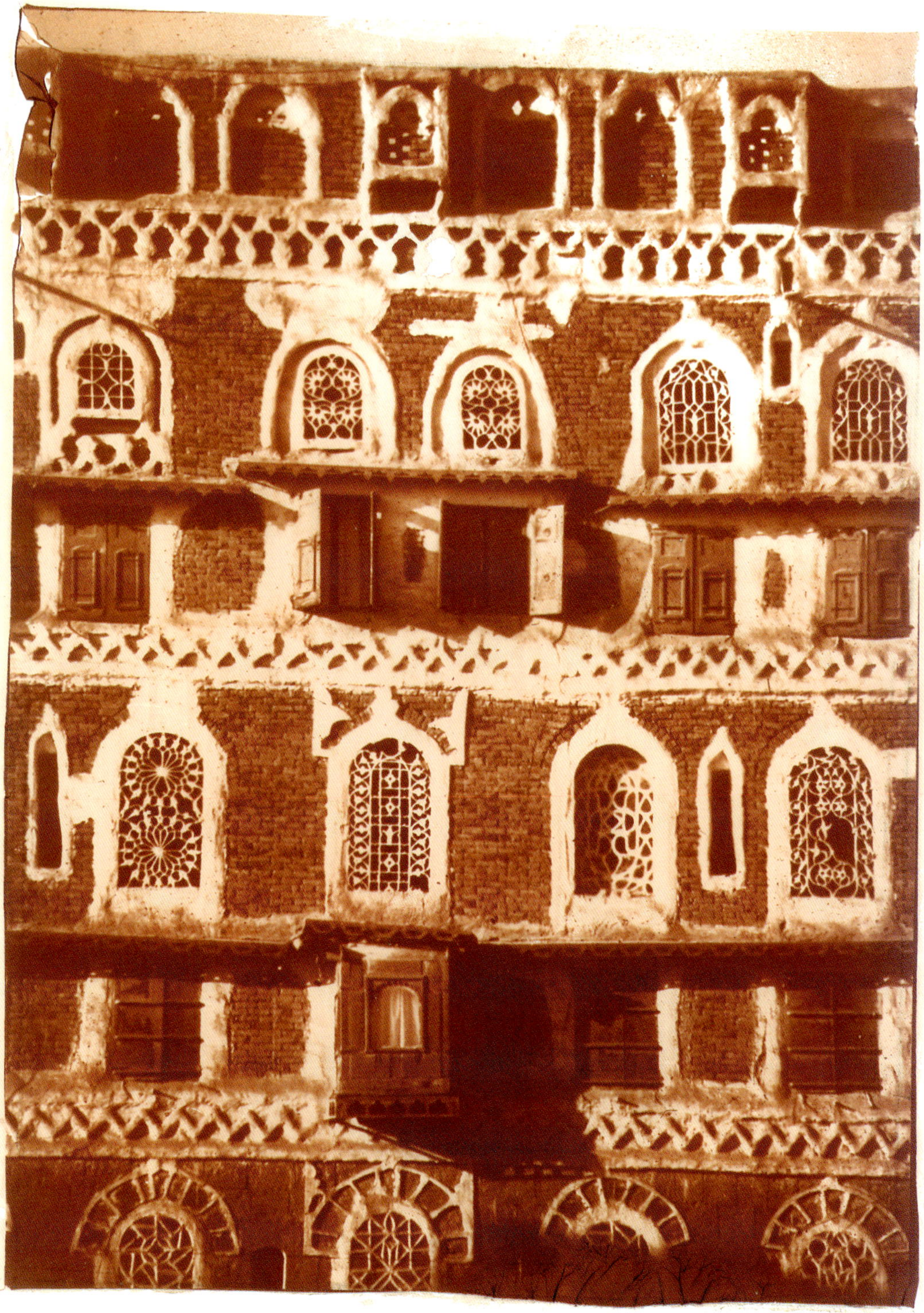

Façade, North Yemen by Randall Webb
Pentax ME Super, 135mm lens, Kodachrome 64 film.
Exposure 1/125sec at f/8

I had the opportunity to visit the city of Sanaa, the capital of North Yemen and, while I was walking around the old quarter, I came across a little square that contained some very traditional buildings. These featured the tiny panes of coloured glass in the windows that are so typical of this region and the buildings themselves were made from mud bricks and were several stories high. I used a long lens to enable me to frame a section of one of them head on so that I avoided converging verticals and it allowed me to achieve this very strong and symmetrical image. The original was shot on colour transparency film but subsequently I decided that I would use it as the basis for a Carbon Print, a photographic process patented as far back as 1864.

Randall Webb

Printing and Processing The first thing I had to do before I could make my print was to produce a black and white negative and I did this by putting the Kodachrome transparency in the enlarger and then printing it onto a sheet of line film that was the same size as I wanted my final print to be, in this case around 11x8ins.

Carbon printing is now a little-used process but was very popular at the end of the 19th century. A piece of plain non-photographic paper is coated with a mixture of gelatin and pigment of any colour to make what is known as carbon tissue. (It is possible to make your own, although this is a time-consuming and fairly laborious process. The beginner would be better advised to either buy the material from Silverprint –email sales@silverprint.co.uk - or, if required in long rolls, direct from Autotype, tel: 01235 771111, which has made the material since the 19th century and is now the only manufacturer from whom it is commercially available. It is now used to make roto-gravure plates for commercial printing and it comes in any colour provided it is terracotta red!).

The carbon tissue is then soaked in a solution of potassium dichromate to sensitise it and then dried. When combined with a negative in a contact printing frame and exposed to sunlight or ultraviolet light, the coating is hardened in inverse proportion to the densities of the negative. This exposed paper is then soaked in cold water and placed face to face with another sheet of paper that has been previously coated with plain gelatin.

Again this can be prepared by hand but I prefer to take a sheet of fibre-based paper and, without exposing it to light, to fix and then wash it so that it has no silver content.

After being left pressed together under a suitable weight—a stack of books is perfect—with the sheet of carbon tissue for a short time this 'sandwich' is placed in hot water. The gelatin softens and the backing of carbon tissue is gently peeled off, leaving an amorphous mass of coloured gelatin on the receiving paper. The image is 'developed' by soaking it in warm water until the unhardened gelatin in the highlights washes off leaving a continuous tone positive image. When all the soluble gelatin has been washed off it is hung up to dry.

The print will have a curious feel to it because the image will be in relief due to the fact that it's been built up from layers of gelatin. It will also have a slightly distorted feel due to the fact that, before it dries, the gelatin will be extremely fluid and it will 'wobble' slightly while being washed.

Pointer Because the image is two stages removed from the line negative, it will be reversed. In this case it wasn't a problem because there was no way of telling which way round the building was, but if you have lettering on view you will need to take account of this by reversing the negative for the initial exposure with the carbon tissue.

"The image is 'developed' by soaking it in warm water until the unhardened gelatin in the highlights washes off leaving a continuous tone positive image."

Vietnamese interior by Barry Cawston
Fujifilm 6x9cm camera, 90mm lens, Kodak T-Max 400 film.
Exposure 1/30sec at f/8

I came across this derelict building in the heart of the jungle close to Ho Chi Min City in Vietnam and, with its characteristically French feel, it was quite bizarre to find it in such a place. I love decaying buildings because they have such a sense of history about them and there is so much scope for interesting photography as nature slowly starts to take them over. I set the camera up so that I could feature both of the main doors into this building in this image. The sunlight coming through the windows just to the side of each door created pools of highlight on the floor which added interest to the scene and broke up the shadows nicely.

Barry Cawston

Printing and Processing I printed this image on to Ilford's Multigrade fibre based matt paper and worked on it quite extensively in the darkroom to achieve this result. The initial exposure for the print was around 20 seconds and for around one fifth of this exposure I placed a single thickness of stocking over the enlarger lens to create some diffusion. After this I burned in the highlights on the floor in front of both doors for a further 30 seconds, diffusing the image for the whole time so that all the details of things such as dust on the floor were removed.

Once the print was processed I decided that I would split tone it in sepia because I love the effect this gives, where the blacks remain the same while the highlights take on a hue of light brown and the mid-tones almost have a colour all of their own, becoming slightly pink in appearance. I wanted to highlight the thin strip of daylight coming between the two halves of the door on the right, to draw the eye to this point, so I started to bleach initially only in this area, using a concentrated mix—1-5 dilution as opposed to the more usual 1-15—and applying it with a cotton bud so that I could work very carefully only in this area.

Once this was done I placed the print in the fix and then washed it thoroughly. Then I put it back in the bleach and waited until the highlights and the mid-tones started to lose density, but I removed and washed the print before the shadow areas were affected. Then, when I placed the print in the sepia toner, only certain parts of it reacted. The shadow areas remained black and the area between the doors took up very little of the brown and consequently retained its light tone.

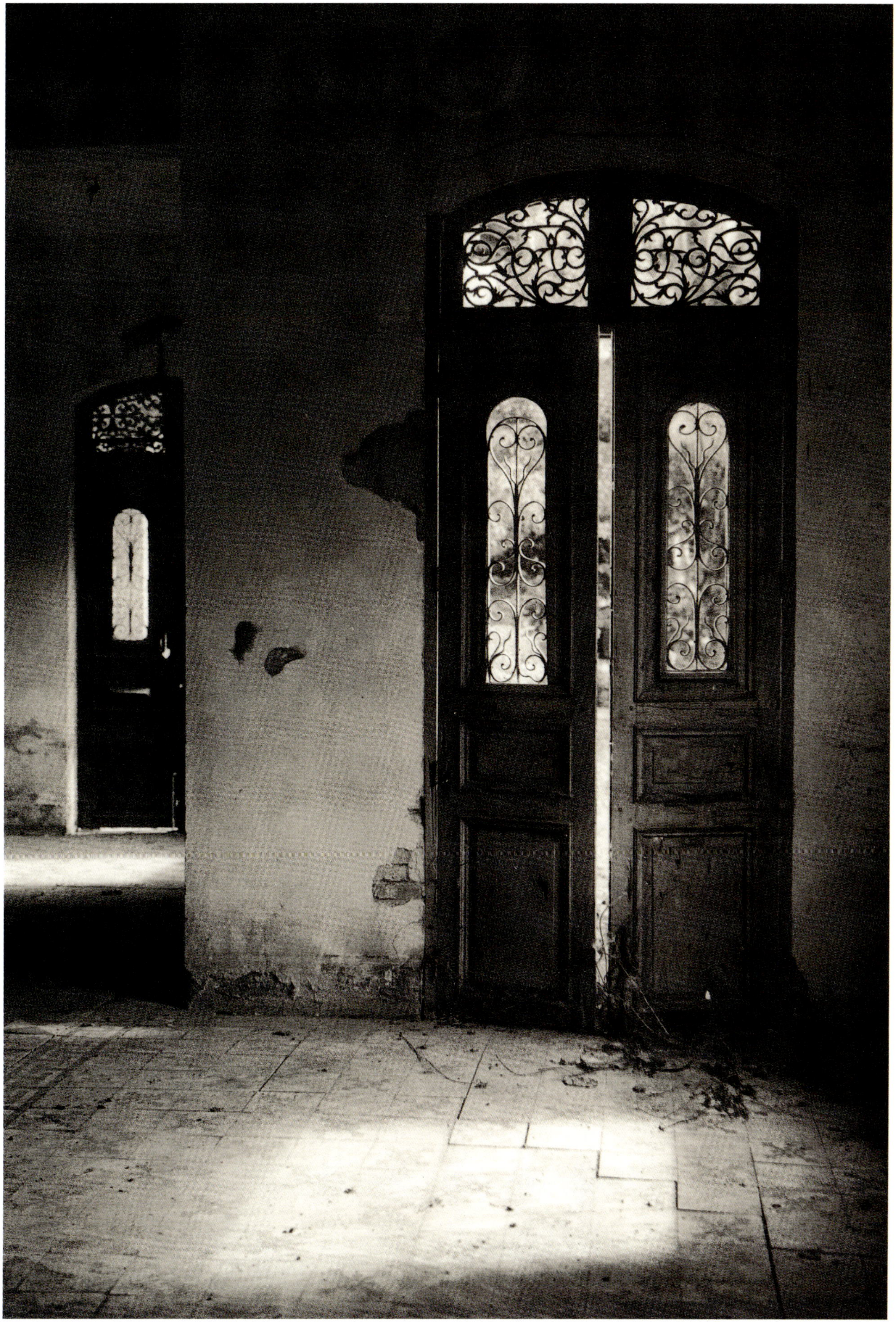

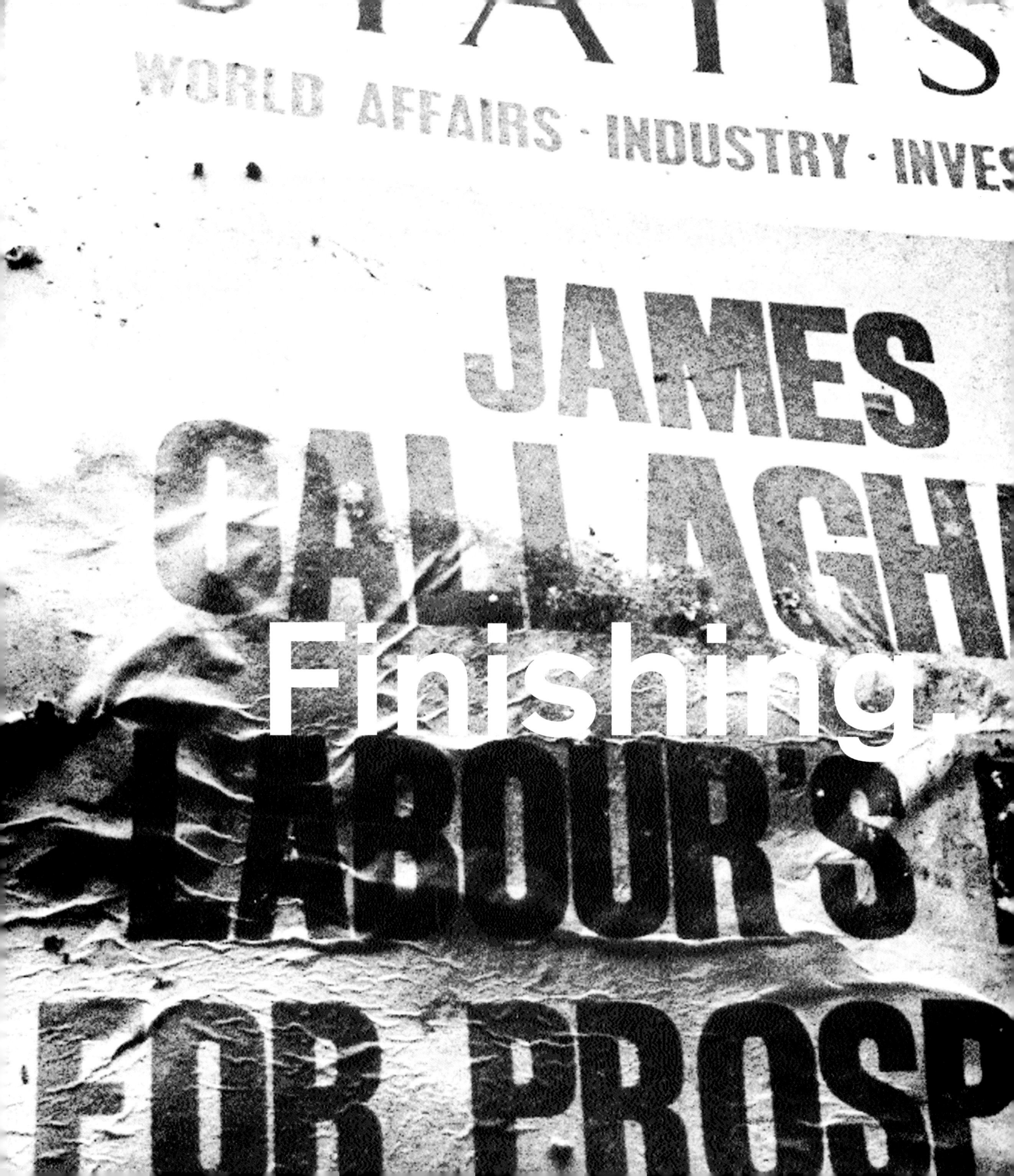
WORLD AFFAIRS · INDUSTRY · INVES
JAMES
CALLAGH
LABOUR'S
FOR PROSP

Finishing.

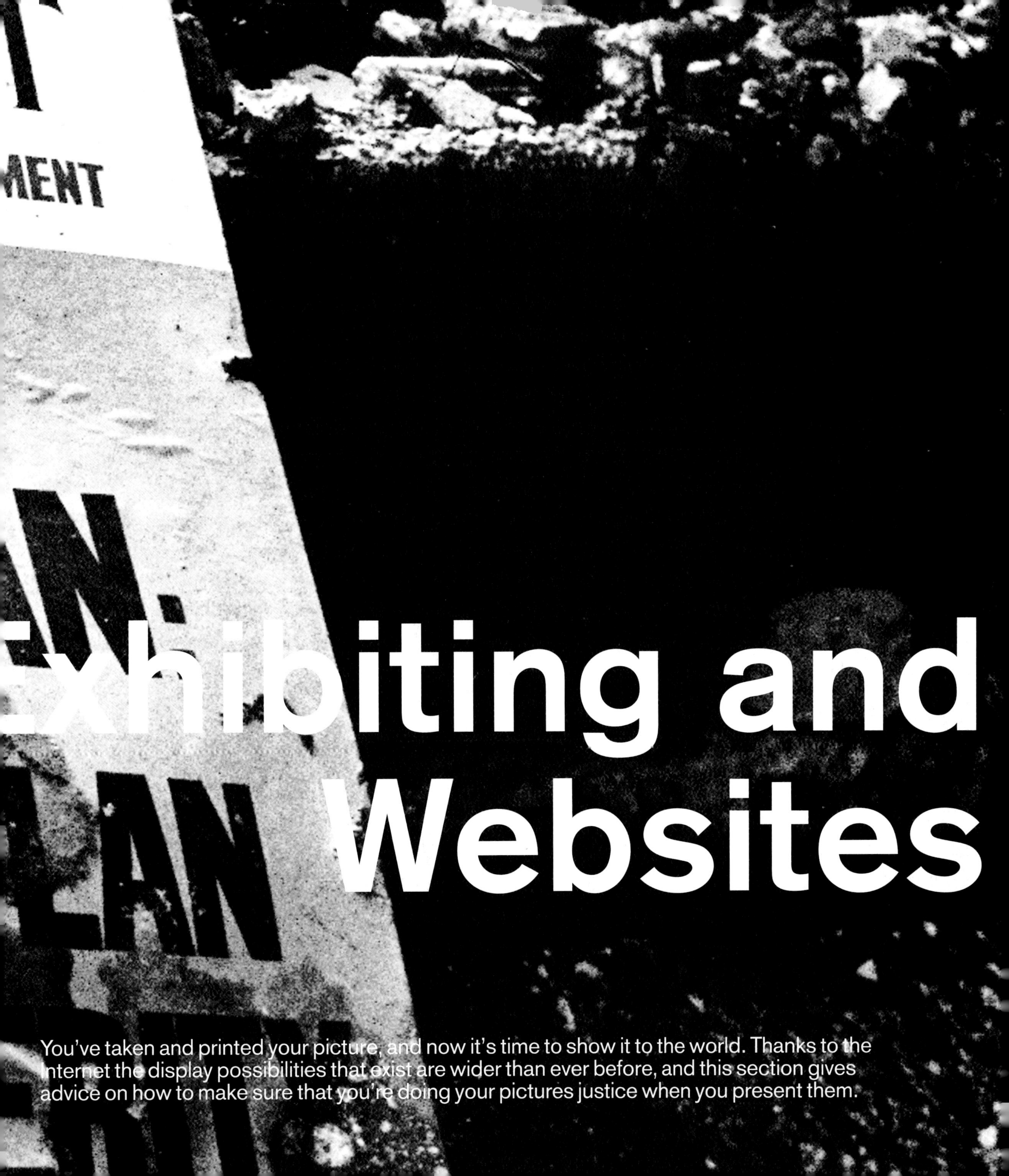

Exhibiting and Websites

You've taken and printed your picture, and now it's time to show it to the world. Thanks to the Internet the display possibilities that exist are wider than ever before, and this section gives advice on how to make sure that you're doing your pictures justice when you present them.

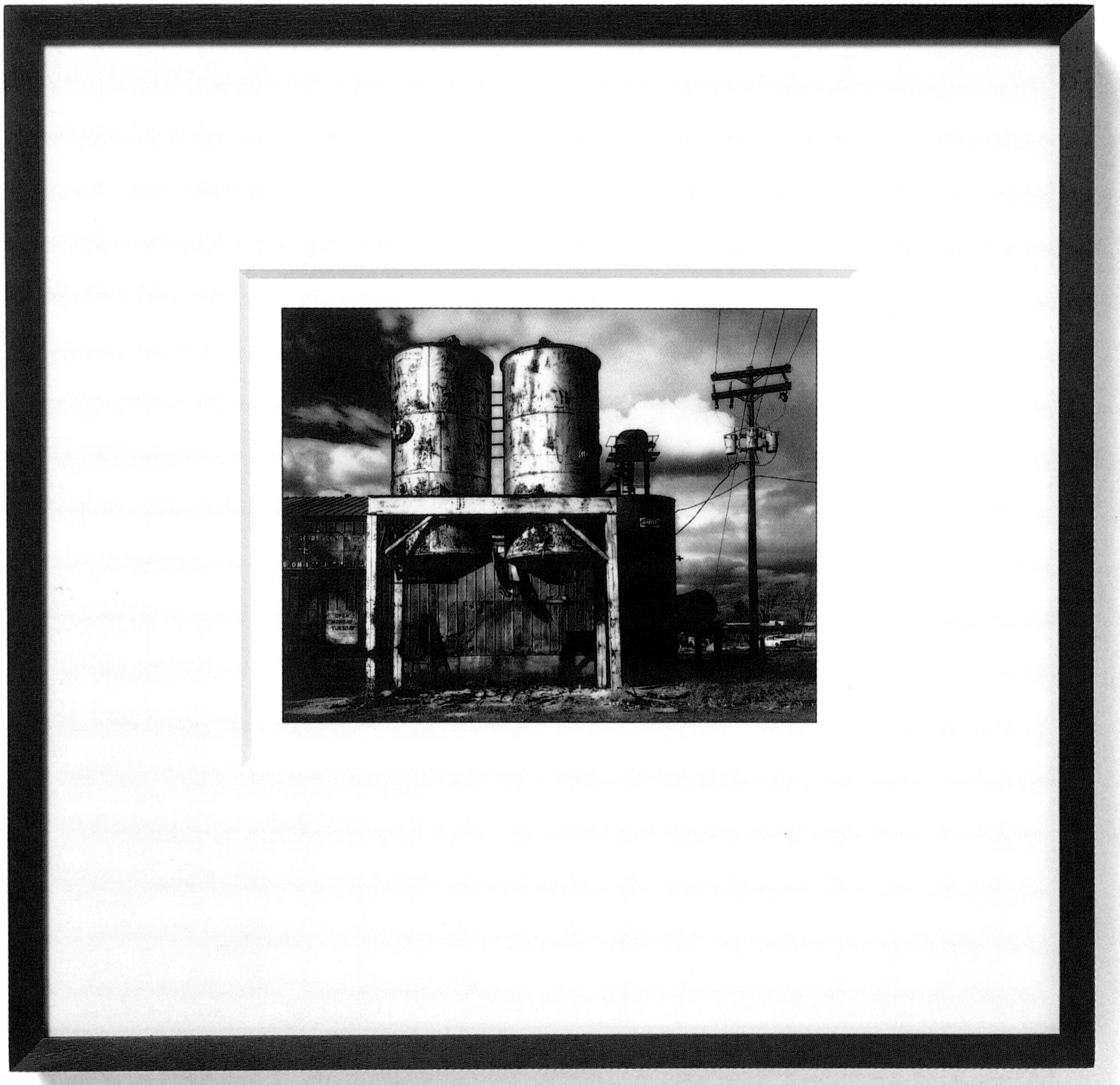

Grain Silos Utah by John Claridge
Deardorff 5x4in camera, 110mm lens, Agfa APX 400 film.
Exposure ½ second at f/22

It's amazing how often photographers put maximum effort into the production and printing of a picture, only to neglect the final framing and mounting stage. And yet the presentation of a picture is a vital part of the whole process, and it's entirely possible that a picture could lose much of the impact that the photographer has worked so hard to achieve simply through lack of care in its finishing.

If you want your picture to last and to be shown off to best effect, there are certain key steps to follow. At the printing stage it's important to ensure that fixing and then washing is extremely thorough. Toning can also add to the permanence of an image: a light Selenium tone is used by many printers, because this has little effect on the normal black and white tones, but helps to make them more stable. Tones such as thiocarbamide and sepia will also add to a print's archival qualities, and the colour they add to a picture is often beneficial as well.

Once a print has been washed and dried, it should be carefully spotted with archival inks to make sure that there are no dust marks or hairs visible. The picture is now ready for mounting.

Mounting The job of the mount is to set the picture off, and to create an area around it that is plain and unlikely to distract. The width of this mount is down to personal choice, though some pictures that are printed as miniatures often benefit from a wider surround in ratio than prints that are larger. Keep the colour of the mount neutral—with black and white images white or light cream is the usual choice—because it will then be able to carry out its job efficiently and well, and the picture itself will remain the centre of attention. Great care needs to be taken over the cutting of the mount: generally specialist tools are required to ensure that a smooth bevelled edge is created. If you try to cut a mount using just a scalpel and a steel edge, the chances are that it will look messy and that you will slice through at least one or two fingers. Visit an art shop and ask for advice from the staff there, and they will recommend the equipment that you need.

The Print Room at the Photographers' Gallery in London handles thousands of valuable photographic prints every year, and often arranges the framing and mounting of pictures for purchasers. Print Manager Fiona Duncan explains the policy on mounts: "Generally when we sell a print," she says, "we mount it in archival acid-free board. One board is used as the backing board, and on this we create three small pockets from archival tape, and these hold the print gently in place. The print doesn't need to be fastened any more securely than this, and this method allows it to be removed easily at a later date if required. Then a window mount needs to be cut so that it frames the picture, and this is connected to the backing board along one long edge using archival tape. This means that it's effectively hinged and can be brought across the picture, and then the picture is ready for framing."

Framing Once again frames are a matter of personal choice, but often it's those that are the simplest in terms of design and colour that work the best. A black frame, for example, can look stunning when it's surrounding a classic black and white picture, whereas one that features a strong colour or an intricate design will start to fight the picture. "The only other colour apart from black that might work on occasion, particularly with vintage black and white prints, is gilded silver leaf," says John Dawson, a Director of John Jones Frames, who carry out much of the framing for the Photographers' Gallery Print Room.

"We would normally suggest that frames shouldn't be more than ½ inch wide for pictures up to around 20x16ins, while above that size the width can rise to ¾ inch without becoming too dominant. The mount should ideally be around three inches in width increasing to three and a half inches at the bottom for prints up to 20x16ins, and again this can rise a little, to four inches perhaps, for larger prints."

The final stage of the framing process is the selection of glass and, for archival purposes, you should select a material that offers UV protection, because this will give your print a longer life, particularly if it's going to be hung in a room that attracts a lot of daylight.
John Jones Framing Department can be contacted on 020-7281 5439

Exhibiting

Car and Croft, Scotland by John Claridge
Deardorff 5x4in camera, 90mm lens, Agfa APX 400.
Exposure 1/4sec at f/22

When I came across this scene in a remote area of Scotland I was just taken with how it all seemed to suggest something from another era. The ancient car that had been left to decompose had become almost like a piece of modern sculpture and, sitting as it was next to this very solid farm building that was bathed in late afternoon light that was full of contrast, it was a great combination. It certainly works for me.

I used an orange filter to darken down the sky and to make it appear slightly more threatening and I increased the mood in the picture by printing it dark, so that I could pull out all the detail in the wall of the building.

This image appeared in a book that I self-published. Called simply One Hundred Photographs, it was a collection of black and white pictures that I had taken, both for myself and on commercial assignments, during a two-year period. Whatever I was doing and wherever I happened to be, I just took pictures and then, when my self-imposed time frame was over, I chose the images that I wanted to use and produced the resulting volume in a limited edition of 3000. It was just a way of showing my work and the book served as an excellent vehicle for holding the photographs together.
John Claridge

Exhibiting John Claridge held his first show of work, a collection of images that he'd taken around his native east end of London, in 1961 at the McCann Erickson Agency in London at the tender age of 17! "All kinds of people, including VIPs from the US and Europe were passing through and they were looking at my work, and it was a really good feeling," he says. Since that time he's shown his work on a regular basis and has also self-published three books: along with 'One Hundred Photographs,' he's also produced 'South American Portfolio,' a selection of personal black and white and colour photographs and 'Seven Days in Havana,' a set of black and white images shot within a specifically defined time frame in the Cuban capital. Further projects are in the pipeline and John finds it a useful way of stretching his creative muscles and of showing work that is free from commercial constraints.

"An exhibition or a book is a really good way of putting yourself on the line and saying to people 'look at this,' he says. "When I was starting out I got tremendous inspiration and pleasure from looking at work from the likes of Walker Evans and Bill Brandt and that's what it's all about really. It's showing something that is special to you and hoping to get a reaction from the people who have made the effort to go and look at it."

Pointer Putting together an exhibition is one of the most satisfying ways of using your pictures, whether it's a show at a major gallery that you're putting on or a small display at your local library. Before you even start you have to make sure that you're really ready to go public: a theme for your work is essential, and, like John Claridge, you must be sure of your own style, because work that's too derivative will be found out immediately.

Making the right selection is the next problem: producing rough prints will help you to see how your pictures work together, and it will give you the chance to get feedback from those whose opinion you trust. In the final analysis, however, you must have the confidence to make your own decisions about what to include, otherwise the exhibition will end up being selected by committee. John is very single-minded about his work and lives or dies by his intuition: "It's all personal choice and it's up to others whether they agree with my selection," he says. "The only person I discuss it with is my wife Janet because I always have too many pictures and have to make decisions about what to include. But I know what I want to say and it's up to me to make the right choices."

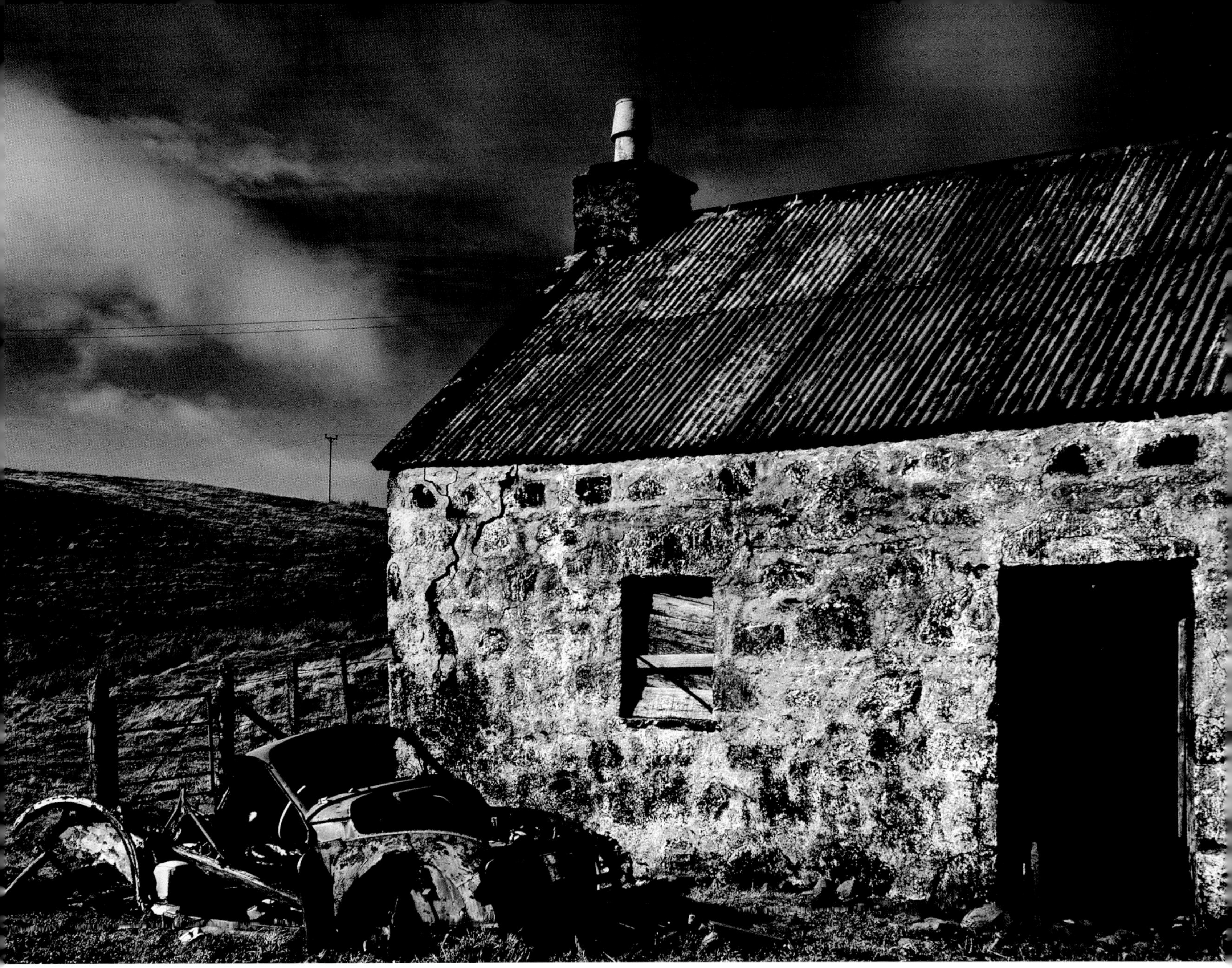

Websites

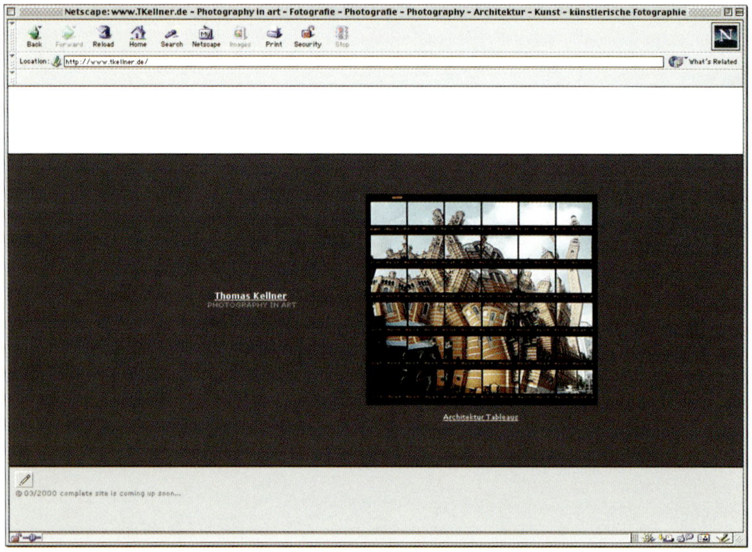

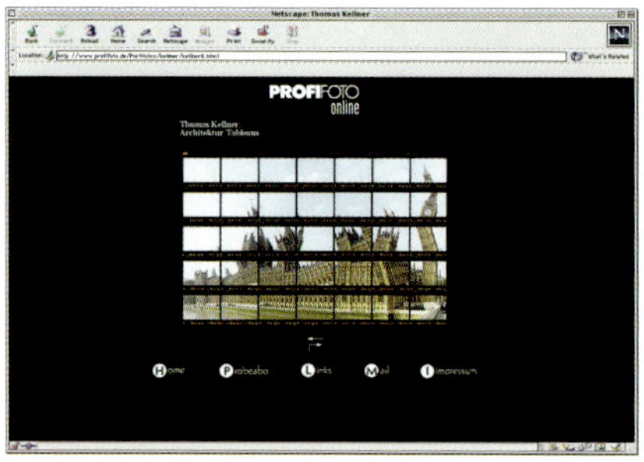

www.tkellner.de

Introduction Over the last couple of years, it seems that everyone you speak to has a website. If you don't have one just yet, however, don't panic, there's still plenty of time to get involved. If anything, it is a perfect time to start designing a website of your own because there are so many out there that it's easy to browse and to see for yourself those that work and others which are less successful.

Therefore, setting up a personal web site now is an exciting and cost effective way of showing your photographs to a potentially unlimited worldwide audience. Best of all, you'll be in charge of the content and the presentation, and so you have far more freedom to express yourself than you would normally expect from a conventional exhibition outlet. All you need is around 10 megabytes of web space from an Internet Service Provider (ISP), usually your internet provider. This service is generally free, and you'll be able to show a large selection of your favourite images, together with any accompanying words you want to include.

What You Will Need The first essential piece of equipment you require is a computer. The very minimum would be a Pentium 160 with Windows 95. Whatever computer you decide on should have at least 32 megabytes of RAM. (Do remember though, your hard drive, i.e. the amount of space in your computer, will slowly be eaten up by the more programmes you load, which will in turn slow down each action you do). You'll find this extra RAM really useful when scanning and editing.

Next you will need a scanner. There are lots on the market and most will do the job. Please note though, the image that will appear is only as good as the resolution of the computer screen displaying it, so it's no good scanning at the highest resolution of your scanner thinking you will get a better displayed image. Typically, screen resolution is 72-96 pixels per inch (ppi). Also, the greater the size of the image, in megabytes, the slower it will take to appear (download) on the internet. The good news for those working in black and white is that mono images will download approximately eight times faster than a colour one.

Once pictures are scanned, you can alter them on an image editing programme, and PhotoShop is widespread. The capabilities of such programmes are vast, but at a simple level, you could create electronic frames and borders, lighten, darken, change image sizes or add a tone. Additionally, you could watermark your images i.e. give them an electronic signature that says they are yours. Although you cannot stop people copying your images from the internet, at least if they appear again, they are watermarked. Remember to save your image: the internet supports gif or jpg, e.g. yourimage.jpg.

As previously mentioned, the time it takes an image to appear over the internet is a function of its file size. For a benchmark, colour images should be approximately 80kilobytes in size, while black and white should be an 1/8th of the file size, when based on an image measuring about 5 x 3cm. It can also be useful, however, to show very small images, known as thumbnails, because these will download in a fraction of the time. Then, if people are more interested and want to see more detail, they can click on the thumbnail, by use of a hyperlink (superscript: A), and a larger version will download. People will be more prepared to wait for something they asked for, but for this system to be effective you'll need to put a meaningful title against the thumbnail.

Now you need to add some text to your pages. If you want to bring text and images together, but don't want to learn pure HTML, you can use programmes such as Front Page or Page Maker, which are simple drop and drag web-editing programmes. Each page you complete needs to be saved as a htm file, e.g. mywebpage.htm, and the first page of your internet site has to be called home.htm, i.e. your home page.

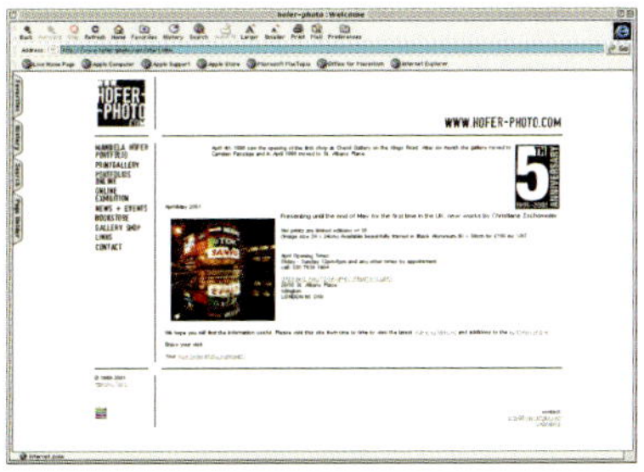

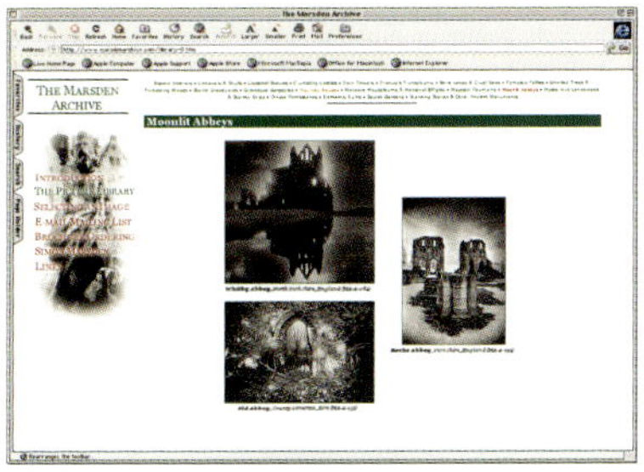

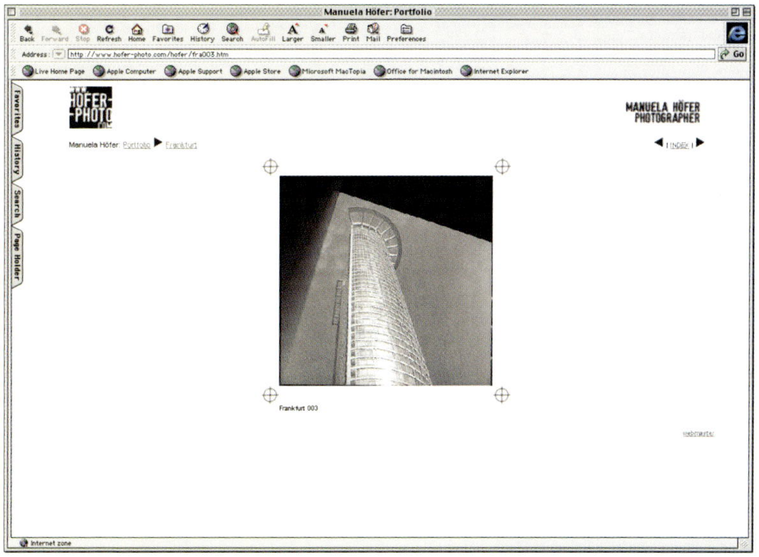

www.hofer-photo.com
www.marsdenarchive.com

How do I transfer my files to the Internet? First you need to register with an Internet Service Provider (ISP). These are widespread now, and normally free. As well as providing you with an e-mail address, they typically supply an amount of web space, e.g. ten megabytes. You will want to give your web site a name, so people can find you. If you register your web site name with your ISP, invariably their name will be the prefix to your site, i.e. www.ispname/you name.com. You could, however, register a unique name, without the mention of your ISP. This will cost around £50 for two years, ie www.yoursite.com. This was the case with www.cityart.net, which was registered to give our web site a professional-sounding name.

Having got your site name registered, you need to transfer your files to your web space. This may sound complicated, but it is actually quite straightforward. You will probably use 'ftp', which stands for file transfer protocol. Basically, all you need to do is dial up your ISP and via a program for 'ftp-ing', transfer your files to your web space. This is protected by your password so only you have access to editing your site.

How will I advertise my site? How will I get visitors? Difficult one! Just type 'photography' into any search engine and see how many sites exist. So how do you get ahead of the competition? Placing adverts in journals can cost an arm and a leg, but there are electronic ways around the problem. For example, you could find a popular site that would complement your own, contact them and then ask whether they will include a link to your site; **www.cityart.com** is one such site that is developing such links. If you feel like writing some web code (HTML), you can also incorporate the META Tags(superscript: A), which are key words that define your web page, in terms of HTML.

Finally, remember to include your email address on your web site, so that if anyone sees your pictures and wants to contact you about them, all they have to do is to click on your address.

Debra Palmer

cityart.net This successful web site, currently getting over 2000 visitors a day, was created by web developer Debra Palmer, and was considered so innovative and attractive to use that it was runner-up in two categories in a major competition for web sites held by **The Times** newspaper. The site, which was created on less than ten megabytes of space, contains 45 examples of investment art in a series of galleries, complete with essential details such as price, condition of picture and so on. It also has links to several other sites of interest to photographers and investors, such as The Royal Photographic Gallery and Photographers in New York, a listing of dozens of top photographers, several of whom have themselves links to other sites.

Biographies

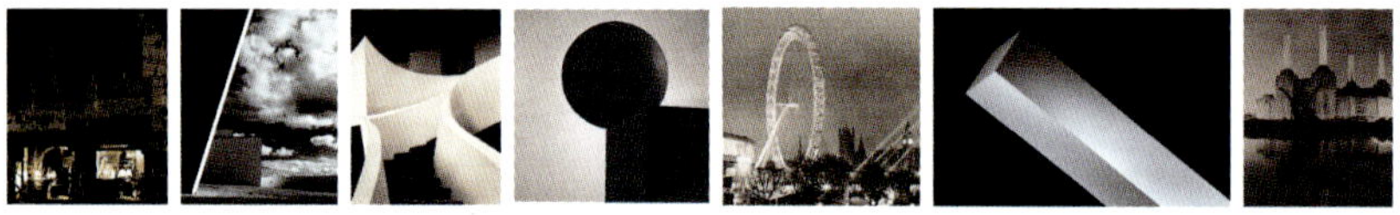

19 29 44 58 74 91 106

Anderson & Low consists of photographers Jonathan Anderson and Edwin Low who have been collaborating since 1990 when they met sharing darkroom space. After one of their early joint works was accepted for exhibition by the Royal Academy of Arts, they decided to embark on a long-term venture together. Anderson & Low have worked together on a wide variety of personal projects, ranging from reportage to portraiture, nudes, architectural studies, landscape, still life and highly disciplined studio-based art prints. Works by the duo, all noted for meticulous attention to form, lighting and printing, have been exhibited worldwide. Their most recent exhibition, **The Athlete**, has been on a world tour for the past two years, taking in venues such as the Royal Commonwealth Society, London, the US Olympic Centre, the National Portrait Gallery of Australia and at the Byron Mapp Gallery in Sydney for the 2000 Olympic Games. One of the images from The Athlete was selected for the John Kobal Award Exhibition at the National Gallery in London and other images from this project have received prizes in both the Sixteenth and Seventeenth Annual Association of Photographers Awards. A further five of Anderson & Low's architectural pictures were selected for the Eighteenth Association Awards and were awarded the coveted Gold Award.

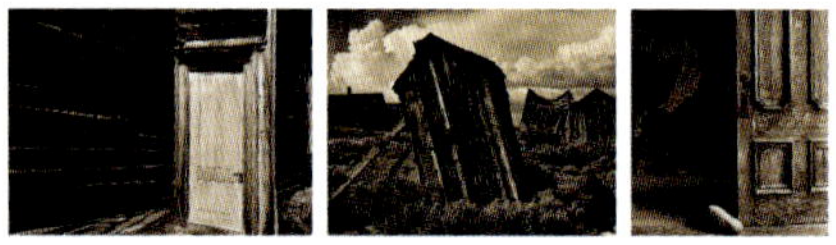

16 84 99

Ron Bambridge started his career in photography in 1975, when he began to assist Vogue fashion photographer Nigel Hartnup. He then moved on to work for a time at London advertising agency Foote, Cone & Belding. When he left here that he decided to set up his own studio in the West End of London and to go freelance. Initially specialising in still life, his personal work turned more towards landscape and location portraiture. Armed with a new portfolio, commissioned work gradually progressed towards more location shoots for clients such as British Airways, Rothschilds, ICI, London Transport, British Gas, The Welsh Development Agency, Peugot and American Airlines. Ron has many awards to his name, including a Highly Commended in the Advertising & People category of the Ilford Awards in 1984, a best photography award in the 1988 National Business Calendar Awards, the Gold Award for the series 'Landscape' in the Association of Photographers Awards 1986, the Merit Award for the series 'People' in the AOP Awards 1988 and the Merit Award for landscape in the AOP Awards 1993. He also was a winner in the still lifes series category, the environmental series category and the environmental colour category in the 1997 London Photographic Awards. He won Silver and Merit Awards in the interior/exteriors category in the 1998 AOP Awards, and was included in the 1999 AOP Awards for his personal series of portraits. He can be contacted on 020-7486 7588, while his work can be viewed on line at: www.contact-uk.com.

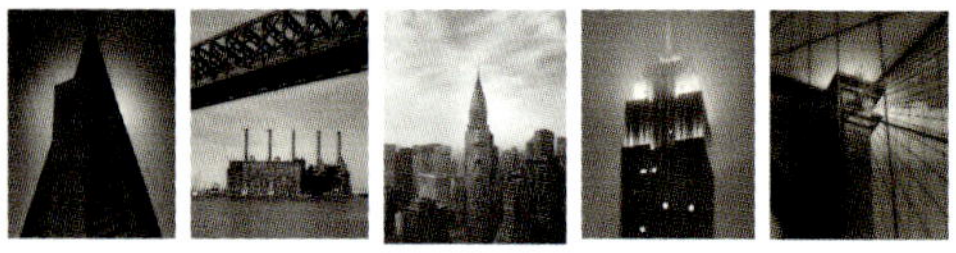

33 37 73 105 123

Tom Baril was born in Connecticut in 1952. He received his BFA from the School of Visual Arts in 1980. In 1979, while still at Visual Arts, he began as Robert Mapplethorpe's printer. Working closely with the photographer he developed the lush quality of Mapplethorpe's definitive works. Baril gained a reputation as a master printer and began printing for a select group of other artists and galleries. Although primarily known as a printer, Baril was quietly making his own pictures. Avoiding the studio, to distance himself from Mapplethorpe's work, he focused on the urban landscape and architecture. Finally moving into the studio with a pinhole camera he began to photograph flowers and make still life photographs of curious objects. Today he continues in the studio making meticulous botanical studies and is also producing unique nature photographs with the pinhole camera. His work is in numerous public and private collections including The Los Angeles County Museum of Art, The Stedelijk Museum, Amsterdam, The Brooklyn Museum New York, The Fogg Museum, Harvard University, and The Center For Creative Photography, Tucson. He has had solo exhibitions in Los Angeles, San Francisco, Chicago, Boston and New York. He currently lives in Manhattan.

76 114 127

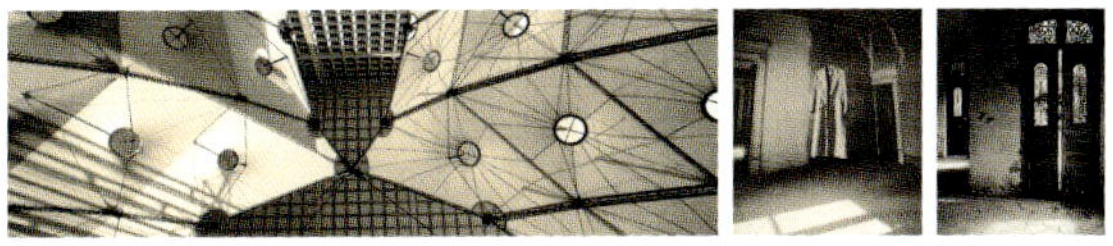

Barry Cawston studied photography at Kitson College, Leeds after becoming hooked during a two-month wander through India in 1986. His professional and personal work is very varied and ranges from architectural photography for English Heritage through to portraits and documentary studies of orphans in Eastern Europe for the European Children's Trust. Almost all of his photography, both black and white and colour, is carried out on negative stock so he considers the darkroom as probably the most important part of the photographic process and the 'alchemical' angle is something that he loves. He tries to match his cameras to his subjects and their mood and so finds himself shooting on everything from 35mm to 5x4in and even 6x12cm panoramic formats as well on old 6x6cm Rolleiflexes and Hasselblads, and he finds that this variety helps him to keep his photographic experience as alive and as new as possible.

23 48 61 95 109 137

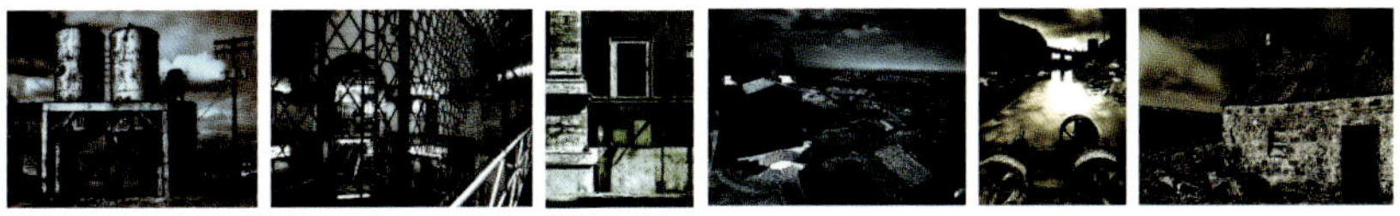

John Claridge was born in 1944 in London's East-End and, from the age of 15 to 17, he worked in the photographic department of a London advertising agency. He decided early on that photography was his vocation, holding his first one-man show at the age of 17, and then working as assistant to American photographer David Montgomery for the next two years. He opened his first studio aged 19 in London's City area, and since that time he's worked for most leading advertising agencies and clients in Europe, the USA and Japan. His work has been exhibited worldwide, and he's been presented with over 500 awards for photography, both editorial and commercial. Selected pictures have been auctioned at Christie's in London, and his work is also held in the permanent collections of the Victoria & Albert Museum in London and The Arts Council of Great Britain Archives. He's published three books: South American Portfolio (1982), One Hundred Photographs (1987) and Seven Days in Havana (2000).

38 47 82 96 119

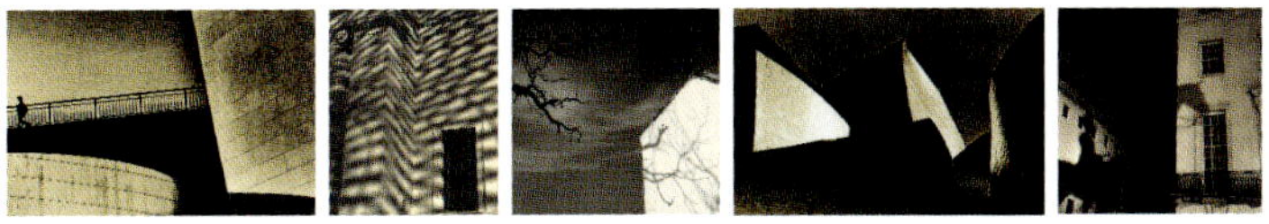

Adrian Ensor is one of Britain's finest black and white printers. He's a previous winner of the Ilford Printer of the Year Award, one of the UK's highest accolades for printers, and his London darkroom attracts orders from many of Britain's top photographers. Over the past eight years Adrian has been building a reputation as a gifted photographer as well, setting himself projects that he finds personally stimulating, and then pursuing them tenaciously. His work has now been accepted by the prestigious Photographers' Gallery print room, where it's offered for sale alongside pictures from some of the world's leading photographers.

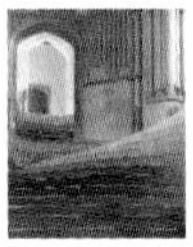

51

Frederick Evans (1853-1943), a former bookseller turned photographer, was a perfectionist, whose photography, both architectural and portrait is remarkable for its purity of line and mastery of light, space and composition. When platinum became scarce after 1914, he stopped printing altogether rather than use an inferior product.

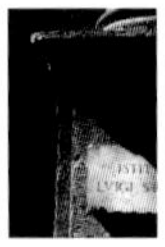
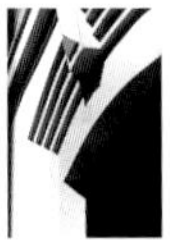
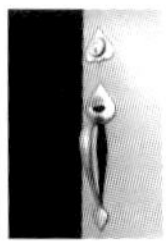
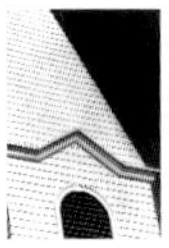
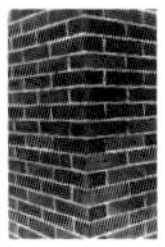

20 57 62 78 92

Ralph Gibson is without question one of the world's greatest photographers. Born in Los Angeles in 1939, he assisted photographic icons Dorothea Lange (1961-62) and Robert Frank (1967-68), before making his own name as a photographer of rare insight and clarity. His work has appeared in numerous books, such as The Somnambulist (1970), Days At Sea (1975), Syntax (1983), Tropism (1987) and, most recently, Overtones (1998) and Deus Ex Machina (1999). Awards have included a Doctor of Fine Arts Award from Ohio Wesleyan University (1997), a Grand Medal of the city of Arles in 1994, a '150 Years of Photography' Award from the Photographic Society of Japan (1989) and a Leica Medal of Excellence Award (1988). The work of Ralph Gibson has been exhibited in some of the world's leading galleries, and his work is held in the collections of international institutions such as the Museum of Modern Art in New York, The Metropolitan Museum of Art in New York, the Whitney Museum of American Art, the National Gallery of Art in Washington DC, The National Museum of Modern Art in Kyoto, The International Centre of Photography in New York, the National Gallery in Ottowa and the Biblioteque National in Paris. His work is represented in the US by the Howard Greenberg Gallery in New York, email howard.greenberg.gallery@worldnet.att.net

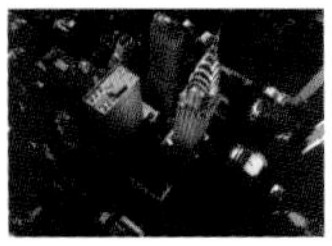

15

Jason Hawkes has specialised in aerial photography for over eleven years and has published twenty books, including titles on London, Britain, Ireland, Provence, Washington DC and South Carolina. His advertising work takes him around Europe and the United States, and has won him awards from D & AD, Campaign and the Association of Photographers. Hawkes runs a specialist aerial photographic library in London, holding over 50,000 pictures, which can be contacted on 020 8960 7525 and viewed at www.jasonhawkes.com. Jason Hawkes is widely recognised as being the UK's leader in his field.

30 112

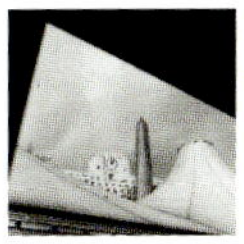
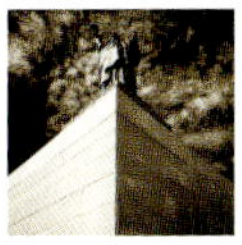

Mauela Höfer, who was born and raised in the German Democratic Republic, is one of only a handful of photographers selling fine-art photography direct to the British public, as well as achieving success selling her images commercially. She has also achieved a worthy reputation as the organiser of the London Contemporary Photography Fair, an annual event that has been held since 1997. In its short lifetime the Fair has already gained European recognition and it attracts photography collectors, curators, agencies, photographers and media journalists from across the world, while also giving unprecedented exposure to many young photographers. Manuela has had her work exhibited in England, France, Germany, the Czech Republic and Hungary, and she has also been published in many photography and art journals across Europe. Her interest in photographing packaging began in 1994 and, after she moved to Britain the following year, she was inspired to continue the series, stunned by the high level of non-recyclable food packaging from supermarkets to sandwich bars. The Manuela Hofer Workshop and Gallery is now established next to the Business Design Centre in London's Islington at 29/30 St Alban's Place, N1 0NX. Manuela's website is www.hofer-photo.com

24 43 65

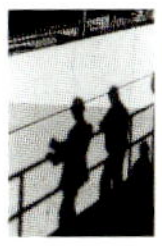
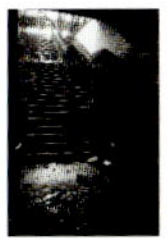
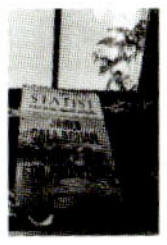

Terry Hope studied photography at Harrow College in west London in the mid-1970s. He moved into photographic journalism in 1981, running the features department of **Camera Weekly** magazine until 1989. After freelancing for a time he became Features Editor and then Deputy Editor of **Amateur Photographer** magazine, one of the world's oldest photographic titles, leaving to freelance again in the summer of 1998. He's now a regular contributor on a variety of subjects to the UK's national press, appearing in such titles as **The Times**, **The Sunday Telegraph** and **The Guardian**, and he continues to contribute interview features to the UK's photographic press. He has extensive connections with some of the world's leading photographers, and collaborated for four years on a regular column that David Bailey contributed to **Amateur Photographer**. He was named IPC Magazines' Commissioning Editor of the Year in 1995 for this, and other, projects. He can be contacted via email on: terry.hope@ntlworld.com

113

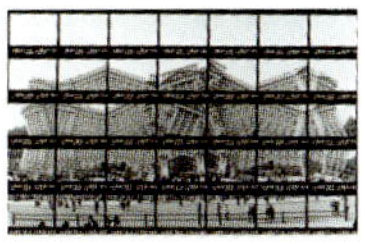

Thomas Kellner was born in Bonn in 1966 and he studied art and photography at the University of Siegen. His first group exhibition came in 1991 with his first solo show two years later and since that time he has shown his work widely at venues throughout Europe and has been widely published. Thomas' work is available from The Manuela Höfer Workshop and Gallery, which is situated next to the Business Design Centre in London's Islington at 29/30 St Alban's Place, N1 0NX. A book of his de-construction images, containing 40 images, is available by emailing through the websites at either www.tkellner.de or www.hofer-photo.com.

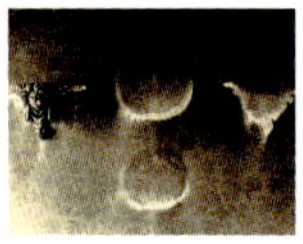 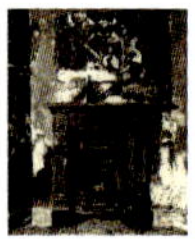

66 100

Gavin Kingcombe concentrated on photography after studying at the London Film School, and now has a studio in west London where he undertakes a variety of commissions for magazines, newspapers and designers. When possible he loves to travel and in the last 18 months he has worked on voluntary expeditions run by the Earthwatch Institute, helping on conservation programmes. For them he has worked on a project set up to protect the endangered wolf population of North West India and another that aims to restore early 20th century glass plate negatives taken by Peruvian photographers. He can be contacted at gavin@gavinkingcombe.com

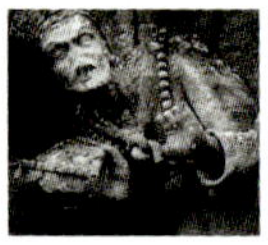 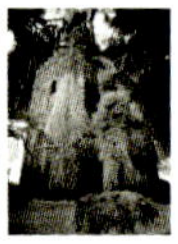

69 86

Simon Marsden is an internationally acclaimed photographer of the fantastic and the supernatural and has devoted his life to photographing ancient ruins and other ghostly sites, capturing in his images the atmosphere of their illustrious past and the eerie presence of the spirits that are still believed to haunt them. His photographs can be found in many prestigious collections, including the Getty Museum in California, the Bibliotheque Nationale in Paris and the Victoria and Albert Museum in London. He has also exhibited in New York, Brussels, Italy and Austria. In 1992 his work was the subject of a one-hour documentary-drama which formed part of the Granada Television arts series Celebration. Books to date include In **Ruins: The Once Great Houses of Ireland**, **The Haunted Realm**, **Phantoms of the Isles**, **Visions of Poe**, **The Journal of a Ghosthunter**, **Beyond the Wall: Germany's Monumental Past** and **Venice: City of Haunting Dreams**. His work can be viewed on his website at www.marsdenarchive.com.

 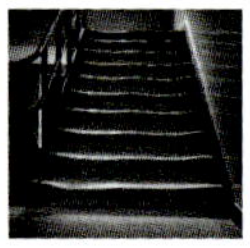

34 52

Simon Norfolk was born in Lagos, Nigeria, in 1963, and from 1988-90 studied Documentary Photography at Gwent College in Newport. He learned photojournalism through working for the far-left press through the early nineties, becoming staff photographer for **Living Marxism** magazine from 1990-1994. He undertook extensive work on fascism and the far-right, especially the British National Party, and also worked over a long period as a photojournalist on anti-racism issues, the Poll Tax and Northern Ireland. He was assigned to eastern Europe at the fall of the Wall, and covered the Gulf War, and his work has been published in all the UK broadsheets and many European magazines. He began his much-acclaimed '**For Most Of It I Have No Words**' project in 1994, and this was premiered at the Impressions Gallery in York at the end of 1998. The show has since gone on to tour around the UK, the US, Canada and Europe. Another exhibition, '**After The Fall: 10 years after the Berlin Wall**,' ran during early 1999 at the Tom Blau Gallery in London. Simon has also been featured in many other exhibitions including the John Kobal Portrait Awards at the National Portrait Gallery in London in 1998 and the Association of Photographers Award Winners Show at The Barbican in London in 1997 and 1998. He was also overall winner of the Amnesty International Photography Contest to celebrate the 50th anniversary of the UN Declaration of Human Rights in 1998, and also gained four runners-up awards.

81

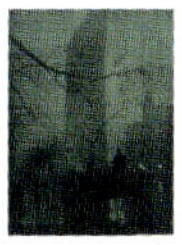

Edward Steichen (1879-1973) began his photographic career as an impressionistic artist and ended it as Director of Photography at the Museum of Modern Art in New York. In between he embraced every form of photography, from abstract, straight, advertising and fashion, bringing his huge enthusiasm and energy to bear to enhance photography as a career, as an art form and as a museum speciality.

120 124

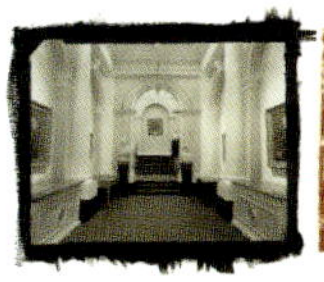

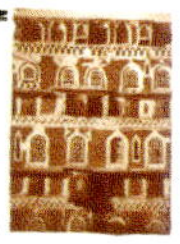

Randall Webb is a freelance photographer and lecturer. He is also a leading authority on the history and practice of photographic printmaking, ranging from the work of Fox Talbot in the 1830s to Andy Warhol in the late 20th century. His interest in early and alternative processing dates from his experiments in 1968 with the now neglected bromoil process. He now runs workshops at museums, art schools and universities on a wide variety of early processes, including salt printing, gum printing, platinum, carbon, photo etching and photo silk screen. Following extensive research, he has recently published a definitive text book on the subject entitled **Spirits of Salts**, in association with Martin Reed of Silverprint – website at http://www.silverprint.co.uk, e-mail sales@silverprint.co.uk. A few years ago he founded the 120 group of photographers, and he exhibits and sells his work which is printed using examples of alternative printing.

Glossary

Backlighting
Light that's coming from a position in front of the camera and illuminating the subject from behind.

Black Reflector
Used to soak up light and to ensure that a selected area retains deep shadow.

Bellows Extension
The amount of distance between the lens and the film plane in a studio camera is variable, and depends on the amount of extension the bellows is subjected to. For close up work, the bellows may be extended to two or three times its usual size, and this will mean that a calculation will be required to allow for extra exposure.

Bounced Flash
Flash that's been reflected from a surface such as a wall or ceiling to diffuse the light.

Cable Release
A flexible device that screws into the camera's shutter release button and activates the shutter without the need to touch the camera.

Camera Movements
Vertical and swing movements that can be made with the lens and the film plane on a studio camera to perform various functions, such as increased depth of field and correction of converging verticals.

Compressed Perspective
Distant perspective that's been brought up close by the use of a telephoto lens.

Dark Slide
A sheet film holder that can usually accommodate two pieces of film, and which is then placed in the back of a studio camera prior to an exposure being made.

Depth of Field
The distance in front and behind the point at which a lens is focused that will be rendered acceptably sharp. It increases when the aperture is made smaller, and becomes smaller when the lens is focused at close quarters.

Dodging
The holding back of certain areas of the negative during printing to reduce print density, allied to the selective increase of exposure to certain areas of the print that require increased density.

Downrating
The opposite to uprating, and primarily done to reduce contrast. The film is shot at a lower ISO rating and, to compensate for what is effectively overexposure, the film is developed for a shorter time

Dual Toning
The technique of placing a print in two separate toning baths to pick up elements of both colours

Extension Tubes
A series of rings that can be used with an SLR camera to position the lens further away from the film plane, and to allow close up pictures to be taken.

Farmer's Reducer
A mixture of potassium ferricyanide and sodium thiosulphate that will lighten selective areas of a print.

Field Camera
A large format camera that has been especially designed to be used on location.

Fill-in Flash
A weakened burst of flash that can be used to subtly fill in the shadows on a subject's face.

Filter Factor
An indication of the amount the exposure needs to be increased to allow for the use of a filter. A x2 filter needs one stop extra exposure, x3 one-and-a-half stops more and x4 two stops more.

Fish Fryer
A rectangular-shaped tent designed to fit over a flashlight and to spread its illumination evenly in the studio.

Fresnel Lens
The front of a fresnel lens consists of concentric rings, each of which forms part of a curved lens surface. These have the same overall convergent effect on illumination as a thicker lens, but the lens loses the heat applied to its inner surface through convection and radiation from its larger external surface area.

Gobo
A device like a flag which can be used in the studio to direct light very precisely into a particular area.

Graduated Neutral Density Filter
A filter that features a denser area towards its top that helps to even out the contrast levels in a picture if the sky is much brighter than the rest of the scene (see Neutral Density Filter)

Grey Card
The Grey Card provides what is assumed to be average density, and a reading taken from its surface will therefore give a good mid-point with a scene of high contrast.

High Key
A picture that consists almost entirely of light tones

Hyperfocal Distance
The distance between the lens and the nearest point of acceptably sharp focus when the lens is focused for infinity

Infra Red film
A film that responds to the different reflecting powers and transparencies of objects in the picture to infra red and visible radiation, producing a series of bizarre tones

Lith Printing Paper
A printing paper that increases the contrast levels in a scene while allowing shadow detail to be retained. Its characteristic feature is a pink tone

Low Key
A picture that consists almost entirely of dark tones

Macro
The term used to describe a close-up picture

Mirror Lock
A lever on an SLR camera that allows the camera's mirror to be locked in the up position before an exposure is made to help reduce vibration

Monopod
A form of support for the camera that utilises one leg, which makes it very easy to set up and move

Neutral Density Filter
Used to cut down the light reaching a film by a stated amount, and absorbs all wavelengths almost equally, ensuring no influence on the tones each colour will record as on black and white film

Polaroid Type 55 film
One of the oldest Polaroid film materials available, which gives the photographer both a print and a negative

Rangefinder Camera
A camera that features two separate images in the viewfinder that come together as the lens is focused

Reflector Brolly
A highly reflective umbrella that attaches to a flashgun to bounce the light back on to a scene

Selenium Toning
A brief immersion in selenium toner diluted at about one part concentrate to 15 parts water should not change print image colour but it will improve the archival permanence of the print. The toner must be used in well ventilated conditions

Spot Meter
A meter that is designed to give an accurate meter reading in difficult lighting conditions by gathering information selectively from three to four areas of a scene

Thiocarbamide toning
A two-bath process that can, according to relative strengths of the components in the toning stage, give a variety of tones ranging from dark brown to yellow brown

Uprating
Rating a film at a speed higher than its nominal rating, and then compensating for the underexposure that takes place by increasing film development

Variable Contrast Paper
Photographic paper that can produce different levels of contrast depending on the filtration it receives

White Reflector
A board or sheet that is positioned to bounce light into areas of shadow

Zone System
The system perfected by Ansel Adams that divides a scene up into areas of differing tones, to allow metering to be more precisely carried out. Consistent metering, combined with close control of negative development, ensures that a perfect negative can be obtained, allowing a pre-conceived result to be produced.